The Social and Cultural History of Palestine

Essays in Honour of Salim Tamari

Edited by Sarah Irving

EDINBURGH
University Press

Edinburgh University Press is one of the leading university presses in the UK. We publish academic books and journals in our selected subject areas across the humanities and social sciences, combining cutting-edge scholarship with high editorial and production values to produce academic works of lasting importance. For more information visit our website: edinburghuniversitypress.com

Edinburgh University Press Ltd
The Tun – Holyrood Road
12 (2f) Jackson's Entry
Edinburgh EH8 8PJ

Typeset in 10.5/13 Gentium Plus by
IDSUK (DataConnection) Ltd, and
printed and bound in Great Britain by

A CIP record for this book is available from the British Library

ISBN 978 1 3995 0361 7 (hardback)
ISBN 978 1 3995 0363 1 (webready PDF)
ISBN 978 1 3995 0364 8 (epub)

Contents

Figures

The Contributors

Nadi Abusaada is an architect, urbanist and historian. He is currently an Aga Khan Postdoctoral Fellow in the Department of Architecture at the Massachusetts Institute of Technology (MIT). Nadi completed his PhD and MPhil degrees at the University of Cambridge and his BA (Hons) at the University of Toronto. He is also the co-founder of Arab Urbanism, a global network dedicated to historical and contemporary urban issues in the Arab region.

Dotan Halevy is a Polonsky Postdoctoral Fellow at the Van Leer Institute, Jerusalem. His research, including his recent PhD from Columbia University, focuses on the cultural, social and environmental histories of the late and post-Ottoman Middle East.

Sarah Irving is Lecturer in International History at Staffordshire University and a Leverhulme Early Career Fellow researching the history of the 1927 Palestine earthquake. Recent publications include the memoirs of Palestinian priest and nationalist Niqula Khoury, translated and annotated with Karène Sanchez Summerer and Charbel Nassif, and *Cultural Entanglement in the Pre-Independence Arab World: Arts, Thought and Literature*, edited together with Anthony Gorman (2021). She is also editor-in-chief of the journal *Contemporary Levant*.

Amin Khalaf is co-founder and former president of Hand in Hand, the Centre for Jewish-Arab Education in Israel. He is currently a lecturer in education at Ono Academic College and David Yellin College of Education, Jerusalem.

Rawda Morkus-Makhoul is a researcher in the social history of Palestinian rural women, rural economy, Palestinian agricultural history and development, and education, mainly during the British Mandate. Her doctoral dissertation is titled 'Rural Palestinian Women in the Economy of Mandatory Palestine', at Ben Gurion University of the Negev.

Issam Nassar is Professor of History at the Doha Institute for Graduate Studies. A historian of the Ottoman period in Palestine and Greater Syria, as well as photography in the Ottoman lands, he is author of a number of books and studies in Arabic and English, several of which have been translated into multiple languages.

Karène Sanchez Summerer is Professor of Middle Eastern Studies at Groningen University and principal investigator of the research project 'CrossRoads: A Connected History between European Cultural Diplomacy and Arab Christians in Mandate Palestine' (2018–22, funded by the Dutch Research Council NWO). Her most recent publication is *The House of the Priest: A Palestinian Life (1885-1954)* (2022), co-authored with Sarah Irving and Charbel Nassif.

Chris Sandal-Wilson is Lecturer in Medical History at the University of Exeter, UK. His first book, on colonial psychiatry and mental illness in British Mandate Palestine, is under contract with Cambridge University Press. His research has previously appeared in *Culture, Medicine, and Psychiatry, Jerusalem Quarterly* and *Contemporary Levant.*

Mahmoud Yazbak is Professor of History at Haifa University and the first Palestinian elected as head of the Middle East and Islamic Studies Association of Israel. His publications include *The Orange City, Yafa: Culture and Community 1700-1840* (2018, in Arabic), *Haifa in the Late Ottoman Period: A Muslim Town in Transition, 1864-1914* (1998) and numerous articles in journals, including the *Journal of Palestine Studies, Journal of the Economic and Social History of the Orient* and the *International Journal of Middle East Studies.*

Sary Zananiri is an artist and cultural historian. He has co-edited two volumes: *Imaging and Imagining Palestine: Photography, Modernity and the Biblical Lens* (2021) and *European Cultural Diplomacy and Arab Christians in Palestine: Between Contention and Connection* (2021). He is currently a Postdoctoral Fellow at Leiden University.

Acknowledgements

This book originated with a discussion which involved, amongst others (and in alphabetical order), Issam Nassar, Norig Neveu, Karène Sanchez Summerer and Sary Zananiri. Its completion was made possible with their ideas, help and support, as well as those of Philippe Bourmaud, Dotan Halevy and Chris Sandal-Wilson, and of the anonymous reviewers. My own involvement was generously funded as part of a Leverhulme Early Career Fellowship. In the most fundamental sense, however, this volume could not exist without the wisdom, generosity and tireless scholarship of Salim Tamari, to whom it is dedicated.

Acknowledgements

Introduction: The Social and Cultural in the Historiography of Mandate Palestine

Sarah Irving

When I began approaching fellow researchers of Palestinian history and society with the request to contribute to this volume in honour of Professor Salim Tamari, the enthusiasm with which the idea was met was almost overwhelming. Few scholars have influenced so many with their work – its form, content and methodology – but also with the generosity and thoughtfulness with which Tamari has welcomed and supported those following in his footsteps, giving his time, wisdom, expertise and boundless knowledge of twentieth-century Palestine.

The idea for this collection was conceived over drinks after a gruelling but invigorating three-day workshop of the Crossroads project on European cultural diplomacy and Arab Christians in Palestine at Leiden University, during which Salim's gentle but precise critiques, vast range of knowledge, scurrilous stories about prominent figures and endless good humour and charm were a constant presence. The main desire of the friends and colleagues in the 't Gerecht bar and those who came later to the project was and is to say: Thank you, Salim, for your intellectual contributions, your tireless searching-out and foregrounding of Palestinian voices, and your inexhaustible kindness and patience. This is not the first act of homage to your work, and we are sure it will not be the last.

Beyond this, however, the collection seeks to highlight, through contributions from both established and newer scholars of Late Ottoman and Mandate Palestine, the breadth of Salim Tamari's influence on how we view this period in Palestinian history, how we write about it, and the methods and sources that we use. Different contributors do so in different ways, foregrounding varying aspects of Tamari's legacy. This introduction thus begins with a brief overview of recent writing on Palestinian history, considering some of the main themes which have developed in recent decades, particularly the strands through which we can see Tamari's work woven. These include his emphasis on social history, informed by his grounding in sociology, and the place of diverse and often subaltern characters; his use of biography and tireless publication of memoirs and diaries by Palestinians whose voices lend richness and detail to our understanding of the

Palestinian past; his stress on the First World War as an event of immense rupture in the Levant, but one through which cultural and social continuities run, insistent on the strength of Palestinian identities and ways of life; and his foregrounding of Jerusalem in Palestinian life at a time when global political currents have threatened to back Israel's efforts to fully annex its eastern half and claim the city as the capital of a mono-ethnic state.

Salim Tamari and Scholarship on Palestine

Salim Tamari has always insisted that he is not a historian, but a sociologist. He is Emeritus Professor of Sociology at Birzeit University; the many visiting fellowships he has held at universities ranging from Cambridge to Georgetown and Berkeley to Ca' Foscari have often been in the social sciences; and his PhD, from the University of Manchester, is in sociology. And yet, as a historical sociologist whose work mainly focuses on Palestine in the first fifty years of the twentieth century, his impact has perhaps been strongest on history and historians; indeed, Rashid Khalidi, one of the other towering figures of Palestinian scholarship, has referred to Tamari as the 'the preeminent Palestinian historical sociologist'. What this perhaps means for Tamari's work is that, whilst it operates in the historical domain, it circumnavigates the classic concerns of political history – elite men, states and power relations on the national and international level. Instead, it remains determinedly focused on the ordinary people of Palestine, their experiences, identities and passions, and how these were interwoven with and affected by the events of history on a grand scale, especially World War I, the end of the Ottoman Empire, the British Mandate and Zionist immigration, as well as socialism and communism, intellectual currents in fields such as ethnography and history, and technological change.

This focus on the ordinary, the quotidian and the subaltern means that one of the contributions for which Tamari is best known – especially in connection with the Institute of Jerusalem Studies, its parent body, the Institute for Palestine Studies, and the journal *Jerusalem Quarterly* – is his editing, translation and publication of memoirs and biographies. Autobiographical writings such as Ihsan Turjman's World War I diaries and Wasif Jawhariyyeh's memoirs, together with Tamari's introductions to them, have become, it is fair to say, canonical in Palestine Studies.[1] Their frank, sometimes faintly scandalous, accounts of everyday life in the late Ottoman and Mandate periods have played a significant role in humanising the figure of Palestinians in recent history and in enriching our understanding of Palestinian life and thought in the first half of the twentieth century. Among an academic literature often focused on the big political questions of colonialism, nationalism and Zionism, these autobiographical volumes, as well as shorter articles and chapters introducing or foregrounding figures – such as the doctor Tawfiq Canaan, 'Aref Shehadeh (better known as the politician, writer and civil servant 'Aref al-'Aref, but presented by Tamari in an earlier incarnation as an Ottoman soldier and Russian POW), or communist, trade unionist and fighter against fascism in Spain Najati Sidqi – add food, music, love, scholarship, travel, behind-the-scenes political, sexual and professional shenanigans, intellectual history and a plethora of other themes to the mix.[2] Tamari never ignores the political – indeed, the backdrop of World War I and the entry and impacts of imperial Britain into the Levant are a constant presence throughout his works – but via his pen we meet the people who experienced, resisted, complied with, subverted and wrote about the momentous changes that overtook Palestine in this period. In short, we meet the people who lived this history, not just the processes of which they were a part.

Beyond the humanising effect of this, writings such as those by Turjman and Jawhariyyeh are – as indicated by the frequency with which they are now cited – mines of valuable primary detail for scholars and students working on these periods. But more than that, even before the current burst of awareness of the need to decolonise Palestinian Studies, these works put the words and thoughts of Palestinian historical actors into the public domain, not just as interesting case studies or 'local colour', but as people whose thoughts, views and analyses of their circumstances should be taken seriously and used to inform our own engagement with their social and political environments.

Tamari's celebratory but critical approach to Palestinian society and culture in the first half of the twentieth century has also helped to set and build trends within both academic and popular writing on Palestine. Volumes such as *Mountain Against the Sea* and *The Great War and the Remaking of Palestine* stand alongside the work of Beshara Doumani and Rashid Khalidi in presenting a diverse and rich vision of Palestinian society, one which was, especially in the pre-war era, a constantly shifting mix of ethnic, religious, regional and political identities.[3] Muslims, Christians and Jews all have their places in this image of Palestine, and these three categories are not necessarily those experienced as most important in the day-to-day lives evoked. This vision of Palestinian history, influenced perhaps most by Tamari and by Zachary Lockman's application of relational history in the Mandate Palestinian case, is now widely accepted, built on, reshaped and sometimes implicitly critiqued by recent scholarship. And yet there is nothing naïve or idyllic in Tamari's portraits of late Ottoman and Mandate society. As'ad al-Shuqairi is introduced as the shaykh who 'achieved notoriety' for his fatwas in support of the Turkish execution of Arab nationalists in 1916,[4] before allowing himself to be used as a catspaw of Ottoman propaganda; 'Isa al-'Isa, proprietor of the newspaper *Filastin* and in the 1930s author of an autobiography promoting his nationalist credentials, is revealed as having knowingly, prior to World War I, published pseudonymous columns by a Zionist politician who promoted the agricultural innovations to be found on Zionist settlements.[5] Tamari's human beings are eminently human: they are honourable, generous and brave, but also scheming, violent and hypocritical. Palestinian Jews are a fundamental part of the country's society, but political Zionism and its project of replacement and removal of the indigenous population is a clear and present danger. Both credit and criticism are applied where they are due, and the Palestine of Tamari's accounts is a place that is profoundly alive – imperfectly, excitingly, challengingly so.

While the subjects of Tamari's writings fall almost entirely within a broad category of Palestinian (and, indeed, often intervene in debates over the development of this as a category that was both politically pertinent and individually meaningful between the beginning of the twentieth century and the *Nakba*), his approach and methodologies locate this work as part of international trends in history writing and, in particular, microhistory. The flourishing of microhistory as a genre since its foundations by the likes of Carlo Ginzburg and Natalie Zemon Davis has been traced to various origins:[6] disquiet with positioning of the national at the centre of history writing; the potential for tracing individual lives across borders and periodisations in order to destabilise conventional distinctions; and the rise of transnational and global histories since the turn of the millennium. In some respects, then, Tamari's work is of a kind that is very much in vogue. It clearly occupies an early, if not pioneering, role in the rehabilitation of biography as a respectable form of history writing and in the validity of tracing the intimate details of the personal and individual as a historical methodology which both contributes to the multi-stranded richness of our understandings of the past and disrupts an excessive focus on histories of the nation-state and its power relations.

Yet, Salim Tamari's sustained focus on Palestinian lives poses an implicit challenge to the standard narrative of microhistory in a global context. One might argue that to reject national frameworks wholesale is a luxury available to those who do not belong to a nation the very existence of which is often denied,[7] and whose movement, including access to archives and travel in the course of their scholarship, is often curtailed as a result of the identities emblazoned on their official documents.[8] This argument implicitly enters into broader debates critiquing discourses of cosmopolitanism or nomadism in the sense used by the likes of Deleuze and Guattari or the Italian philosopher Rosi Braidotti, especially in respect to the strains of eurocentrism and blindness to white privilege embedded in some of these ideas. The details of these theoretical disagreements lie beyond the scope of this book, but suffice it to say that Tamari's example – the sense of both the scholar and his work – overlaps with that of the likes of Edward Said and other critical Palestinian voices. It overlaps in that it combines a scepticism regarding the value of the nation as an analytical category while simultaneously suggesting the political value of the notion of national liberation and the potential for emancipation within nationalist movements which may in other respects be reactionary.[9]

The final facet of Tamari's work that I will mention here similarly highlights the fundamentally political nature of his scholarship, his persistent and fierce yet almost gently expressed defence of Palestinian life and culture. This is the importance of Salim Tamari in foregrounding Jerusalem as a Palestinian city, past and present, both in his scholarship and in the institutions, particularly the journal *Jerusalem Quarterly*, in which he has played a central role as founding member. As Yair Wallach recently phrased it, 'Tamari and *Jerusalem Quarterly* have been instrumental in dismantling the idea of Jerusalem as, until the British Mandate, an ancient, backward, fanatical backwater of a city'.[10] The strand runs through all the aspects of Tamari's scholarship mentioned above; the Jerusalem personalities and lives brought to light, the focus on cultural and social richness, internal variation and interplay, and the blend of historical depth with political and emotional immediacy. This is decolonial scholarship in its truest sense, not only pushing insistently for the value of Palestinian voices and ideas in understanding and analysing history, but also reinforcing the intellectual and institutional barricades against the efforts of the Trumps, Netanyahus and Ir David Foundations of this world.

The ways in which the chapters in this volume pay explicit and implicit homage to Salim Tamari's work are myriad in number. Firstly, Mahmoud Yazbak presents a *longue durée* view of Jaffa, very much in Tamari's tradition of focusing on the social and cultural, rather than state, aspects of Palestinian history, and with the same insistence on the continuities of Palestinian society between the Ottoman and Mandate periods. Karène Summerer-Sanchez's portrait of the director of the Alliance israélite universelle school in Jerusalem, Albert Antebi, both highlights Tamari's direct impacts on the choices and directions of scholarship on Palestine; she follows his method of uncovering and exploring multiple strands of cultural and intellectual history through the study of a single life-story. Dotan Halevy similarly adopts a microhistorical technique, tracing the policies of the Mikveh Israel agricultural school towards its Palestinian students across the Ottoman and Mandate eras, using these to comment on the shifting activities of different forms of Zionism within Palestinian society. Sary Zananiri, meanwhile, takes up Tamari's pioneering interest in photography as a rich source for studying the changing dynamics of Palestinian society, again either side of the Great War, while Nadi Abusaada uses similar approaches towards materials such as maps and textbooks to engage one of Tamari's key themes – that is, changing conceptions of Palestine as a land and homeland and its borders and relations with other geographical imaginaries such as Southern Syria. Rawda Morkus-Makhoul then returns to Tamari's sociological roots, combining these methods with historical sources and analysis to provide an explicitly decolonial picture of the working lives of Palestinian *fellahat* in the

Mandate period. Chris Sandal-Wilson takes up Tamari's studies – best known from *Mountain Against the Sea* – of Palestinian nativist ethnography, comparing it with similar themes as treated by the French ethnographer Antonin Jaussen and relating the contents of such scholarship to the Mandate administration's policies on mental illness, particularly among Islamic communities. Sarah Irving's study of donations made to the fund to help victims of the 1927 Jericho earthquake pays homage to Tamari's technique of tracing multiple strands and networks from a single incident. And finally, Issam Nassar, a long-standing collaborator with Salim Tamari on books and articles, particularly biographies and works on Palestinian photography, offers an exploration of the ways in which Palestinian, Zionist and other photographers presented the Nakba and its aftermaths in their work.

Notes

1. Tamari, *Year of the Locust*; Tamari, Nassar and Elzeer, *The Storyteller of Jerusalem*; for summaries of life-writing in Palestinian and broader Arabic literatures, see Irving, Nassif and Khoury, *House of the Priest*, and Reynolds (ed.), *Interpreting the Self*.
2. 'Lepers, Lunatics and Saints'; 'With God's Camel'; 'The Enigmatic Bolshevik'.
3. Tamari, *Mountain Against the Sea*; idem, *Great War*.
4. Tamari, *Great War*, p. 67.
5. Ibid., pp. 106–8.
6. Most famously in volumes such as Zemon Davis, *The Return of Martin Guerre*; Ginzburg, *The Cheese and the Worms*; see also Gamsa, 'Biography and (Global) Microhistory'; Ghobrial, 'Introduction'.
7. Amara, 'Language, Identity and Conflict'; Peled-Elhanan, 'The Denial of Palestinian'; Rosemary Shinko, 'Discourses of Denial'.
8. Kraft, 'Palestinians Uncover'; Hammond, 'Palestinian Universities'.
9. Said, *Culture and Imperialism*, pp. xii–xiv et passim; 'Yeats and Decolonization', esp. pp. 74–76; *Peace and Its Discontents*, pp. 16–20 et passim; see also Hasso, 'The Women's Front'.
10. Yair Wallach, 'The Missionary School, the Museum, and the Tramway: The Networks of Late Ottoman Jerusalem', conference paper at *The Market for Biblical Antiquities, 1852–2022*, online/Agder University, 9–10 March 2022.

Bibliography

Amara, Muhammad. 'Language, Identity and Conflict: Examining Collective Identity through the Labels of the Palestinians in Israel'. *Journal of Holy Land and Palestine Studies* 15, 2 (2016): pp. 203–23.

Peled-Elhanan, Nurit. 'The Denial of Palestinian National and Territorial Identity in Israeli Schoolbooks of History and Geography 1996–2003'. In *Analysing Identities in Discourse*, ed. Rosana Dolón and Júlia Todolí, pp. 77–107. Amsterdam: John Benjamins, 2008.

Gamsa, Mark. 'Biography and (Global) Microhistory'. *New Global Studies* 11, 3 (2017): pp. 231–41.

Ghobrial, John-Paul. 'Introduction: Seeing the World like a Microhistorian'. *Past and Present* 242, supplement 14 (2019): pp. 1–22.

Ginzburg, Carlo. *The Cheese and the Worms: The Cosmos of a Sixteenth-Century Miller*. Baltimore: The Johns Hopkins University Press, 1980.

Hammond, Keith. 'Palestinian Universities and the Israeli Occupation'. *Policy Futures in Education* 5, 2 (2007): pp. 264–70.

Hasso, Frances. '"The Women's Front": Nationalism, Feminism and Modernity in Palestine'. *Gender and Society* 12, 4 (1998): pp. 441–65.

Irving, Sarah, Charbel Nassif and Karène Sanchez Summerer. *The House of the Priest: A Palestinian Life (1885–1954)*. Leiden: Brill, 2022.

Kraft, Dina. 'Palestinians Uncover History of the Nakba, Even as Israel Cuts Them Off From Their Sources'. *Ha'aretz*, 20 April 2018, https://www.haaretz.com/middle-east-news/palestinians/.premium.MAGAZINE-hidden-stories-of-the-nakba-1.6010350, accessed 31 December 2021.

Reynolds, Dwight F. (ed). *Interpreting the Self: Autobiography in the Arabic Literary Tradition*. Berkeley: University of California Press, 2001.

Said, Edward. 'Yeats and Decolonization'. In *Nationalism, Colonialism, Literature*, pp. 69–97. Minneapolis: University of Minnesota Press, 1990.

Said, Edward. *Culture and Imperialism*. New York: Vintage, 1993.

Said, Edward. *Peace and Its Discontents*. New York: Vintage, 1996.

Shinko, Rosemary. 'Discourses of Denial: Silencing the Palestinians, Delegitimizing Their Claims'. *Journal of International Affairs* 58, 1 (2004): pp. 47–72.

Tamari, Salim. 'With God's Camel in Siberia: The Russian Exile of an Ottoman Officer from Jerusalem'. *Jerusalem Quarterly* 35 (2008): pp. 31–50. Tamari, Salim. *Mountain Against the Sea: Essays on Palestinian Society and Culture*. Berkeley: University of California Press, 2009.

Tamari, Salim. *Year of the Locust: A Soldier's Diary and the Erasure of Palestine's Ottoman Past*. Berkeley: University of California Press, 2011.

Tamari, Salim, Issam Nassar and Nada Elzeer. *The Storyteller of Jerusalem: The Life and Times of Wasif Jawhariyyeh, 1904–1948*. Northampton: Interlink, 2014.

Tamari, Salim. *The Great War and the Remaking of Palestine*. Berkeley: University of California Press, 2017.

Zemon Davis, Natalie. *The Return of Martin Guerre*. Cambridge, MA: Harvard University Press, 1983.

CHAPTER 1

Jaffa before the Nakba: Palestine's Thriving City, 1799–1948

Mahmoud Yazbak

The story of the city of Jaffa in the modern era begins with a tragic crime. This was committed by the French army of occupation, led by Napoleon, when it invaded and occupied Jaffa for a short period on 6 March 1799. The city of Jaffa refused to surrender to the invaders, and when the French army entered it, it wreaked havoc and destruction, expelling the inhabitants and plundering the city. Contemporary sources describe the massacre committed by Napoleon's army against the people of Jaffa; Abd al-Rahman al-Jabarti, an Egyptian diarist, estimated the number of Yafis killed by the French army at 4,000.[1] A shocking description of the massacre was also written by the physician Étienne-Louis Malus, who accompanied the French army; he noted that 'the soldiers spread over all parts [of the town and] slaughtered men, women, old people, children, Christians, Turks; all this horrible inhuman picture was the victim of their fury'.[2]

Unfortunately, travellers or other contemporary narrative sources do not shed light on how local society reacted to Napoleon's massacre, but local records affirm the theme of this chapter: the city's resilience in the face of conflict and change. Indeed, as Salim Tamari has concluded, Jaffa re-emerged as a preeminent city in Palestine after each major catastrophe it faced during the nineteenth and mid-twentieth centuries.[3] But the *sijill* of Jaffa's *mahkama* or shari'a court is the only local source that touches on the question of how the society of Jaffa rebuilt itself after the shocking Napoleonic massacre. This information is found in the first volume that was written by the court after the withdrawal of the French troops from Jaffa. During the forty days of the French occupation of Jaffa, the shari'a court stopped its activity; the French troops set fire to it, and its *sijill* volumes were burned. The first volume of the *mahkama*'s *sijill*, which the *qadi* (judge) started to record immediately after the French withdrawal, contained many edicts and regulations sent from Istanbul, urging the local authorities in Jaffa to reorganise local government. The *sijill* entries also reflect the priorities of the population using the services of the local court immediately after the French withdrawal. This information clearly indicates that local society quickly returned to normal life, despite the trauma of the occupation and the depredations of Napoleon's troops.

The first entry of the *sijill* appeared on 14 Muharram 1214 AH/18 June 1799, with an order from Ahmed Pasha al-Jazzar (the *wali of* 'Akka) to preserve a box of letters left by the French troops in Jaffa.[4] Through the entries of the *sijill's* first volume we can trace how the local people behaved when they faced the dangers of invasion and occupation. It took only three weeks after the French withdrawal for the local shari'a court and other governance institutions to renew their activities. Those who had fled the town during its occupation started to return to their homes and businesses immediately after the French withdrawal. The owners of looted houses and those who had lost their property were the first to visit the shari'a court, in order to document their material losses. Many others used the court to document the inheritance of relatives who had been killed during the invasion and occupation.[5] Thus we witness how, immediately after the bloody invasion, people focused on how to ensure their daily living and basic needs. But not long after the occupation, people started to come to the court to register more ordinary social and economic cases, signalling the gradual return of life in Jaffa to some kind of normality. One month after the French withdrawal, a marriage was registered,[6] as well as cases of buying and selling.[7] These cases clearly indicate the return to normality which continued uninterrupted until World War I.

In addition to many descriptions and records in the *sijill* volumes concerning homes and stores looted by the French soldiers, the *sijill* entries draw a clear view of Jaffa's daily life at the beginning of the nineteenth century. One entry relates to land usage near the town's walls, which sheds light on Jaffa's social and political realities. The lands owned by the people of Jaffa were mostly cultivated as orange groves (*bayyarat*) and vegetable gardens. Many of these orange groves had been destroyed by the French troops, who camped in them during the siege of Jaffa.[8] The groves quickly returned to their flourishing state and generated large returns on the investments of the city's merchants and members of the elite, the *a'yan* or notables. The orange groves represented an investment opportunity which attracted entrepreneurs from different regions, especially Jerusalem, Nablus, Gaza and Ramla, who put large sums into this high-yielding sector of the local economy.[9]

After the French withdrawal, Jaffa witnessed a speedy return of refugees to their homes, along with newcomers, causing a major housing shortage. As a result, homeowners began renting out spare rooms. For example, a certain manager of the Wahbi Muharram *waqf* (endowment) rented out two large homes, containing eleven rooms in one case and twelve in the other, to twenty families who had migrated from northern Egypt to Jaffa.[10] The number of migrants – from Palestinian villages surrounding Jaffa, Nablus, Ramla and Gaza and from Egyptian villages, especially from the Delta region and Sharqiyya – increased during the first decade of the nineteenth century, deepening the housing crisis in Jaffa. They primarily came looking for work in the orange groves. This crisis created a new type of housing among the poorer strata of society, bringing together many families who were not connected by kinship and who were strangers to one another but shared a courtyard and facilities. This type of living became familiar in Jaffa, especially within the walled town. In other words, the privacy so often considered a feature of the Islamic city was blurred by economic and social necessity.

After the French withdrawal from Jaffa, the Ottoman authorities restored buildings that had been destroyed by the French, especially the city's castle, to restore peace to its people and persuade them to return to their city.[11] As Jaffa recovered from the Napoleonic invasion, the city suffered from a power struggle between Ahmed Pasha al-Jazzar and his heir Suleiman Pasha, the governors of 'Akka, and the governor of Jaffa, Muhammad Abu Maraq.[12] This conflict ended in 1805, when Muhammad Abu Nabbut took over the city of Jaffa. Abu Nabbut restored calm and tranquillity to Jaffa and put it on the path to development and change to become one of the most important cities on the Syrian coast in general and the Palestinian coast in particular. Some months after Napoleon's massacre, William Wittman arrived in Jaffa, accompanying the Ottoman and British troops on their way to fight the French. His description gives a sense of the status quo ante on which Abu Nabbut would build up the city:

> ... on the successful progress of the French in Syria, the principal and more wealthy of the inhabitants fled to Jerusalem, with their effects and merchandise, in consequent of which trade was altogether at a stand during our stay there. In times, however, of greater tranquillity, its commerce cannot be otherwise than flourishing, since, independently of the advantages of a sea-port, it maintains an intercourse by land with Damascus, Jerusalem, and several other places of no little importance in its vicinity.[13]

Abu Nabbut ruled the city of Jaffa until 1819,[14] a relatively long period in this era. He sought to raise his administrative position from *mutasallim* (the rank of ruler of a *sanjak* in the Ottoman system) to *wali* (the rank of a provincial governor, like al-Jazzar) and to change the administrative position of Jaffa from a *sanjak* or *mutasallimiyya* under 'Akka's administration to the centre of a *wilaya* or province in its own right, directly linked to Istanbul. In addition to his exertions to shift its administrative status, as a result of Abu Nabbut's extensive efforts, Jaffa witnessed a clear change in its general features, its appearance, its buildings and decoration; this is still visible to this day, despite the destruction that the city suffered later, especially in the aftermath of the Palestinian Nakba.

Among the most significant developments and architectural monuments of Abu Nabbut, we might mention the Islamic cemetery, which he built outside the city walls, on land previously known as *al-barriyya* or the wilderness,[15] the construction of markets inside Jaffa's walls and the expansion of the orchards outside the walls, as well as the building of a shipyard and new breakwater at the port. He also oversaw the renovation and fortification of the city's walls and the digging of a trench that surrounded the city from the land side,[16] and the restoration of the seven mills at Ras al-'Ayn (10 km to the east of Jaffa), the revenues of which were used to support a library and the students of a new school at Jaffa's Great Mosque.[17] Abu Nabbut also commissioned several important building projects, the results of which can still be seen in present-day Jaffa, including the reconstruction of the Great Mosque of Jaffa, known as al-Mahmudi, in memory of his son Mahmud,[18] and two *sabils* or water-fountains, the Mahmudiyya Sabil, also known as the Sabil Al-Juwwani, one of the masterpieces of Ottoman art (Figure 1.1).[19] Furthermore, he reconstructed the al-Shifa Sabil, also known as the Sabil al-Barrani, and later as the Sabil of Abu Nabbut, which is located on the road to Jerusalem 3 km outside Jaffa (Figure 1.2).[20]

The increased security and urbanisation witnessed by the city of Jaffa encouraged both the return of those inhabitants who had fled the French onslaught and the appearance of many immigrants to the city. As result, the city started to become overcrowded. Within the walls of Jaffa, a number of neighbourhoods were formed, the best-known amongst them including al-Qal'a (the castle), Sheikh Ibrahim, al-Naqib, al-Burj (the tower), al-Nasara (the Christians), al-Rum (the Greek Orthodox), al-Arman (the Armenians), al-Fellahin (the farmers),

Figure 1.1   The Mahmudiyya Sabil (al-Juwwani). Image courtesy of the author.

Figure 1.2   Sabil al-Shifa (al-Barrani). Image courtesy of the author.

al-Tabiya (named after a local mosque), al-Sidra (the name of a famous tree from the Qur'an), al-Marah (a place for animals to rest), al-Rumayla (the sandy land), Bibi (after the name of a famous family living in the neighbourhood), al-Zawiya (a Sufi convent), al-Shaykh Raslan al-Bakri, al-Ashrafiyyah, al-Hashshash (a family name), al-Zanat (also the name of a family) and Shaykh Jum'a. In addition to the growth of residential areas, the sources refer to the return and revival of the economic facilities that had existed in the city before the Napoleonic invasion, including three soap factories and three sesame oil presses. In 1810, two additional soap factories were established. Meanwhile, foreign countries began to appoint consuls in Jaffa to look after their growing commercial interests.

Jaffa Oranges

Since the beginning of the nineteenth century, Jaffa's economic features had crystallised in two main branches: the port as a crossing point connecting the coast to the Palestinian interior, and the cultivation of and trade in oranges and other citrus fruit. Abu Nabbut showed a special interest in both branches and personally owned a large fleet of feluccas – the boats that transported goods and travellers to and from the quayside to the large ships anchored in the deeper waters offshore. He also invested and encouraged investment in the cultivation of orchards, which began to extend outside the town's walls to cover large areas of the plains extending towards the cities of Ramla in the east and Gaza to the south.[21]

As the importance of Jaffa oranges increased, shaping the city's economy, investments were concentrated in the hands of rich merchants who were able to manage complex commercial networks. Usually, the branches of these commercial networks extended between the ports of Damietta, Jaffa and Istanbul. The Jaffa orange merchants in these Mediterranean ports owned large warehouses and used a number of agents to take care of their far-flung commercial interests.

The orange groves were the most important investment for Jaffa merchants, and usually this was very profitable, but it drained a lot of money before yielding a return. In order for an orchard to start generating profits, the investor was forced to buy a large plot of land and establish a very expensive irrigation system, which included digging a well, constructing a large pool to collect water and excavating channels to transport water to the trees. The owner of the orchard also hired between three and five specialised workers (biyyari) who were employed to maintain the groves throughout the year. During the fruit-picking period, a large number of additional workers were hired. In order to yield profits, the investor had to create a sophisticated marketing network. Usually, Jaffa citrus fruit found its way to the Egyptian market, and the success of this marketing depended on the experience and efficiency of commercial networks and agents in Egypt.[22]

Orange dealers and orchards depended on their local connections to protect their large investments in orange cultivation and trade. At the beginning of the nineteenth century, most of the Jaffa merchants' orchards were located near the 'Auja River, far from the city and near the areas under the control of the Abu Kishk tribe, the most powerful in the Jaffa region, who also operated the water mills located along the river's course. In order to conduct their business, Jaffa's merchants developed economic links with the chiefs of the tribe, hiring caravans of Abu Kishk camels to transport oranges from the orchards to the port and employing a number of tribe members to guard the orchards.[23]

With Ibrahim Pasha's invasion of and nine-year rule over Palestine from 1831 onwards, the control of the Mamluk families in Palestine, which followed al-Jazzar's reign and included Abu Nabbut in Jaffa, came to an end.[24] Unlike the Napoleonic invasion that brought destruction and massacres to Jaffa, Ibrahim Pasha's forces did not harm either the infrastructure or the city's residents. During the period of Egyptian rule, the number of immigrants to Jaffa increased. A large number of Egyptian peasants migrated to the Jaffa region, joining their predecessors. As the number of orchards increased and their areas expanded, the demand for agricultural workers increased, which attracted many Egyptian immigrants, and new villages appeared outside the walls of the Old City and in the Jaffa countryside. These new villages were called sakanat, and in the beginning they were inhabited by these immigrants. The most famous of these sakanat were Sakanat al-'Abid (village or settlement of the Black Africans), most of whose inhabitants came from Sudan, and Sakanat Irshid to the north of the old town.[25] When they were first set up, most of these *sakanat* were inhabited by workers employed in the orchards and businesses related to the orange trade. Over time, some of these *sakanat* became neighbourhoods of Jaffa. All of them were destroyed by the State of Israel after the Nakba, and no trace of them remains.

After the departure of Ibrahim Pasha and Egyptian rule from Palestine in 1840, Jaffa oranges became a major export product, mostly sold to the Egyptian and Anatolian markets, especially Istanbul. The rapid expansion of this cultivation as a result of the increasing demand for Jaffa oranges was reflected in the influx of large investors and the richest people from the Palestinian interior as well as the wider Levant to invest enormous amounts in this field.[26]

As investment in the citriculture sector required large sums of money, the orchards belonged exclusively to major investors. Since the 1830s, there had been investors who belonged to major merchant families of Nablus and Jerusalem and who established branches in Jaffa. Many Christian immigrants, especially from Lebanon, joined this sector as well, and they counted among the most important investors, helping to establish orchards and the citrus trade. The Jaffa orange groves extended over vast areas of the district's lands to the east and even beyond the city of Ramla.

Until the 1870s, most investors continued to reside within the walls of Jaffa, and they usually invested also in other commercial sectors. An investor in the orange sector usually had to wait around seven or eight years before the orchard started to yield a consistent profit. Orange cultivation consumed large initial sums to provide the necessary abundant quantities of water, as the trees needed constant irrigation during the seven summer months. Year-round water supplies derived from two sources in the Jaffa area: from the 'Auja River, described above, and from groundwater. To extract groundwater, a well was dug to a depth ranging between 3 and 20 m. The irrigation system included a device for drawing water known as *saqiya* (a type of waterwheel), which was usually driven by a camel or other animal. The water drawn by the *saqiya* poured into a storage pool. The water then flowed from the pool by means of channels dug throughout the orchard, and from these channels into a small hole that surrounded each tree. Establishing and maintaining such an irrigation system throughout the year required a large initial investment and a substantial number of workers. In addition, the owner of the grove had to spend large sums of money to weed the land and keep agricultural pests away.

Despite these costs, an 1881 report by the British Consul from Jaffa noted that investments in orange groves were considered the most profitable.[27] At the beginning of the 1880s, the staff of the American Consulate in Jaffa estimated the number of groves around Jaffa to be 500, and the number of trees at least 800,000.[28] During the three decades between 1850 and 1880, the land occupied by orchards around Jaffa had quadrupled.[29]

From the available statistical sources on the export of oranges since the mid-nineteenth century, one can see that in 1856 about twenty million oranges were exported.[30] By 1873, the number of orange orchards belonging to Jaffa had reached 420, producing about 33.3 million oranges. The local market consumed one-sixth of this quantity, and the rest was exported to Egypt and Asia Minor.[31] Since 1875 Jaffa has exported large quantities of oranges to Europe (mainly France, Germany, Austria and Russia). Exports to Europe – that is, over long distances – increased significantly when oranges began to be wrapped and packed in wooden crates to preserve them during the complex transportation process.

Despite these improvements, not all types of oranges were suitable for export. The smooth orange, in the shape of an egg and with a thick peel, was more suitable for long-distance transport than others. The smaller, thin-skinned oranges, known as *baladi*, were mostly consumed in the local market. In 1880, Jaffa's production was estimated to be around thirty-six million oranges.[32] Since oranges were an export product, destined for international markets, and have a much shorter shelf life than soap or olive oil, the orchards had to be established relatively near to a port to quickly transport the product from there to the boats. As Jaffa was the only export port for central and southern Palestine, the city of Jaffa was affected both by the increase in the volume of foreign trade and by

Figure 1.3   Picking and packing oranges in wooden crates, c. 1900–1920. Courtesy of Library of Congress, G. Eric and Edith Matson Photograph Collection.

the waves of pilgrims coming to Jerusalem. The development of the port and of means of communication with Jerusalem thus became the main concern for merchants in Jaffa, its local government and foreign consuls. With the rapid growth of the capital cycle, the transit of goods and passenger traffic in the 1870s and 1880s, the need for a new operating system for Jaffa's docks could no longer be ignored.[33] In 1864, a French company built a modern lighthouse for the port,[34] and the Ottoman government took the initiative to make some improvements to the ship berths, but these steps soon became inadequate. In the face of government inaction, a number of Jaffa businessmen broke away and set up a local association. In 1875, they bought a small steam engine from Marseilles and installed it in the port of Jaffa to facilitate movement and communication between land and ships anchored at sea.[35]

Since the 1850s, Jaffa and Jerusalem merchants had repeatedly asked the local government to build a highway between the two cities. Several attempts were made to improve the road conditions so as to facilitate the transit of goods and people between the two cities, which were separated by an uneven and insecure road through steep hills. In 1867, after the central government had finally been convinced of the importance of this project, it began constructing the road, which was officially opened in 1868. Vehicles began running daily: in the 1890s around thirty to forty wagons ran daily, transporting passengers. At the same time, demands from merchants and investors to build a railway between Jaffa and Jerusalem also increased, with construction finally beginning in 1890.

The economy of Jaffa depended mostly on import and export trade and on work related to pilgrims going to Jerusalem. Since the middle of the nineteenth century, the importance of these economic sectors had increased, and Europeans also started to participate in the operation and management of these businesses. From the late 1890s onwards, Zionist investors also started to pay attention to the citriculture sector. Estimates from the 1870s indicate that about 5,000 people from Jaffa worked in the orchards during the orange-picking, -wrapping and -packing season. Moreover, there were about 3,000 permanent workers who worked in the orchards throughout the year.[36]

The continuous growth of trade in general, and of the orange sector in particular, revived Jaffa and sped up its development. Although the city was surrounded by walls and a moat with a single gate, the great merchants, beginning in the mid-nineteenth century, took the initiative to build large and luxurious homes in their groves around the city walls and extending along the main roads linking Jerusalem, Gaza, Nablus and Ramla. Under pressure, especially from the merchants, the local government agreed to open another gate in the city walls. Five years later, it also demolished part of the wall. In 1874, the government removed all the walls and defences that surrounded Jaffa and sold the stones to construct the buildings that were being erected along al-Hilweh Street, which was built in 1875 and had until then been the site of the wall and the moat. This street became the new commercial centre of Jaffa. Until then, Jaffa had been described as a Greek theatre because it was built on a hill that slopes steeply towards the sea. But in only a few short years after the walls had been removed, the city's shape changed, and it began to extend towards the east on the flat land, towards the orchards. And the more the city expanded eastwards, the more the Jaffa citrus groves extended towards the city of Ramla.

The orange groves were mostly owned by urban investors, but a major shift occurred in the mid-nineteenth century. The owners of the older groves did not practice the orange trade themselves, but usually sold their produce to intermediaries. The owners of the new groves were mostly merchants, and they considered the grove as just one of their total investments and another branch of their trade. To increase their profits and speed up the marketing of their product, the new owners developed complex business networks. This network began in the orchard itself, where the owner needed an expert to manage the affairs and maintenance of the orchard, and to hire workers for picking and packaging, as well as other teams for packing the wooden crates to protect the oranges during the long-distance transportation process.

The orange merchants and investors in the wells around Jaffa were among the city's largest owners of capital, and they also were among the first to take up new technologies to increase their profits and production. They contributed substantially to the development and modernisation of the Palestinian economy and the transfer of modern technologies. The technology of modern irrigation systems was one of the first to be absorbed in the early 1890s. An official report from 1890 stated that sixty steam engines to draw water were operating at full capacity in the Jaffa orchards. Despite the high cost of steam engines, the demand for them increased after new markets opened for Jaffa oranges.[37] And the increase in demand and high profits encouraged rich investors to increase their investments in this field. Reports indicate that the orchard area surrounding Jaffa expanded from 7,500 *dunams* in 1890 to 12,000 in 1904 and more than 30,000 in 1914. At the same time, the increase in the number of orange crates exported from Jaffa was very dramatic: from 260,000 in 1895 to 500,000 in 1905, and then a jump to 1.5 million in the 1913/14 season. Of these, 1,200,000 crates, or 80 percent, came from groves that were owned by Arabs, and the rest were owned by the German Templars or the Jewish sector.[38]

Aspects of Cultural and Social Life in Jaffa: 'Oh, You Take Me to Rubin or Divorce Me!'

Jaffa's economic position was reflected in its social and cultural life. The seasonal visit to the shrine of the Prophet Rubin (Biblical Reuben) constituted a legacy that reflected the extent of the social and cultural openness of Jaffa before the

Nakba. It was not a coincidence that a famous saying, related to the city's heritage, became the feminist saying: 'Oh, you take me to Rubin or divorce me'. This means that the wife required her husband to choose between taking her to participate in the celebrations of the Prophet Rubin or divorcing her.

The shrine (*maqam*) of the Prophet Rubin is located near the mouth of the Rubin River, south of Jaffa. This shrine had a *mawsim*, or season – that is, a public visit at a set time of the year, for a specific period.[39] The Rubin season became a key element of social life when economic conditions in the city improved. It extended over a whole month, corresponding to the end of the orange-picking season, which usually occurred during September. The sources indicate that thousands of Jaffa residents annually participated in this *mawsim*, which in the city's cultural heritage acquired the character of a resort. During the *mawsim*, people set up thousands of tents on the sandy lands surrounding the shrine of Nabi Rubin near the seashore and the banks of the river. In essence, visitors or vacationers set up a temporary tent city, with a population of between 30,000 and 50,000, for a whole month. During the Rubin *mawsim*, Jaffa was empty for a month, with most of its residents gathering on the banks of the Rubin River.

During the Rubin Mawsim, markets were set up for all kinds of goods; cafés and restaurants sprang up; and places of entertainment abounded. In this *mawsim*,

Figure 1.4   The *ziyara* to Rubin Mawsim, 1930s. Image courtesy of Library of Congress, G. Eric and Edith Matson Photograph Collection.

theatrical groups presented their shows. Some were local groups, but troupes came from as far away as Beirut, Damascus and Cairo to entertain the vacationers. It is notable that these shows were presented sequentially and alternately for both men and women. In advertisements for theatrical performances, advertisers would announce separate show times for women and men. From the 1930s onwards, movies were also shown in the open air for the enjoyment and entertainment of vacationers. Famous singers from all over Palestine and even from Egypt and Lebanon came specifically for the Rubin celebrations.

Rubin Mawsim provided women in particular with an opportunity to break free, even if only temporarily, from the social and cultural frameworks that confined them within four walls and from going out into the public space. It gave them an opportunity to participate in a recreational activity that mixed genders yet was socially acceptable. This waiting and yearning for the season every year occupied the minds of many women in Jaffa, as expressed in the memoirs of Salwa Abu Al-Jebeen.[40]

What must be emphasised here is that the Rubin Mawsim, which had originated as a religious season, changed its character to become popular, while religion became a secondary consideration. Thus, Rubin Mawsim gradually became a Jaffa social season, allowing Christians and Muslims to participate and enjoy its recreational atmosphere as members of one community and one city, men and women.

The civil or secular nature of men and women spending their time in the Rubin Mawsim space reflected the social changes in Palestinian civil society in general and Jaffa society in particular, which began in the late Ottoman era. The popular desire for temporary liberation from the monotony, demands and pressures of daily life in the city, as well as the resort to a long summer vacation to renew themselves and their activities near the seashore and the riverbank, indicates more than anything else the manifestations of modern and urban life in Jaffa before the Nakba. While Jaffa remained an Arab city during the Mandate, not a mixed city, it provided a vivid example of the meanings of modernity, urbanisation and cosmopolitanism in pre-1948 Palestinian society.[41]

After the year of the Nakba, 1948, the Nabi Rubin Mawsim was interrupted after Jaffa and its rural hinterland, as well as the neighbouring cities of Ramleh and al-Lud, were subjected to ethnic cleansing and the expulsion of more than ninety-seven per cent of their population outside the borders of their homeland. As for the shrine of Rubin itself, it was taken over by a Jewish group and judaised.[42] The nearby mosque was demolished, although some of its traces are still visible.

Cultural Manifestations

By the late Ottoman period, the port and the train linked Jaffa to the world beyond Palestine and to the country's interior. In addition, Jaffa society enjoyed a diversity of cultures and languages among its inhabitants because of the uninterrupted migration to it. From the end of the Ottoman era, numerous cultural and literary institutions and associations were established in Jaffa, with dozens springing up before the Nakba.

Among these, the Islamic Sports Club, established in 1926, was noteworthy, with its active members including both Christians and Muslims.[43] Its activities included literary events, and it was visited by many Arab poets from Iraq, Egypt, Syria and Lebanon. The club hosted sports events and established teams in many different fields, the most important of which were a boxing team, basketball, table tennis, weightlifting, billiards and football. In partnership with the Supreme Muslim Council, the club set up a small football ground near the al-Qishleh building and later, in partnership with the municipality, in Ard al-Bassa built a large stadium that could accommodate 10,000 spectators.

The Orthodox Youth Club was also famous in Palestine. It was a cultural and sports club, founded in 1924, and hosted many activities, including cultural and literary lectures and theatrical performances. It also established sports teams that competed at the national level. The club's basketball, table tennis, billiards and football teams were all national champions, and it possessed a world-class football stadium called the Orthodox Club Stadium, located next to the Orthodox College near Tallat al-'Araqtanji. Other well-known associations in Jaffa included the Muslim Youth Association, the Arab Club, the Student Club, the Olympic Club (a sports club), the Youth Club, the Literary Forum and dozens of other clubs and associations.

Many women's associations from Jaffa also became famous, such as the Orthodox Women's Association, which was founded before World War I.[44] The Women's Solidarity Association was concerned with culture in general and emphasised the role of women in society, hosting many famous writers from the Arab world in the 1930s and 1940s.[45] The Arab Women's Association similarly promoted the public role of women;[46] in addition to its literary and cultural activities, the association established a workshop to teach girls the arts of tailoring and sewing. Other well-established women's groups included the National Women's Association and the Arab Women's League.

The first theatres appeared in Jaffa at the end of the nineteenth century, such as al-Zarafiyya Theatre, al-Bannur Coffee Theatre, Parisiana Theatre and al-Halwani Café Theatre.[47] From the 1920s onwards, there appeared new venues that also included movie theatres, including the al-Tubaji Cinema, named after its owner Abdul Rahman Al-Tubaji. The city's cultural clubs also established spaces where theatre plays and films were shown, including the Sports Club Theatre and the Arab Club Theatre. Many theatrical groups performed over two seasons during the year: the summer season began at the Rubin Mawsim, while in the winter they performed on the Jaffa theatre circuit. Many Egyptian troupes visited Jaffa and performed in the city's theatres.[48] Jaffa's cafés were also famous for setting up smaller theatres within them, such as the Abu Shakush coffee theatre.

In the 1920s and 1930s, a group of cinemas was also established in Jaffa, the most important and luxurious of which was the Al-Hamra Cinema; the beautiful building still stands today. This was a favourite destination for Jaffa's families. Other cinemas emerged, including the Nabil, Apollo, al-Sharq, al-Rashid, Farouk, al-Salahi, Tubaji, Fanqul and 'Aden Cinemas.[49]

Alongside the arts and entertainment, Jaffa equally played an important role in the Palestinian press. *Al-Taraqqi* was the first newspaper to be published in Jaffa, in 1907.[50] In 1908, *al-Asma'i*, a bi-monthly social magazine, was launched. *Al-I'tidal* newspaper was published in 1910, and in the same year *al-Huriyya* magazine was established. In 1911, the weekly newspaper *al-Akhbar* joined them. The year 1911 also saw the foundation of the most important Palestinian newspaper of the pre-Nakba era, *Filastin*, established by the brothers 'Isa and Yusif al-'Isa. In all, between 1910 and 1948, about fifty newspapers and magazines were published in Jaffa.[51]

This boom in press publications based in Jaffa was accompanied by the emergence of a large group of modern publishing and printing houses. Among these, we might mention the al-Matb'a al-Wataniyya (National Press), Matba'at Filastin (Palestine Press), Matba'at al-Nasr, Gharabi Press, al-'Asriyya (Modern) Press and others, some of which operated until the year of the Nakba. Between 1918 and 1948, the number of printing and publishing houses in Jaffa reached thirty-eight.

All of this was accompanied by an expansion of the number of libraries, including the al-'Asriyya Library, the Al-Sifri, the al-Tahir, al-Maktabah al-'Ilmiyya al-Filistiniyya (the Palestine Scientific Library) and many others. Two public libraries were also famous, namely the Islamic Khazanah Library and the Abu Nabbut Library, the latter having been founded at the beginning of the nineteenth century by Abu Nabbut at the Mahmudi Mosque, as mentioned above.[52]

Jaffa's active and lively cultural life would not be complete without the presence of dozens of cafés that used its halls for artistic and musical performances. Great singers of the 1930s and 1940s from Egypt and other countries came to Jaffa and sang on its stages, such as Umm Kulthum and the musician Muhammad 'Abd al-Wahab. In his encyclopaedia, Ali al-Bawwab collected the names of seventy-five cafés in Jaffa before 1948.[53] In addition to these, night clubs appeared, where song and music were performed by bands both local and from Egypt, Syria and Lebanon. Among the most famous of these was the al-Zarifiyya nightclub near the Clock Square, the Abu Shakush, the Parisiana, the al-Dalu, the Ghantus and the Taj Mahal.

The End

The pulse of life in Jaffa stopped and was cut off from its past as well as from its wide cultural connections across the Arab world when Israeli forces occupied it in 1948. Jaffa, like the rest of Palestine, was devastated, stone buildings were demolished, the orchards were cut down, the waterways and the waterwheels were destroyed. The people who had made the Rubin Mawsim became refugees, and Rubin's sands became a training camp for Israeli army units. No Arabic printing or publishing houses survived; theatres were demolished; only the Al-Hamra Cinema remained; it was confiscated, and those among the people of Jaffa who were able to stay in their homeland which became Israel were forbidden to use it.

The Zionist establishment worked hard to judaise Jaffa's spaces and erase its glorious past,[54] so that it would appear to the stranger as if Jaffa had never been there.

Notes

1. Al-Jabarti, *Aja'ib al-Athar*, vol. 2, p. 261. See also *sijill* of the *shari'a* court of Jaffa, vol. 1, p. 1, and many other entries.
2. Malus, *L'agenda de Malus*, p. 135.
3. Tamari, *The Great War*; see especially pp. 46–50, dedicated to Jaffa.
4. Sijill of Jaffa, vol. 1, p. 60, 14 Muharram 1214 AH\18 June 1799.
5. Sijill, vol. 1, p. 60, 17 Muharram 1214 AH/21 June 1799.
6. Sijill, vol. 1, pp. 60–61, 18 Muharram 1214 AH/22 June 1799.
7. Sijill, vol. 1, p. 61, 19 Muharram 1214 AH/23 June 1799.
8. Sijill, vol. 1, p. 60, 17 Muharram 1214 AH/21 June 1799.
9. Sijill, vol. 1, p. 65, 1 Safar 1214 AH/5 July 1799.
10. Sijill, vol. 8, p. 24, 1 Dhi al-Hijja 1211 AH/27 May 1797.
11. Wittman, *Travels in Turkey*, p. 205.
12. For a detailed story of this conflict, see Yazbak, *Madinat al-Burtuqal*, pp. 46–83.
13. Wittman, *Travels in Turkey*, p. 127.
14. Sijill, vol. 4, pp. 238–39, 9 Jumada 1234 AH/5 April 1819.
15. Sijill, vol. 2, p. 230, 1 Dhi al-Qi'da 1220 AH/21 February 1806.
16. Sijill, vol. 4, p. 93, Mid Sha'ban 1232 AH/30 June 1817.
17. Manuscript of al-Sabil al-Mubarak, p. 44.
18. Sijill, vol. 2, pp. 282–83, 15–19 Dhi al-Qi'da 1223 AH/1–5 January 1809.
19. Manuscript of *al-Sabil al-Mubarak*, al-Najah University, Nablus, Manuscripts division no. 234.
20. Sijill, vol. 48, p. 260, 5 Rabi' 2 1297 AH/16 March 1880.
21. For detailed information on Abu Nabbut's investments in orchards cultivation see Sijill, vol. 1, p. 21; vol. 2, p. 31, p. 179. See also Mustafa Kabha and Nahum Karlinsky's *The Lost Orchard*. In this study, Kabha and Karlinsky tell the story of the Palestinian citrus industry from its inception until 1950, tracing the shifting relationship between Palestinian Arabs and Zionist Jews.
22. Yazbak, 'Penetration of Urban Capital', pp. 252–65.
23. Yazbak, 'A Mamluk Household in Jaffa', pp. 33–45; Yazbak, *Madinat al-Burtuqal*, pp. 210–11; Sijill, vol. 9, p. 70, 28 Rabi' Thani 1256 AH/28 June 1840.

24. Yazbak, 'Palestinian Commercial Networks', pp. 7–10.
25. Other famous *sakanat* were al-'Ajami, al-Maslakh, al-Jabaliyya, Abu-Kbir, Darwish, Abu Taha, al-Hulwa, al-'Arayna, al-Danayta, Abu Humam, al-Manshiyya, al-'Azm, Hammad, Sumayl, Tal-al-Rish, Karm al-Tut and al-Ghazazwi.
26. Yazbak, 'Palestinian Commercial Networks', pp. 12–14.
27. Ibid., vol. LXXI, Jaffa, May 1882; Thomson, *The Land and the Book*, p. 519.
28. Owen, *The Middle East*, p. 178.
29. Schölch, *Palestine in Transformation*, p. 92.
30. Public Record Office (hereafter PRO), Foreign Office (hereafter FO) / 78, vol. 1419, Jaffa, 17 May 1856.
31. Great Britain, Parliamentary Papers, vol. LXVII, Jerusalem, February 1874; Schölch, *Palestine in Transformation*, p. 92.
32. Great Britain, Parliamentary Papers, vol. XC, Beirut, 19 March 1881.
33. Ibid., p. 135.
34. Parliamentary Papers, vol. LXI, Jaffa, May 1864; PRO, FO,78, vol. 1834, Jaffa, 9 November 1864.
35. Schölch, *Palestine in Transformation*, p. 136.
36. Parliamentary Papers, vol. LXXIV, Jaffa, February 1880.
37. Kabha and Karlinsky, *The Lost Orchard*, Chapter 2, pp. 73–105.
38. Franghia, 'Report on Irrigation', p. 2.
39. For a detailed study of the Nabi Rubin *ziyara*, see Yazbak, 'The Muslim Festival'.
40. Abu al-Jibin, *Shahadat Taliba*, p. 29.
41. Hammami, 'Gender, Nakba and Nation', p. 261.
42. Benvenisti, *Sacred Landscape*, p. 274.
43. Al-Bawwab, *Mawsu'at Yafa al-Jamila*, p. 1179.
44. Ibid., p. 1194.
45. Dhiyab et al, *Yafa 'Itru Madinah*, p. 179.
46. Al-Mawsu'a al-Falastiniyya, Damascus, Hay'at al-Mawsu'a al-Falastiniyya, vol. 2, 1990, p. 216.
47. The activity of a coffeehouse theatre is detailed through a complaint preserved in the Ottoman Archives. Başbakanlık Osmanlı Arşivi (hereafter BOA), DH.MKT. 1234\77\4.
48. *Majallat al-Fluka*, December 1996, vol. 27, pp. 15–25.
49. Al-Bawwab, *Mawsu'at Yafa al-Jamila*, vol. 2, p. 1205.
50. *Al-Mawsu'a al-Falastiniyya*, vol. 3, pp. 13–18.
51. Yahushuwa', *Al-Sahafa al-'Arabiyya*; see also Sulayman, *Ta'rikh al-Sahafa*.
52. For detailed research about Abu Nabbut's library, see Yazbak, *Madinat al-Burtuqal*, pp. 112–14; *Al-Mawsu'a al-Falastiniyya*, vol. 4, p. 287; Haykal, *Ayyam al-Siba*, p. 161.
53. Al-Bawwab, *Mawsu'at Yafa al-Jamila*.
54. On the judaisation of Jaffa and resistance to it by Palestinian inhabitants, see especially the work of Yara Sa'di-Ibraheem in 'Jaffa's Times' and 'Settler Colonial Temporalities'; see also Shaindlinger, 'Wishful Landscapes'.

Bibliography

Abu al-Jibin, Salwa. *Shahadat Taliba min Yafa* (Testimony of a Schoolgirl from Jaffa). Amman: Dar Ward, 2009.

Al-Bawwab, Ali Hasan. *Mawsu'at Yafa al-Jamila* (Encyclopaedia of Beautiful Jaffa). Beirut: al-Mua'ssassah al-'Arabiyya, 2003.

Benvenisti, Meron. *Sacred Landscape: The Buried History of the Holy Land Since 1948.* Berkeley: University of California Press, 2000.

Dhiyab, Imtiyaz. *Yafa 'Itru Madinah.* Beirut: Dar al-Fata al-'Arabi, 1991.

Franghia, Georges. *Report on Irrigation and Orange Growing at Jaffa.* London: Foreign Office, Miscellaneous Series, no. 300, Reports on Subjects of General and Commercial Interest, 1893.

Hammami, Rema. 'Gender, Nakba and Nation: Palestinian Women's Presence and Absence in the Narration of 1948 Memories'. In *Across the Wall: Narratives of Israeli-Palestinian History*, edited by Ilan Pappé and Jamil Hilal, pp. 235–68. London: I. B. Tauris, 2010.

Haykal, Yusuf. *Ayyam al-Siba: Suwwar min al-Hayat wa-Safahat min al-Tarikh.* Amman: Dar al-Jalil, 1988.

Al-Jabarti, Abd al-Rahman. *Aja'ib al-Athar fi al-Tarajim wa-al-Akhbar* (4 vols). Cairo: National Library Press, 1997.

Kabha, Mustafa and Nahum Karlinsky. *The Lost Orchard: The Palestinian-Arab Citrus Industry, 1850–1950.* Syracuse: Syracuse University Press, 2021.

Malus, Étienne Louis. *L'agenda de Malus: Souvenirs de l'expédition d'Égypte, 1798–1801.* Paris: Honoré Champion, 1892.

Owen, Roger. *The Middle East in the World Economy, 1800–1914.* London: I. B. Tauris, 1981.

Sa'di-Ibraheem, Yara. 'Settler Colonial Temporalities, Ruinations and Neoliberal Urban Renewal: The Case of Suknet Al-Huresh in Jaffa'. *GeoJournal* 87, 2 (2020): pp. 661–75.

Sa'di-Ibraheem, Yara. 'Jaffa's Times: Temporalities of Dispossession and the Advent of Natives' Reclaimed Time'. *Time & Society* 29, 2 (2020): pp. 340–61.

Schölch, Alexander. *Palestine in Transformation, 1856–1882: Studies in Social, Economic and Political Development.* Washington: Institute for Palestine Studies, 1993.

Shaindlinger, Noa. 'Wishful Landscapes: Protest and Spatial Reclamation in Jaffa'. *Comparative Studies of South Asia, Africa and the Middle East* 39, 2 (2019): pp. 313–27.

Sulayman, Muhammad. *Ta'rikh al-Sahafa al-Filistiniyya 1876–1976.* Ramallah: al-Ittihad al-'Am lil-kuttab, 1988.

Tamari, Salim. *The Great War and the Making of Palestine.* Berkeley: University of California Press, 2017.

Thomson, W. M. *The Land and the Book: Or Biblical Illustrations Drawn from the Manners and Customs, the Scenes and Scenery of the Holy Land.* London: T. Nelson, 1901.

Wittman, William. *Travels in Turkey, Asia-Minor, Syria and Across the Desert into Egypt During the Years 1799, 1800 and 1801, In Company with the Turkish Army and the British Military Mission to Which are Annexed, Observations on the Plague, and on the Diseases Prevalent in Turkey*. London: Richard Phillips, 1803.

Yahushuwaʻ, Yaʻqub. *Al-Shafa al-ʻArabiyya Fi Filastin Fi Nihayat al-Intidab al-Baritani ʻAla Filastin 1930–1948*. Shafa Amru: Dar al-Mashriq, 1983.

Yazbak, Mahmoud. 'The Muslim Festival of Nabi Rubin in Palestine: From Religious Festival to Summer Resort'. *Holy Land Studies* 10, 2 (2011): pp. 169–98.

Yazbak, Mahmoud. 'Palestinian Commercial Networks in Transformation, 1750–1900'. *Sociology Study* 2, 11 (2012): pp. 805–18.

Yazbak, Mahmoud. *Madinat al-Burtuqal: Yafa, Hadara wa-Mujtamaʻ 1700–1840*. Beirut: Mu'ssasat al-Dirasat al-Filastiniyya, 2018.

Yazbak, Mahmoud. 'Penetration of Urban Capital into the Palestinian Countryside: The Beginnings, Jaffa in the 1830s'. In *Life on the Ottoman Border, Essays in Honour of Nenad Moačanin*, edited by Vjeran Kursar, pp. 252–65. Zagreb: University of Zagreb, Faculty of Humanities and Social Sciences Press, 2022.

Yazbak, Mahmoud. 'A Mamluk Household in Jaffa: The Case of Abu Nabbut (1805–1819)'. In *From the Household to the Wider World: Local Perspectives on Urban Institutions in Late Ottoman Bilad al-Sham*, edited by Yuval Ben-Bassat and Johann Buessow, pp. 33–45. Tübingen: Tübingen University Press, 2022.

CHAPTER 2

To 'Strengthen Mediterranean Resistance'? Albert Antebi and the Porous Boundaries of Cultural Identification in Ottoman Jerusalem, 1896–1919

Karène Sanchez Summerer

In correspondence with his superiors from the Alliance Israélite Universelle (AIU) in Paris in 1913, the organisation's Jerusalem school director Albert Antebi/ Ibrahim Entaibi[1] underlined the need to strengthen, in his opinion, a 'Mediterranean resistance', echoing the expression of a French minister, against the German paradigm of parts of the Zionist movement.[2] He pointed out the need to reinforce the economic development of Palestine, envisaging it as much as an Ottoman and Jewish reality as a French one, within the framework of an ongoing capitulations system and in line with enterprises begun in the early 1880s, such as the Rothschild-sponsored colonies.[3] This letter highlights the ways in which Antebi saw the entangled relations within which he existed in Palestine in the first two decades of the twentieth century: through Franco-German national and cultural competition in the region; the contest between cultural and political or 'Oriental' and European schools of Zionist thought; and economic-cultural versus political-national models of Jewish integration into the wider society of the Ottoman Levant.

This article focuses on the period between 1909, in the aftermath of the Young Turk revolution, and Antebi's death in 1919, during which he remained the 'consul of the Jews'[4] for many Arab Palestinians, members of the Jewish communities and French actors of the Jerusalem scene, as well as French Jewish actors in Paris. Homo ottomanicus *par excellence* for many,[5] Abraham Albert Antebi (1873–1919) was director of the Alliance Israélite Universelle (AIU) vocational school in Jerusalem from 1896 to 1913, representative of the Jewish Colonisation Association (ICA) from 1899 to 1913, land buyer for Baron Edmond de Rothschild and for the Lovers of Zion (founded in Russia in the 1880s to encourage emigration to Palestine), advisor to Cemal Pasha from early 1915 to October 1916, friend of Meir Dizengoff (founder and first mayor of Tel Aviv) and of Said Effendi al-Husayni (mayor of Jerusalem 1902–6 and deputy to the Ottoman Parliament), godfather of Amin el-Husayni (the later

Haj Amin), 'liberator' of David Ben Gurion and Isaac Ben Zvi, soldier of Mustafa Kemal and dragoman of the French embassy in Constantinople.

While discussing with Salim Tamari at the 2014 MESA meeting the ability to identify and assess quirky references to the cultural 'anatomy' of 'Homo ottomanicus', of both elite and anonymous figures, we evoked the understudied impact of the French cultural paradigm among Arab Palestinians and German cultural endeavours in the same period. As we discussed the documentary *1913, Seeds of a Conflict*,[6] we briefly discussed Albert Antebi and the rumour, among some in the Latin parish of that period, that he might have been a spy for the French during World War I (as the Dominican Antonin Jaussen turned out to be).[7] I became even more interested in Albert Antebi while writing a monograph on French cultural policy in British Mandate Palestine and discussing the qualification of 'mission' for Jewish institutions such as the AIU.[8] Furthermore, reading articles by Israel de Haan from the Dutch newspaper *Algemeene Handelsblad*, discussing his opposition to political Zionism,[9] I noted the names of Orthodox members of Antebi's network whom I had encountered in the AIU archives. When discussing my contribution to this volume with Sarah Irving and Sary Zananiri, I kept in mind my conversation with Salim Tamari at MESA and decided to explore further the AIU archives in Paris, although I was not able to verify some of the information on the period 1917–19 in the Ministry of Defence archives, due to COVID-related restrictions.

This article builds on these considerations to focus on the complication of defining Albert Antebi within the framework of language and nationalism in Ottoman Jerusalem, and his overlapping affiliations within an overarching project for the Mediterranean under the auspices of the French. In a period when identifications were fluid and loyalties sometimes overlapping, the figure of Antebi lies between exclusive identification modes (for example, religious groups) and inclusive ones (Ottomanism or local urban identities like Jerusalemite). This is rendered even more complex by his positioning within different groups, as he was never fully integrated into either the governing AIU elite from France or the Sephardic elites in Jerusalem. Antebi's colonising activities are incomprehensible without recalling that the First Aliyah was partially influenced by French Jews.[10] The life and the activities of Albert Antebi were closely linked to a French network in Ottoman Palestine and to the French elites of AIU in Paris and Palestine. Raised and educated within the framework of the Alliance, Antebi identified with the project of 'regenerating' the Jews of the East through work. Yet, he was not a simple missionary of the Alliance in Ottoman Syria. Hyperactive and visionary, he was involved in crucial dossiers of Ottoman Jerusalem and Palestine, deeply implicated in local developments, to the great displeasure of his Parisian superiors who constantly called him to order, until the final rupture on the eve of World War I. He thus constitutes an important figure for understanding the mechanisms of Palestinian and Levantine societies at the beginning of the twentieth century.

In the recent historiography on Ottoman Palestine, Albert Antebi appears in articles and books analysing Jewish emancipation under Turkish rule and the activities of those Ottoman Sephardic Jews who supported the growth of the New Yishuv (predominantly from the first and second Aliyot 1882–1903 and 1904–14).[11] Recently, Louis Fishman has shown how, along with other Arab Sephardic elites, he was unsuccessful in building ties with Arab Palestinians, via debates in the press, and Roberto Mazza has traced his involvement in Cemal Pasha's unsuccessful endeavour to sell the Western Wall.[12] Strangely enough, he does not appear in Kaspi's volume about the AIU and remains almost completely absent from French historiography,[13] as if his marginal and contentious positioning within the AIU resulted in his absence from analyses of the institution.

Although Albert Antebi deserves a proper academic biography, this article proposes the more limited project of rethinking his contribution to the Jerusalem scene, looking at the less-known French paradigm in the recent historiography on late Ottoman Jerusalem, and helping to situate him in relation to the developing 'Palestinism' of the day.[14] I also attempt to better understand the extent to which political Zionism placed a barrier between him and his fellow Palestinians, particularly Arabs, whether Christian or Muslim, to highlight the fluidity of his identification during this period and the impact of his French cultural paradigm on his perceptions of Palestine, its different communities and scenarios, as well as the tensions there on the eve of World War I. This article therefore first contextualises Antebi's life, his activities as AIU school director and his networks; it then analyses his economic plan for Palestine under the auspices of France, the evolution of his positioning after 1913, when he redefined his 'Mediterranean resistance' against German influence, and its complications and failure before his death in 1919.

Contextualising Albert Antebi, a Man of Influence in Ottoman Jerusalem and the Mediterranean

Salim Tamari's works have underlined the importance of social biographies as invaluable ways of understanding the past,[15] 'adding richness and complexity, an emphasis on human agency and a prominent strand of humanisation to narratives of the region's history'.[16] The analysis of Antebi's positioning between 1908 and 1919 enriches our understanding of Jerusalem's Ottoman past, the complex and contradictory pictures which exist of it, illustrating the fact that 'individuals are rarely uncomplicated representatives of their social groups'.[17] To dig further into Antebi's French connections via cultural and national lenses makes it possible to interpret the many layers in his overlapping identifications and 'entangled loyalties'.[18]

The period between 1909 and 1919 corresponds to a moment when discussions on issues such as Zionism, Ottomanism, Arab Palestinian nationalism, colonialism, education, language use and growing identification among Jewish communities intersected with the ways in which Albert Antebi envisioned the past, present and future of Jerusalem, and this challenged his loyalties. The rise of political Zionism raised new questions for the diverse Jewish communities of Jerusalem and, more broadly, of Palestine. During his lifetime, Antebi dealt with and discussed with his French peers Arab Palestinian nationalism, the rise of different branches of Zionism, the politicisation of workers, the quarrels over schooling, the separation of church and state in France (with its consequences for Jews and the Consistory)[19] and the ambiguity of a secular France in its foreign cultural agenda.

The complexity of tracing Antebi's actions also comes from his multiple and at times apparently contradictory relations with many actors of Ottoman Jerusalem's scene, reflecting the complex webs of Ottoman Palestinian society and the intertwined social, intellectual and professional relationships across lines of ethnicity, whose boundaries were unstable and permeable.[20] Far from being united, the various Jewish communities had a relationships with Antebi,[21] his networks exemplifying how 'Jews operated within manifold networks, some parallel, some interlinked, some conflicting with each other'.[22]

This calls for a caveat when deciphering Antebi's actions: tracing his actions in Ottoman Jerusalem, his network and interactions with various French and francophone interlocutors implies exploring the ways in which he sometimes saw himself as part of a larger Jewish transnational network and at times was ascribed specific identities, trying to trace the instability and mutability of identities. At different moments of his life in Jerusalem, Antebi inscribed himself into different emerging collectives. Antebi at times shared, at times rejected the views of his peers in the AIU who, rooted in one of the pan-Jewish diaspora organisations, 'perceived local communities, and to a lesser degree acted, as [if they were] a single community'.[23] The tone and the positioning within these archives alternate, according to the recipient, the period, the type of network involved in the narrative, among others, between self-perception and external perspectives.

These analyses of his biography add granularity to our understanding of Ottoman Jerusalem. Beyond the tensions between the 'Oriental Antebi' (as he was often referred to at AIU headquarters in Paris) and the French institution, Antebi's agency is clearly visible in multiple settings. In spite of the greater formal weight of the head office, locally Antebi constantly made decisions, sometimes in the name of AIU without Paris' knowledge, sometimes influencing official policy. Within this Jerusalem 'war of languages',[24] this multilingual middle-class man kept his overarching vision for Palestine under the auspices of France while quickly grasping the emulation and competition between his various interlocutors. Throughout his reports, requests and analysis, Antebi proved strategic at many levels; he challenged his French hierarchy and the very heart of their approach to Palestine, offering facts, alternative narratives and analysis, reaching a broad public audience in France and trying to put economic develop-ment at the heart of the AIU's mission, alongside educational development. In a sense, then, he appropriated and transformed a French idea into an indigenous (Jewish) plan for Palestine.

Beyond a lachrymose conception of history, or a simplistic presentation of an agent of cultural colonialism, or a utopian interfaith vision,[25] mainly depicting France, like other European nations present in Palestine, as disturbing a climate of coexistence by their colonial actions, Antebi's writings suggest his entangled identification and the spaces to manoeuvre in the Jerusalem scene. He witnessed the processes that led to progressive segregation at different levels in Ottoman Jerusalem society.[26] Being at odds with his hierarchy in Paris, he advocated for integration via economic planning (mainly an educational curriculum including business-oriented courses, allocation of public works to French Jews, purchase of land and creation of industries to provide immigrants with work),[27] for all Jews settling in Palestine to learn Ottoman Turkish and become Ottoman citizens, but envisaging this integration via a special kind of French protection. The way in which he qualified the various Jewish communities borrows from different reg-isters, partially from the French elite and from the AIU.[28] Ultimately, Antebi was part of the larger AIU network in the Ottoman Empire, aiming to create a mod-ernising, French-oriented, Jewish Ottoman elite, but he campaigned also for the AIU and French networks in Palestine to take into account and adapt to the local context, which, ultimately, they refused to do. In spite of this rejection and his resignation, he remained faithful to the French 'idéal des Lumières', as he wrote until his death. It is therefore necessary to adopt a connected approach, between a historiography analysing Middle Eastern Jews as part of Middle Eastern societ-ies within a relational scope, by looking at Antebi's action as a Levantine Jew operating in a province of the Ottoman Empire, but equally placing his actions within the scope of Western European Jewish philanthropic organisations, thus investigating his agency on several levels. In a sense, Antebi asserted for the French language a wider role than solely that of the 'language for the develop-ment of Oriental Jews', as the AIU headquarters viewed it.

The archives of the AIU in this period evoke many aspects of daily life in late Ottoman Jerusalem and Palestine,[29] including the intellectual relationships between different communities, colonial cultural agendas, the first and second Aliyot and their impact on the Palestinian landscape, the common grounds and differences between French and German colonialism and their translation into language and cultural policies. Within the scope of this article, they also con-stitute primary sources to access some of Albert Antebi's thoughts about 'com-munity', 'nation' and 'linguistic nationalism'. They allow us to delve into Antebi's personal positioning towards language and cultural options in Ottoman Palestine and the Sephardim's reactions to socio-political developments in Palestine, as well as their attitude to the role of France vis-à-vis Jewish communities via the education system. His correspondence, whether intimate letters with colleagues or more formal exchanges with the directorship of AIU, allow us to go further than the programmes of AIU, taking into account his experiences on the ground.

A Damascus-born, French-educated Director of AIU Jerusalem

Albert Antebi was born in Damascus to a rabbinic family of Sephardic ancestry, originally from Aintab, with far-reaching links to French Jewish elites; indeed, the case of his grandfather led to the creation of the AIU itself in 1860.[30] Antebi attended a rabbinic school in Damascus and the AIU school, and he was fluent in several languages – that is, Arabic, Hebrew, French, English and Ladino. His AIU school director early on sent him to study the craft of blacksmithing in France, at an AIU school in Le Marais (Paris) and at the École d'arts et métiers in Chalons-en-Champagne, and he remained inspired by what he defined as the 'French ideals' of emancipation through education, in spite of the context of the Dreyfus affair.

Albert Antebi arrived in Jerusalem in 1896 as director of the Alliance vocational school, and he remained in this role until early 1914.[31] Other French Jews were present in the city, but his network extended to the majority of the French nationals in Palestine.[32] The Alliance's intention was – as Jacques Bigart, AIU general secretary, was to express in a conference given in Paris on 24 May 1913 at the Université Populaire Juive – to 'regenerate the Orientals by the Orientals'. Antebi's acceptance of the position of director follows his ideas not only about French emancipation, but also about his economic development plan within this particular Ottoman province.[33] The Jerusalem vocational school which Antebi directed can be seen as providing a type of missionary work in an environment perpetually described by Antebi as hostile or ungrateful, but, at the same time, the place from which he could propose concrete pedagogic and economic plans for Palestine.[34] Hyperactive, Antebi was involved in many aspects of urban and communal Ottoman Jerusalem life – and Palestinian, too, to the great displeasure of his Parisian AIU superiors. He was thus an important interlocutor for the French consuls, many of whom did not represent the Catholic elements in the French administration.[35] However, Antebi appears different from other AIU schoolteachers. Having graduated from a vocational school and not qualified as an agricultural expert (as was Joseph Niego, the director of the Mikveh Israel farm-school near Jaffa),[36] he also stood out from the rest of the AIU profiles due to his lack of literary training.[37] In this AIU network in Paris, he seems to have encountered contempt from his peers. This came in response not only to his educational profile and his Arab Syrian origin, but also to his economic endeavours for his pupils and the Jewish population more generally.

These concurrences between philanthropic movements in Jerusalem were later transformed by different cultural agendas and territorial and economic support for Jewish communities.[38] This cultural and linguistic competition also explained the framework of the future scenarios envisaged for Palestine by different groups within the Jewish communities and the Zionist movement.

An 'Homme de l'Entre-deux' (Go-between) in Fin-de-siècle Jerusalem[39]

As Antebi was not from Palestine, he has been portrayed as 'playing the role of an arbiter between the Jewish community, Arabs, and Istanbul' and 'without particular loyalties'.[40] If the first is true, the second is less evident, but looking into relevant archival sources at the AIU and cross-analysing them with what has been previously written, deduced from the Zionist archives, it seems that Albert Antebi was a man of overlapping identifications and loyalties, with a strong link to France. Within the paradigm of the multiple Jewish agendas in Palestine, Antebi appeared to be at the crossroads of the porous boundaries of global French, international, Jewish issues, linked to a trans-imperial network, Jewish and non-Jewish internationalism, and local networks in Palestine. Albert Antebi was an expert at the crossroads of the two legal orders of Ottoman Jerusalem: the reformed Ottoman law of the Tanzimat period and Capitulations law.[41] As an expert in Ottoman land law, he became an indispensable interlocutor for reform-minded Ottoman officials and a skilful practitioner in the provincial institutions set up since the Vilayet Law of 1864. He also became an essential intermediary for the French consuls in Jerusalem, an expert on the status of consular protection in the field of Jewish institutions and individuals. Very few held such a position in Palestinian Jewish life and beyond in Palestinian society from 1900 to 1919, hence the continual recourse to his mediation by various interlocutors.

From his correspondence with the AIU, a trans-community of sociability between Ottoman Jerusalem elites appears: the Arab Muslim aristocracy of Jerusalem seems to have had no objection to sending their children to Alliance schools (to learn French), and Jewish notables did the same with the Christian missionary schools.[42] Antebi was linked by close friendship to the Dominican Marie-Joseph Lagrange, founder of the École Biblique, and to the Husayni family, which held the offices of mayor and mufti of the holy city.[43] At the same time, he knew when to turn towards England and even more so towards Germany.

In his exchanges with the AIU, he appears to be well-acquainted with the representatives of an older religious Jewish community. In the name of strict respect for religious orthodoxy, he at the same time struggled with this community's members, as they were opposed to the so-called modernisation led by the Alliance.[44]

Despite his official anti-Zionist political stance, Antebi was not against Jewish immigration to Palestine, and he was a key figure in facilitating Jewish settlement and securing lands for their expansion within the Ottoman Empire.[45] Indeed, his role as an intermediary between the Ottoman administration, the local Jewish Yishuv and the Arab population made him into what many have described as a model Ottoman citizen. Antebi was a central figure in both promoting Jewish immigration and strengthening the various Jewish communities of Palestine.[46] When the Arab Congress demanded 'the closure of Palestine and Syria to the Jews',[47] Antebi was more than ever in favour of a strategic rapprochement with France, evoking a 'peaceful, intellectual, moral and economic penetration, only achievable by the AIU and France'. He presented Palestinian Catholics as being in the bosom of Italy (he wrongly shared the opinion present among the vast majority of French missionaries with whom he was in contact, that they were a minority within the Catholic sphere); the Orthodox with Russia; and the Protestants with Germany and Britain. Thus, the association with Levantine mechanisms went haywire from the time of the Young Turk Revolution onwards, and power rivalries became exacerbated with a growing involvement of *protégé* clienteles: Antebi defended a Franco-Rothschildian view against a German-Zionist one, seen as the enemy.

With the reinstatement of the parliamentary constitution, the Ottoman Empire was celebrated as a civic 'family of nations'.[48] Multiple nationalisms emerging in the empire 'did not denote working for an independent state, but rather for achieving measures of cultural autonomy'.[49] As recently shown by Louis Fishman, in the period following the 1908 Young Turk Revolution, the adoption of Hebrew as a national language did not contradict support for the Ottoman homeland. Antebi continued to play the role of mediator between Jews and Arabs, on multiple social and political levels. His unique role in bridging the growing divide between Jews and Arabs became an impossible mission in the late Ottoman era.[50]

When plans were made by Cemal Pasha for large-scale, even comprehensive, expulsions of Zionist and pro-Zionist activists, Antebi's connections with the Ottoman administration softened, albeit temporarily, due to Cemal's decision.[51] Antebi also served as representative of the Jewish Colonisation Association. During his first decade in Palestine, he was staunchly opposed to the Zionist Organisation, which called for an independent Jewish state in Palestine; however, with the post-1908 realigning of political Zionism towards a more pro-Ottoman stance, much of his animosity towards the movement lifted.

Did Antebi distinguish between *migrants* and *settlers* and their goals? He did so by distinguishing their activities, but to what extent? How he then reacted differently with respect to the help he provided for land purchases needs to be further explored via a systemic cross-analysis of several archival collections. He underlined the consequences of political Zionism in the growing rise of anti-semitic attitudes.[52] This distinction later on seems to have impacted his thoughts on a Mediterranean connection in opposition to the German alliances of the European Zionist movement.

'To Strengthen the Mediterranean Resistance'? Loyalties, Nationalism and the Blurring of Identification after 1913

Albert Antebi, in his correspondence with Paris during the twelve years prior to his resignation, several times mentioned his desire to go back to France and escape the exhausting Jerusalem milieu. Yet, he remained director of the AIU until 1914, driven by pedagogical desire and the materialisation of his economic endeavours for Palestine under the auspices of France. Antebi was moving between two systems of influence, the French and the German,[53] negotiating tirelessly between them when tensions rose. He enrolled one of his children in a school in Germany, and he felt at ease in this 'Babel in Zion'.[54] The AIU, in its 'universal' goals, did include German members.[55] In addition to political support for Jewish communities and victims of intolerance, the 'moralisation' and 'modernisation' of Eastern Jewish communities became the two keywords of the alliance's ideology, according to which education should allow the 'regeneration' of Jewish communities 'brought down by centuries of oppression'.[56]

Antebi, however, did not see the network of AIU schools solely as the incarnation of the message of Franco-Judaism, but as an incentive to economic independence and integration in local Ottoman societies. He was logically not inclined to promote only the French language, nor to propose the model of the emancipated French Jew in Palestine. He thus remained detached from the milieu of the Parisian Jewish scholars.[57]

The competition between French and German supporters culminated in physical assault and death threats by a German representative when Antebi refused to comply with the request to expel Muslim pupils from the AIU school.[58] Tensions arose more sharply between France and Germany after 1908, when their institutions and networks of influence, in particular those with commercial influence, translated into a competing use of language with national goals, less related to understanding Eastern Jewry and the work to be done with them.[59] Antebi, along with the French representative, resented what he regarded as a German undercover plan for Palestine via the use of the Zionists' agenda.[60] The French reaction shows the full variety of their answers: the AIU headquarters, in the midst of a quarrel with Antebi, decided to close the boarding section of its vocational school and fire Antebi for being too involved in local politics, contravening their 'neutrality' in Palestine; however, the French government representative regretted this decision as 'diminish[ing] one of the main factors of French influence in Jerusalem, where Jews currently represent at least 2/3 of the population'.[61]

Antebi was all the more bitter because, on 18 April 1912, the first stone of the Haifa Technical College, planned by the Zionists allied with the Hilfsverein,[62] was laid in the presence of the German consul. Planning, funding and building the college, later known as the Technion, had been the cause of vicious infighting between various Zionist factions, and it would remain so for years to come.[63] Antebi sent even more reports to the AIU in Paris, analysing this unexpected rapprochement between the two former enemies. The AIU headquarters continued to promote the ideal of universalism, but Antebi, while identifying with some of the AIU concepts inherited from the French Revolution, also pointed out their interpretation on the ground in Ottoman Jerusalem and the limits of this supra-national ideology.[64]

A Jewish Economic Independence under the Auspices of France, 1908–16

In many of his letters and reports, Antebi pointed out the need for Jews to build up their economic resources and to contribute to the larger community. From the beginning of his role within the AIU he campaigned for more commercial topics and lessons within the curriculum, focusing more on knowledge of the Ottoman Empire and its culture; he campaigned to invest in land acquisition, agricultural and industrial projects so as to create small local enterprises. For Antebi, the acquisition of lands was the motor of this economic independence, as only with enough lands and Ottoman citizenship would Jews be able to play an economic role locally.[65] Antebi used his French connections to become a land-broker in Palestine, as the representative of charitable organisations run by wealthy Jews such as Baron Edmond de Rothschild.[66]

An admirer of French republicanism, Antebi wanted Jewish economic autonomy in Palestine under the auspices of, and in close coordination with, France. He was convinced of the 'concordance' of 'the Jewish interest, of the universal and Palestinian Jewish policy' with 'the interests of the extension of French civilisation and genius',[67] although he himself had been expelled from the École des Arts et Métiers in Châlons-sur-Marne when his Jewishness became known. He wrote:

> I desire to achieve the conquest of Zion by economic means, not politically; the Jerusalem I would cherish is the historical and spiritual Jerusalem, not the modern and temporal Jerusalem. I want to be a Jewish deputy in an Ottoman parliament, and not in the Jewish temple of Mount Moriah. Ottoman Jews should have the same rights, responsibilities and hopes as the Jews of England, Germany and France. I wish to create powerful Jewish economic centres embedded in universal democracies. I do not wish to be a subject of a Judean autocracy.[68]

Although inspired by the French Third Republic, he remained convinced that political equality for the Jews could not be achieved in the Ottoman Empire, but that economic independence would reinforce their integration and rights as Ottomans.

A transition to rapprochement with practical Zionism, still largely outside the field of political Zionism, can be observed, but it appears that his relationship with the working-class leadership of the second Aliyah was extremely bad. As an Ottoman Levantine, Antebi could not tolerate the sectarian exclusivism of those from Russia who demanded the removal of non-Jews from Jewish institutions and Jews from non-Jewish institutions. In this respect, he was representative of a Sephardic population that shared a common Arab-Ottoman culture with non-Jews, and his Levantine Francophilia was that of somebody who sought a strengthened Jewish presence in the Holy Land while rejecting the exclusivist nationalism imported from Europe.

Antebi's activities in support of the Jewish colonies must be placed within the context of the first Aliyah, which was influenced by French Jews, as attested to by regular references to Zadoc Kahn (chief Rabbi of France) and Edmond de Rothschild in the correspondence.[69] Co-founder of the Jewish Colonisation Association and a friend of Zadoc Kahn, he elaborated an earlier project for the economic development of Palestine to make it as much a Jewish reality as a French one, within a framework that would maintain the Capitulations, in line with the settlement enterprise begun in the early 1880s. This did not contradict debates in the new Hebrew press after 1908, which promoted the idea of modern Jewish nationhood as part of the Ottoman family of nations and debated the appropriate forms of collective representation for the Jews of Palestine.[70]

Some of Antebi's ideas were embraced by Zionists, some of whom saw economic power as a way to achieve political influence. But to German Zionists contesting his activities in the Jewish settlements, he responded by arguing that the AIU had developed some of the ideas of the Zionist programme twenty years earlier, informed by a deep knowledge of the local population, unlike the political Zionist groups. He reiterated his views on economic integration into an Ottoman society that would also employ and benefit Arab Muslim and Christian local communities and, thus, on the necessity of mastering Arabic and Ottoman Turkish.

According to Antebi, Palestine would be the last province to be taken from Turkey, and if this did happen, it would be declared international. By virtue of trade and its geographical position, he believed that a possible partition would allocate it to France or Britain, but he also pointed out that in terms of direct influence and local activity, by number of nationals and activity, Germany and Russia were in the lead.[71]

Furthermore, at this point the cross-community sociability of the elites was being challenged as the wider political milieu became fragmented.[72] Within the context of the hesitations and confusions of World War I in this region, Albert Antebi's world was that of the Capitulations and the Tanzimat reforms. In parallel, to achieve his goals, Antebi was acquainted with the Anglophone Jewish milieu, responsible for the *Caisse des Prêts*, a local funding apparatus of the ICA, which granted low-interest loans to Jewish artisans in Jerusalem and its environs and to new colonies, a subject which needs further exploration.[73]

1913, a Turning Point towards a 'Mediterranean Resistance'?

On 2 March 1913, the French Minister in Serbia, Léon Coullard Descos, in one of his reports on Bulgaria, estimated that 'Zionism clear[ed] the way for the Germanic descent; the Alliance [AIU] strengthens the Mediterranean resistance'.[74] Enver Pasha's stint as military attaché in Berlin between 1909 and 1911, his fascination with the Prussian army and his warm relationship with the German state strengthened the German presence throughout the Ottoman Empire. Within the AIU and ICA, the balance of power thus shifted in favour of the German Zionists, rather than the Austro-Hungarian Empire.[75] Antebi continued to envisage the AIU's development via the French paradigm and to place greater confidence in France. For him, Jews were the pawns of the powers that they served, sacrificed by them sooner or later. Although the French consul backed his analysis, Antebi was denounced in May 1913 by the AIU's Paris headquarters, accused of placing his children in the Sisters of Saint Joseph school (certainly a Catholic school, but above all a French one).[76] On 20 July 1913, writing to the Alliance, he expressed his exhaustion with the complaints and the lack of support from some of his superiors, and he declared that he 'laid down his arms and demanded [his] release' in order to devote himself to local political and industrial activities. During the latter half of 1914, Antebi no longer represented either the ICA or the AIU.[77] The fact that he worked for the interests of both old and new Jewish settlements in Palestine, the contradictions between philanthropy and estate, representative of both and the Jewish Colonisation Association (founded by Baron Hirsch) led him into an untenable situation.

The break-up of the alliance between the Zionists and the Hilfsverein to build the Haifa Technical School and the ensuing battles in November 1913 confirmed Albert Antebi in his perception of the battle over ideology and language in Jewish Palestine. He remained determined to fight under the auspices of France: for him, 'France alone can serve Jewish Palestinianism, without competition and without monopolisation, respecting its entity and its genius'.[78]

However, the main outline of such common activities would be easy to envisage:

French savings monopolise Turkey's public works, French Jews have a preponderant influence in the Paris Stock Exchange; why not capture a small inflow from this Palestinian Jewish financial source with the active and sincere collaboration of the real forces of Palestine, the acquiescence of the indigenous intellectuals, the sympathy of the French government. [...] We must act, because Germany and Russia are doubling their zeal to consolidate their respective positions in Palestine. Woe to the Jews if one of these two powers should seize this country. [...] I foresee for Palestine a system of regionalisation for the district of Jerusalem and a French protectorate for its other cities and towns. [...] France is the obvious heir of Turkey in Syria; [...] for once by chance, sentiment and reason unite to achieve this marriage of interest and inclination.[79]

Antebi proposed to the AIU and Edmond de Rothschild the creation of a *Comité France Palestine*, with the help of Prime Minister Aristide Briand, to implement some of his economic initiatives under the auspices of France. But his offers was declined by the AIU headquarters, while Rothschild, who visited Palestine in early 1914, was much influenced by Zionism by then.[80] In its replies, the AIU headquarters repeatedly proclaimed its neutrality and remained at least partly blind to what Zionism represented on the ground.[81] The French idea of the nation translated into the idea that the AIU considered being Jewish a religion, not a race or a 'people'; thus, the AIU continued to argue for the universality of its mission and the necessity to be 'politically neutral', which Antebi opposed fiercely.[82] At the same time, the reports of the Central Committee during this period highlight debates about confessional polarisation in Jerusalem.

In January 1914, the local Sephardic newspaper *HaHerut* published several short articles on Antebi's economic vision for Palestine and promotion of investments in agriculture and industry.[83] Just months later, after the beginning of the war in August 1914, Enver Pasha abolished the Capitulations, and Antebi's French paradigm thus faced revision.[84] And on 15 January 1915, *HaHerut* published an interview with Cemal Pasha, warning the Jews of Palestine to Ottomanise or leave. The next day, he summoned about thirty Jewish notables whom he had decided to exile to Brousse (Bulgaria). Antebi pleaded their cause and managed to gain Cemal's confidence and appointment as his adviser. Within this role, Antebi intervened in favour of Ben Gurion and Ben Zvi, his opponents, and managed to avert their exile or imprisonment.[85] Antebi was, however, denounced in the growing climate of exclusive identifications, because of his links with France; Ottoman officials were linked to the Germans, and in spite of Antebi's choice of a German school for one of his children he fell into disfavour.[86] Later, Enver Pasha sent him to the Caucasus front, where he fought alongside Mustafa Kemal.[87]

Conclusion

Albert Antebi was an important node in transnational thought on Palestine at the turn of the twentieth century and a mediator between several of the competing national, religious and ideological factions in Ottoman Jerusalem. His correspondence with the AIU suggests a flamboyant man, generous with his time and entangled with different interlocutors, with a wide network in Ottoman Jerusalem and the Mediterranean, caught up in multiple overlapping identities and loyalties.

Although understudied, his writings in French and his correspondence with the AIU deserve more attention, as they address many important topics on Ottoman Jerusalem, the so-called Arab Jews of Palestine, the various identifications, loyalties and linguistic battles of the era, early cultural diplomacy, colonialism and the economic agenda, which appear in his exchanges with many actors of the Jerusalem *fin de siècle* and the years before and after World War I. The figure of Antebi invites us to revisit the subject of the agency of Oriental Jews within French cultural politics and their plans for integration into local society as these shifted politically, culturally and economically. It also invites to envisage the impact of French Jewish politics in Ottoman Palestine through connected lenses, not through that of a single organisation in isolation from broader European, international and Palestinian contexts. Antebi, like other French Jewish actors within the AIU, was well integrated into transnational, transimperial networks and transnational mobility.[88]

Albert Antebi's activities halted only in March 1919, when he died at the age of forty-five, struck by typhoid fever. Before dying, he set up a structure for thousands of Muslim, Jewish, Greek and Armenian refugees driven out by World War I, chartering numerous French ships for them.[89] After his death, his wife Henriette Antebi would spend twenty-five years as director of the ENIO (École normale israélite orientale), training French Jewish teachers to be sent around the Mediterranean. She opposed the Zionism of the first director of the AIU school for girls in Jerusalem, Mathilde Levy-Haarscher,[90] and her husband Isaac Levy, director of the Anglo-Palestine Bank.

Salim Tamari's various studies have underlined the necessity to revisit social history and the long-lasting effects of cultural entanglements and biographies, connected to local, spatial and social realities. In the same spirit, this chapter's modest contribution invites us to explore in greater depth the multiple facets of Antebi's biography, part of a moment of 'interstitial society',[91] exploiting the space created by the push of imperialisms and the evolution of the Ottoman Empire, before nationalisms took over. Some of Antebi's successors within the various Jewish communities hardly understood Arabic and French, but they did master English . . .

Notes

1. I will refer to him using the French version of his name, which he himself used as his signature in the vast majority of the archival sources consulted.
2. Archives des Affaires étrangères, Nouvelle série Turquie, n°138, 02/03/1913, Léon Coullard-Descos (Ministre de France en Serbie).
3. Halperin, *The Oldest Guard*.
4. Lemire, *Jérusalem 1900*, p. 145.
5. Anastassiadou and Heyberger, *Figures anonymes, figures d'élite*.
6. http://1913seedsofconflict.com
7. Sanchez Summerer, *French in the Holy Land*. On the figure of Jaussen, see Chatelard and Tarawneh, *Antonin Jaussen*; Mazza and Ouahes, 'For God and La Patrie', pp. 145-64; Sandal-Wilson, this volume.

8.   Neveu, Sanchez Summerer and Turiano, *Missions and Preaching*.
9.   https://www.dbnl.org/tekst/haan008feui01_01/index.php
10. Kaplan and Malinovitch, *The Jews of Modern France*.
11. Fishman, 'Arab Jewish Voices in Ottoman Palestine'; Campos, *Ottoman Brothers*; Jacobson and Naor, *Oriental Neighbors*; Laskier, 'The Sefaradim and the Yishuv', pp. 113–26.
12. Mazza, 'The Deal of the Century?' pp. 696–711.
13. See, for example, Kaspi, *Histoire de l'Alliance israélite universelle*. His grand-daughter, Elizabeth Antébi, has written a novel inspired by the life of her grandfather, *L'homme du sérail*, but without archival references. Her MA research (Diplôme de l'École Pratique des Hautes Etudes, section des Sciences Religieuses, 1996), *Albert Antébi ou la religion de la France (1873-1919)*, in spite of the sometimes-hagiographical tone, includes appendices with several letters by Albert Antebi from private collections and reproduces partially some of the many letters of Albert Antebi preserved in the AIU archives (volume II). Antebi was a prolific letter-writer, and his letters are an important resource for the study of this period.
14. Palestinianism as the 'essence of what it meant to be a Palestinian before the rise of nation-state nationalism, when in the late Ottoman era a modern notion of patriotism for Palestine began to be expressed among the local Arab population', describing the sense of "connectedness" and "commonality", which led them to join together to take action, to defend, preserve and place claim over their perceived homeland, without having national aspirations towards establishing an independent state'. See Fishman, *Jews and Palestinians*, p. 16.
15. Tamari, *The Storyteller of Jerusalem*; *Year of the Locust*.
16. Irving, Nassif and Sanchez Summerer, 'The House of the Priest', introduction.
17. LeVine and Shafir, *Struggle and Survival in Palestine/Israel*.
18. Khalidi, *The Iron Cage*, introduction; Admiraal, conference at Leiden University, 14 October 2021, 'Celebrating Maimonides in Cairo: Jewish Historiography, Egyptian nationalism and Global Crisis', and her dissertation 'Entangled Loyalties in the Middle East'.
19. The *Consistoire central de France* was founded in 1808 by Napoleon on the model of the Catholic Church in order to organise the Jewish religion. For the concept of a Jewish mission in the Orient, see Vilmain, 'A Jewish Mission?'
20. On this permeability, see Firges and Graf, 'Introduction'.
21. On the heterogeneous communities constituting the so-called *yishuv* (understood differently by the Orthodox Ashkenazim, who emphasised the pious character of community, and Jewish nationalists, who championed colonisation at the end of the Ottoman period and how they were embedded within local, regional and global networks, p. 289), see Wallach, 'Rethinking the Yishuv', pp. 275–94; Jacobson, *From Empire to Empire*, pp. 82–116.
22. Wallach, 'Rethinking the Yishuv', p. 289.

23. Wallach, 'Rethinking the Yishuv', p. 289; Levy, 'Historicizing the Concept', p. 465; Levy, 'The Arab Jew', pp. 79–103.

24. Sanchez Summerer, 'Les langues entre elles', pp. 119–43.

25. Cohen, 'The Golden Age', pp. 28–38; Sharkey, *A History of Muslims, Christians and Jews.*

26. This went as far as physical threats, for example, on 17 December 1899, when German Jews attacked him after he refused to reject Arab pupils and employees from his AIU school; AAIU, III E 10, 2420/25.

27. AAIU, Israel XI E 32, 4950/9.

28. Such as, for example, criticising the *halukka* (diaspora Jewish charity and patronage towards Palestinian Jews) while at the same time indulgently benefiting from it with his family in Damascus.

29. Part of the archives were found in the vocational school (in the mid-1970s). Damage to a wall revealed a boarded-up room containing the school's archives from its creation in 1880 until the eve of World War II. Georges Weill and Simon Schwarzfuchs brought them to the Central Archives for the History of the Jewish People, with which the Alliance has a deposit agreement for its school archives outside France (discussion with the AIU archivist, June 2021).

30. His grandfather, Jacob Antebi, chief rabbi of Damascus, was one of the victims of the blood libel associated with the 1840 Damascus Affair, when he was arrested and falsely accused of being part of a group that kidnapped two men and murdered them to use their blood to make matzo for Passover. His father was a teacher at AIU schools in Syria and later in Cairo.

31. The AIU school was founded by Nissim Behar in 1882 (school for boys); in 1897, the vocational school opened its doors, and only in 1906 the school for girls. Albert Antebi was sent to Jerusalem to assist Nissim Behar, in charge of the AIU schools' network; Antebi replaced him (1882–97) as the AIU delegate.

32. On the Ratisbonne brothers, French Jews who converted to Catholicism and acquired the Ecce Homo where they installed the Sisters of Sion in 1862, see Sanchez, 'Ouvrir les trésors de la charité', pp. 207–38.

33. See Vilmain, 'A Jewish Mission in the Orient?' In 1860, the founders of the AIU were inspired by Michelet, for whom the mission of France to the world replaced the Christian mission. This did not prevent German, Italian, Russian and other Jews from joining. At the same time, the Alliance was clearly an off-shoot of the Franco-Judaism that was still being constructed at the time. Religion was now a private matter, and the Jews had given way to the Israelites and renounced forming a separate nation. However, the Alliance is also Jewish in its conception of a particular universal. Jules Carvallo, one of the founders of the Alliance, stated as early as 1853: 'Israel was given to the world to bless and improve it; but it has a duty to fulfil; it is to unite, to defend itself, to preserve the lives of those whom God has reserved for this great purpose'; quoted by

Simon-Nahum in Kaspi, *Histoire de l'Alliance*, p. 42. Finally, the 'universality' of the Alliance is an Occidentalism.

34. Back in 1898, he had been proud that the AIU vocational school was chosen to help with the restoration of the Dome of the Rock for the Kaiser's visit.

35. Antebi influenced the 1904 report to the French government about the Jewish 'clientèle' of France (Consul Auguste Boppe to Minister Delcassé), Archives du ministère des Affaires étrangères, Nouvelle série Turquie, n°131. Following the consul Boppe, the new consul Georges Outrey (1905–8) was openly anti-Dreyfus and tried to block many of Antebi's initiatives.

36. See Halevi's chapter in this volume.

37. Joseph Niego (1863–1945) had been born in Adrianople (Edirne) into a family of rabbis and studied at the Montpellier School of Agriculture. In 1890, he was appointed director of the AIU farm-school near Jaffa, Mikveh-Israel, and became an agronomist. Albert Antebi was often in contact with him to settle tax and settlements problems; AAIU, Israel XLVIII E 128 b-d, Israel XLIX E 128 e-g, Israel L E 128 h-j, Israel LI E 128 k-l. In 1903, Niego was appointed Inspector for the Jewish Colonisation Association (ICA) and ICA representative in Constantinople. In 1908, he became president of the B'nai B'rith Lodge of Constantinople. Albert H. Navon, *Les 70 ans de l'École Normale Israélite Orientale (1865–1935)*, Paris, 1935, pp. 127–28.

38. On the context of emancipation and assimilation, the transformation of Western European Judaism and the development of a philanthropy directed towards the Jewish communities of the Mediterranean basin, see Vilmain, 'A Jewish Mission to the Orient?' Starting from private initiatives such as those of Moses Montefiore, this phenomenon became institutionalised in the second half of the nineteenth century, around associations such as the Alliance Israélite Universelle founded in 1860 and its counterparts, the Anglo-Jewish Association (1871), the Organisation Reconstruction Travail in Russia (1880) and the Hilfsverein der Deutschen Juden (1901), dealing differently with the adherence to the idea of 'civilisation'.

39. Heyberger and Verdeil, *Hommes de l'entre-deux*.

40. Campos, *Ottoman Brothers*, p. 219.

41. All Jews were members of a single *millet* (non-Muslim ethno-religious corporate body), especially important when it came to liaising with imperial authorities regarding taxation, conscription, population registration and land registration; see Campos, *Ottoman Brothers*, and Wallach, 'Rethinking the Yishuv'.

42. Letter 364, cited by Antébi, *Albert Antébi (1873–1919)*, 1996, vol. II.

43. No specific correspondence was found in the archives of the EBAF (École biblique et archéologique de Jérusalem), nor at IDEO (Institut Dominicain des Etudes orientales), where the personal archive of M.-J. Lagrange is kept; interviews with Héléna Rigaud, archivist of the EBAF and J.-F. Perrénès, Prieur of EBAF, May 2021.

44. His reports to the AIU from 1902 to 1912 show Antebi's concerns to take into account how this modernity promoted by the Paris elites was understood in Ottoman Jerusalem, how he should promote it and adapt it for what he referred to, often, as a successful future in Palestine.

45. CZA, J85; Antebi helped the Lovers of Zion and Dizengoff, but never supported the international socialist movement.

46. Campos, *Ottoman Brothers*, p. 219, and Fishman, *Jews and Palestinians*, p. 150.

47. AAIU, IX E.27, Albert Antebi to Frank, 18 October 1909. Albert Antebi observed that a group was being formed among the local population to prevent sales of land to Jews.

48. Campos, *Ottoman Brothers*, p. 210.

49. Following the 1908 Young Turk revolution, the term 'shared homeland' became a common term to denote the unity of Ottoman citizens regardless of religion, ethnicity and often linguistic divisions. After 1908, the Ashkenazi and Sephardic 'communities were linguistically merging together through the adoption of Hebrew as the main language of the Jewish Yishuv'; Fishman, *Jews and Palestinians*, pp. 9, 19; Der Matossian, *Shattered Dreams of Revolution*, pp. 73–95.

50. Campos, *Ottoman Brothers*; Jacobson, *From Empire to Empire*; Gribetz, *Defining Neighbors*; Tamari, 'Ishaq Al-Shami', pp. 10–26; Evri, 'Partitions and Translations', pp. 71–93.

51. AAIU Letter 505, cited in Antébi, *Albert Antébi (1873–1919)*, vol. II.

52. AAIU, H. Frank to Antebi, 8 November 1908, AIU VIII E.25 Antebi, of the Jewish Colonial Association (XX). 'The Zionists had made the Muslim population ill-disposed to all progress accomplished by the Jews and the ill-will had spread to the Administrative Council, the law courts and government officials, many of whom especially at lower levels were drawn from the population'. Antebi to President of JCA, 31 August 1913, JCA 2681. Albert Antebi reported that, since accounts of speeches by Ruhi Khalidi and Shukri al-Assali had spread among the peasants, anti-Jewish feeling had spread.

53. On an international level outside Palestine, France and Germany confronted each other in Morocco (in 1906, during the Conference of Algeciras, and in 1911 when a German war ship was in Agadir harbour). On this German sphere in Jerusalem (both Protestant and Catholic), see Irving, 'Elias Nasrallah Haddad', pp. 9–29; Irving, *Intellectual Networks*; Goren, 'Echt katholisch und gut deutsch'.

54. Halperin, *Babel in Zion*.

55. AAIU, ICA IV H14-16, VH 17 and Germany IV A4-5. Within the Central Committee, growing tensions occurred between the German and the French members, the latter worrying about losing the majority of the seats within the AIU Central Committee and resenting the Germans' support of Zionists' political project in Palestine. (The Deutsche Conferenz Gemeinschaft [DCG] was created to rationalise the fundraising for the AIU in Germany; Zionists

exploited the tensions about its autonomy to gain power with the DCG); Rodrigue, 'Totem, Taboos and Jews', p. 15.

56. Kaspi, *Histoire de l'Alliance Israélite Universelle*, annexes 2 and 3 ('Exposé des motifs' and 'Appel de 1860'), pp. 455-62.

57. On this unique political and cultural stance, the French conjunction on academic career, Jewish communal and social activism, see Rodrigue, 'Totem, Taboos and Jews', p. 6.

58. AAIU, Allemagne IV A4, A5 and A8. Several letters expose the many complaints about factional dissent between Jews and in particular the German Zionists' antipathy towards Jews from Arab lands against their Arab cultural background. Collège des frères des écoles chrétiennes de Jérusalem archives: list of Jewish Oriental family names (until the early 1930s); Sanchez Summerer, *French in the Holy Land*.

59. France itself seemed to have played a curious double game: the French consul proposed to take the Zionist gymnasium under his protection, perhaps in the hope of rallying this clientele to France.

60. Archives des Affaires étrangères, Nouvelle Série Turquie, n°134, new ambassador, A. Bompar to the Ministry of Foreign Affairs, 05/09/1912, A. Ministry of Foreign Affairs, accompanied by an article published in *el-Munadi*, 2 September 1912, Zionists and the new governor of Jerusalem Mahdi Bey, Osmanische Lloyd, 'German Interests in Palestine Are, in Many Respects, Identical to Those of the Jewish Settlements'.

61. Archives des Affaires étrangères, Nouvelle Série Turquie, n° 135; AAIU, Israël IX E 28: the secretary of the AIU, Jacques Bigart, and the central committee wanted to dismiss him, but the rabbis and Jews of Jerusalem would not let them do so.

62. Archives du ministère des Affaires étrangères, Turquie, Nouvelle Série, The French consul in Jerusalem, Gueyraud, to the Minister of Foreign Affairs, S. Pichon, n° 133, 21/07/1910. 26-30/12/1909; hard-line German and Russian Zionists debated the intensive land purchase policy in Palestine and some interlocutors such as Azmi Bey 'mastered neither Arabic nor French'.

63. Alpert, *Technion.*

64. Wilke, 'Das deutsch-französische Netzwerk', pp. 173-99.

65. AAIU, Israel XI E 32, 4950/9.

66. He co-founded the Chamber of Commerce (Campos, *Ottoman Brothers*, p. 176).

67. AAIU, Israel X E 31, 4916/5.

68. Letter of 4 August 1908, private collection, cited in Antébi, *Albert Antébi (1873-1919)*, vol. II.

69. Kahn (1830-1905) had been Chief Rabbi of France and a major support of the AIU; Rodrigue, 'Totem, Taboos and Jews'.

70. All Jewish factions in Palestine, regardless of their ethnic and ideological positions, stated their adherence to the Ottoman civic project and articulated their

vision for Jewish society within this framework; see Ben-Bassat, 'Rethinking the Concept of Ottomanisation', pp. 461–75. Antebi even promoted the idea of a bilingual newspaper in French and Arabic that would support the sultanate and constitution and defend regional and municipal economic interests; AAIU Israel VIII 25, 2/8/1908, 04/08/1908.

71. AAIU, Israel X E 31, 1446/8.

72. We can mention, among others, a pro-French and anti-Zionist group among the Arab Palestinians (the al-'Isa family and *Filastin* newspaper); a pro-French group among the Jews (with Antebi as its leader); a pro-English group among Arab Palestinians; a pro-German group among the Jews; an Ottoman administration that was challenged by Arab autonomy; Arabs who considered allying themselves with the Zionists against the Ottomans; and Zionists who made proposals to each other.

73. Halperin, *The Oldest Guard.*

74. Archives des Affaires étrangères, Nouvelle Série Turquie, n° 138.

75. AAIU, ICA file IV H 14-16, V H 17. Germany IV A 4-5; Germany V A 6-8: during decisive elections of new members of the Central Committee, in which he almost was not re-elected, Salomon Reinach (AIU vice-president) to AIU representative Bigart or Leven (Blau, Netter, members of the Hilfsverein); all foreign members of the central committee, even Americans, should come to Paris at the expense of the AIU, the goal being to eventually win the majority over to the Parisians.

76. AAIU, Israel VIII, E24, 3520/5, 22/05/1913; Antebi stresses that the St Joseph sisters are not proselytes, that they do not work on Saturdays as the majority of their pupils are Jewish and that they are praised by the French government for their work.

77. Archives AIU, Israel E X 31: a financial compensation to hand over the services to his successor at the vocational school in March 1914. Since the president of the AIU at the time, Narcisse Leven, was also the president of the ICA, and as both administrations were headquartered in Paris, it is likely that through these connections Antebi was divested of his functions in both organisations simultaneously, but most probably stayed linked to them, in one way or another, via family and friendship links.

78. AAIU, Israel X E 31, 4916/5.

79. AAIU, Israel X E 32, 4950/9. Within the French Consulate itself, attitudes were radically different between the traditional pro-missionary consul and his chancellor, anti-Catholic and Freemason.

80. AAIU, Israel XI, E 32, 4950/9 and 637/3; in February 1914, Rothschild still asked Antebi to buy all the lands around the Ophel area, as the Baron envisaged to create an Archaeological School similar to the École Française d'Athènes; Antébi declined.

81. Kaspi, *Histoire de l'Alliance Israelite universelle*, pp. 246–61.

82. This ultra-universalist stance was further impossible to maintain for the Central Committee after Reinach's resignation in 1912; see Rodrigue, 'Totem, Taboos and Jews'.
83. AAIU Israel XI, E 32, 254/5. Antébi also mentioned the Bank Perrier of Paris and its concessions in Jerusalem (electricity, water supply) that seem to have stopped with World War I.
84. AAIU, XXI, E 68.
85. AAIU, Israel XXI E 69, Annexe A III.
86. CZA, A 208.
87. Antébi, *Albert Antébi (1873-1919)*, p. 107, private collection of letters.
88. On the French Mediterraneans, see Lorcin and Shepard (eds.), *French Mediterraneans*.
89. Antébi, *Albert Antébi (1873-1919)*, p. 107, private collection of letters, n° 507, 508, 509.
90. AAIU, Israel XX, E 063-067.
91. Ilbert, *Alexandrie, 1830-1930*.

Bibliography

Admiraal, Lucia. *Entangled Loyalties in the Middle East: Discussions on Fascism, Nazism and Antisemitism in the Arabic Jewish Press 1933-1948*. Unpubl. PhD dissertation. Uva Amsterdam, 2021.

Anastassiadou, Meropi and Bernard Heyberger, eds. *Figures anonymes, figures d'élite: Pour une anatomie de l'Homo ottomanicus*. Istanbul: Isis, 1999.

Antébi, Elizabeth. *L'Homme du sérail*. Paris: Nil Editions, 1996.

Bar-Chen, Eli. 'Two Communities with a Sense of Mission: The AIU and the Hilfsverein der Deutschen Juden'. In *Jewish Emancipation Reconsidered: The French and German Models*, edited by Michael Brenner, Vicki Caron and Uri R. Kaufmann, pp. 111–21. Tübingen: Mohr Siebeck, 2003.

Bocquet, Jérôme, ed. *L'Enseignement français en Méditerranée: Les missionnaires et l'Alliance Israélite universelle*. Rennes: Presses universitaires de Rennes, 2010.

Cabanel, Patrick, ed. *Une France en Méditerranée: Écoles, langue et culture françaises, XIXe-XXe siècles*. Paris: Creaphis, 2006.

Chatelard, Géraldine and Mohamed Tarawneh, eds. *Antonin Jaussen, Sciences sociales occidentales, patrimoine arabe*. CERMOC: Beyrouth, 1999.

Cohen, Mark. '"The Golden Age" of Jewish Muslim Relations: Myth and Reality'. In *A History of Jewish Muslim Relations: From the Origins to the Present Day*, edited by Abdelwahab Meddeb and Benjamin Stora, pp. 28–38. Princeton: Princeton University Press, 2013.

Campos, Michelle. *Ottoman Brothers: Muslim, Christians, and Jews in Early Twentieth-Century Palestine*. Palo Alto: Stanford University Press, 2011.

Dierauff, Evelin. *Translating Late Ottoman Modernity in Palestine: Debates on Ethno-Confessional Relations and Identity in the Arab Palestinian Newspaper* Filastin *(1911–1914)*. Göttingen: V & R Unipress, 2020.

Evri, Yuval. 'Partitions and Translations: Arab Jewish Translational Models in Fin de Siècle Palestine'. *Journal of Levantine Studies*, 9 (2019): pp. 71–93.

Firges, Pascal and Tobias Graf. 'Introduction'. In *Well-Connected Domains: Towards an Entangled Ottoman History*, edited by Pascal W. Firges, Tobias P. Graf, Christian Roth and Gülay Tulasoglu. Leiden: Brill, 2014.

Fishman, Louis. 'Arab Jewish Voices in Ottoman Palestine: Caught between the Sephardim and Palestinians'. *Revue d'histoire Culturelle* 2 (2021), http://revues.mshparisnord.fr/rhc/index.php?id=915

Goren, Haim. *'Echt katholisch und gut eutsch': Die deutschen Katholiken und Palästina 1838–1910*. Göttingen: Wallstein Verlag, 2009.

Gribetz, Jonathan Marc. *Defining Neighbors: Religion, Race, and the Early Zionist-Arab Encounter*. Princeton: Princeton University Press, 2014.

Ilbert, Robert. *Alexandrie, 1830–1930: Histoire d'une communauté citadine*. Cairo: Institut Français d'Archéologie Orientale, 1996.

Irving, Sarah. 'Elias Nasrallah Haddad: Translating Visions of Palestine'. *Jerusalem Quarterly* 85 (2021): pp. 9–29.

Irving, Sarah. 'Intellectual Networks, Language and Knowledge under Colonialism: The Works of Stephan Stephan, Elias Haddad and Tawfiq Canaan in Palestine, 1909–1948'. Unpubl. PhD dissertation. University of Edinburgh, 2017.

Irving, Sarah, Charbel Nassif and Karène Sanchez Summerer. '*The House of the Priest': A Palestinian Life (1885–1954)*. Leiden: Brill, 2022.

Jacobson, Abigail. *From Empire to Empire: Jerusalem between Ottoman and British rule*. Syracuse: Syracuse University Press, 2011.

Jacobson, Abigail and Moshe Naor. *Oriental Neighbors: Middle Eastern Jews and Arabs in Mandatory Palestine*. Boston: Brandeis University Press, 2016.

Kaplan, Zvi Jonathan and Nadine Malinovitch, eds. *The Jews of Modern France: Images and Identities*. Leiden: Brill, 2016.

Kaspi, André, ed. *Histoire de l'Alliance israélite universelle de 1860 à nos jours*. Paris: Armand Colin, 2010.

Khalidi, Rashid. *The Iron Cage, the Story of the Palestinian Struggle for Statehood*. Boston: Beacon Press, 2006.

Lardinois, R. and George Weill. *Sylvain Lévi, le savant et le citoyen: Lettres de Sylvain Lévi à Jean-Richard Bloch et à Jacques Bigart, Secretaire de l'Alliance israélite universelle (1904–1934)*. Paris: Honoré Champion, 2010.

Laskier, Michael. 'The Sefaradim and the Yishuv in Palestine: The Role of Avraham Albert Antebi: 1897–1916'. *Shofar* 10, 3 (1992): pp. 113–26.

Leff, L. M. *Sacred Bonds of Solidarity: The Rise of Jewish Internationalism in Nineteenth Century France*. Palo Alto: Stanford University Press, 2006.

Lemire, Vincent. *Jérusalem 1900: La ville sainte à l'âge des possibles*. Paris: Armand Colin, 2013.

Levy, Lital. 'Historicizing the Concept of Arab Jews in the "Mashriq"'. *The Jewish Quarterly Review* 98, 4 (2008): pp. 452–69.

Levy, Lital. 'The Arab Jew Debates: Media, Culture, Politics, History'. *Journal of Levantine Studies* 7, 1 (2017): pp. 79–103.

LeVine, Mark and Shafir Gershon. *Struggle and Survival in Palestine/Israel*. Berkeley: University of California Press, 2012.

Lorcin, Patricia and Todd Shepard, eds. *French Mediterraneans: Transnational and Imperial Histories*. Lincoln: University of Nebraska Press, 2016.

Der Matossian, Bedross. *Shattered Dreams of Revolution: From Liberty to Violence in the Late Ottoman Empire*. Palo Alto: Stanford University Press, 2014.

Mazza, Roberto. 'The Deal of the Century? The Attempted Sale of the Western Wall by Cemal Pasha in 1916'. *Middle Eastern Studies* 57, 5 (2021): pp. 696–711.

Mazza, Roberto and Idir Ouahes. 'For God and La Patrie: Antonin Jaussen, Dominican Priest and French Intelligence Agent in the Middle East 1914-1929'. *First World War Studies* 3, 2 (2012): pp. 145-64.

Navon, Albert. *Les 70 ans de l'École Normale Israélite Orientale (1865-1935)*. Paris: Durchlacher, 1935.

Neveu, Norig, Karène Sanchez Summerer and Annalaura Turiano, eds. *Preaching: Comparing and De-Compartmentalizing the Study of the Missionary Phenomenon (Middle East - North Africa - 19th-20th centuries)*. Leiden: Brill, 2022.

Rodrigue, Aron. 'L'exportation du paradigme révolutionnaire, son influence sur le judaïsme sépharade et oriental'. In *Histoire politique des Juifs de France*, edited by Pierre Birnbaum, pp. 182-95. Paris: Presses de Sciences Po, 1990.

Rodrigue, Aron. *De l'instruction à l'émancipation: Les enseignants de l'Alliance israélite universelle et les juifs d'Orient, 1860-1939*. Paris: Calmann-Levy, 1989.

Rodrigue, Aron. 'Totem, Taboos and Jews: Salomon Reinach and the Politics of Scholarship in Fin-de-Siècle France'. *Jewish Social Studies* 10, 2 (2004): pp. 1-19.

Sanchez, Karène. 'Ouvrir les trésors de la charité aux enfants dévoyés d'Abraham: L'action rançaise des sœurs de Sion en Palestine rançai et mandataire (1860-1948)'. In *L'enseignement française en Méditerranée: Les missionnaires et l'Alliance israélite universelle*, edited by J. Bocquet, pp. 207-38. Rennes: Presses Universitaires de Rennes, 2010.

Sanchez Summerer, Karène. *French in the Holy Land: Language, Diplomacy, Identity and French Education in Palestine (1918-1948)*. Amsterdam: Amsterdam University Press, forthcoming.

Sanchez Summerer, Karène. 'Les langues entre elles dans la Jérusalem ottomane (1880-1914): Les écoles missionnaires françaises'. *Documents pour l'histoire du français langue étrangère ou seconde* 43 (2009): pp. 119-43, http://journals.openedition.org/dhfles/864; DOI: https://doi.org/10.4000/dhfles.864

Sharkey, Heather. *A History of Muslims, Christians and Jews in the Middle East.* Cambridge: Cambridge University Press, 2017.

Tamari, Salim. 'Ishaq Al-Shami and the Predicament of the Arab Jew in Palestine'. *Jerusalem Quarterly File* 21 (2004): pp. 10–26.

Tamari, Salim and Ihsan Turjman. *Year of the Locust: A Soldier's Diary and the Erasure of Palestine's Ottoman Past.* Berkeley: University of California Press, 2011.

Tamari, Salim and Issam Nassar. *The Storyteller of Jerusalem: The Life and Times of Wasif Jawhariyyeh, 1904–1948*, trans. by Nadia Elzeer. Northampton: Interlink Books, 2014.

Vilmain, Vincent. 'A Jewish Mission in the "Orients"? Nineteenth century–1920'. In *Missions and Preaching: Comparing and De-Compartmentalizing the Study of the Missionary Phenomenon (Middle East – North Africa – 19th-20th Centuries)*, edited by Norig Neveu, Karène Sanchez Summerer and Annalaura Turiano. Leiden/ Boston: Brill, 2022.

Wallach, Yair. 'Rethinking the Yishuv: Late-Ottoman Palestine's Jewish Communities Revisited'. *Journal of Modern Jewish Studies* 16, 2 (2017): pp. 275–94.

Wilke, Carsten. 'Das deutsch-französische Netzwerk der Alliance Israélite Univer-selle, 1860–1914: Eine kosmopolitische Utopie im Zeitalter der Nationalismen'. *Frankfurter judaistische Beiträge* 34, 8 (2007): pp. 173–99.

CHAPTER 3

Tales out of School: Palestinian Students in a Jewish Institution, 1870–1937

Dotan Halevy and Amin Khalaf

This chapter analyses a micro-historical case of how Jewish-cum-Zionist institutions turned Palestinians into a foreign element in their own land.[1] Such an end is, of course, central to any settler-colonial project – the alienation of the native people from their soil and, finally, their replacement. Occupying the land, occupying its labour, economic dispossession and cultural-political marginalisation of the Palestinians were (and remained) clear Zionist goals. Yet, day-to-day relations between Jewish institutions and the Arab majority in Palestine until the Nakba often promoted these goals in a subtle, not always effective and not always ideologically consistent manner.

The case offered here demonstrates these dynamics through a close look at encounters that took place within the Jewish agricultural school of Mikveh Israel, founded in 1870 by the French Jewish organisation Alliance Israélite Universelle (AIU). Serving the AIU's broad goals of productivising and regenerating Jewish communities across the Middle East, Mikveh Israel set out to draw Jewish youth into agricultural training. When founded, it was the first institution of its kind in Palestine and among the leading agricultural institutions in the Ottoman Empire as a whole. Yet, although it was established for Jews, until 1937 its student body also included Muslims, Arabs and finally Palestinians. Moreover, Palestinian students were included as a way of promoting Jewish and Zionist interests. This chapter probes why that was the case and tries to reconstruct something of the Palestinian experience in, and of, the school.

The first part examines the school within the landscape of Ottoman Palestine. I argue that indigenous Palestinians took the school to be a local institution and felt that they had full rights to apply to and attend it. Wondering what prevented them from doing so led to a gradual Palestinian comprehension of Zionism's appeal to non-European Jews and its slow penetration into local institutions. The school administration, for its part, considered the admission of non-Jewish students as no more than a tribute to the Ottoman administration. As such, and although the school rejected Zionist ideology at the time, it cultivated a standard of discrimination against the native Arabs. The second part explores how Zionist institutions, during the British Mandate, utilised the school's long-standing reputation to tempt Arab dignitaries to collaborate with them. As the Zionist-Palestinian conflict was brewing during the Mandate years, some Palestinian families still saw this as an important opportunity and insisted on their children attending Mikveh Israel, in an effort to provide them with a path towards social mobility and political contacts.

'A Purely Ottoman School', Or Who Has the Right to Modern Schooling in Palestine?

The story of Palestinian presence in the agricultural school of Mikveh Israel begins with the official Ottoman authorisation to establish the institution – the 1870 *firman* (Ottoman Turkish: *ferman*), granted to Charles Netter of the AIU, by Sultan Abdulaziz (r. 1861–76). Scholars often take Ottoman consent for European endeavours on its soil for granted, as part of its quest for what James Gelvin terms 'defensive developmentalism'.[2] Yet, understanding the social makeup of the particular institution under concern here merits questioning the obvious: why did Sultan Abdulaziz and his successors consent to a French organisation establishing and running an agricultural school for Jews on Ottoman soil?

Indeed, the Ottoman Empire was not passive in accepting AIU's endeavour. The empire was rather loyal to a central pillar in its modernisation project: improving agricultural productivity and profitability. A specialised imperial office dealing with agricultural development was first founded in 1838. It took different shapes throughout the reform era, ultimately maturing into the Ministry of Forest, Mines and Agriculture in 1893.[3] State spending and loans for land reclamation and cash-crop cultivation also featured in the empire's productivisation efforts, culminating in the establishment of the Ottoman Agricultural Bank in 1888.[4] Acclimating the Ottoman peasantry to new crops and means of cultivation also required new technological expertise and the dissemination of scientific knowledge. Thus, the modernisation of agricultural work intersected with the modernisation of the empire's educational system. Ottoman reformers sought to establish a centralised system that would provide its population with access to modern education, develop a collective Ottoman identity and loyalty, and cultivate a class of professional civil servants and military officers to lead future state affairs. The educational reforms also aimed to integrate Muslim and non-Muslim educational institutions and bring foreign schools operating in the empire under state authority.[5] A plan for a generalised system of schools was conceived in 1845, the Ministry of Public Education was founded in 1857, and compulsory education was proclaimed in the 1869 Education Act.[6] Agricultural training was thus highly regarded, as both an instrument of economic modernisation *and* a vessel for modernising education in the rural areas of the empire.[7]

Yet, despite the novel intentions, the Ottoman Empire lacked the funds and trained pedagogues to accomplish these objectives, and 'many educational policies of the early nineteenth century simply remained on paper'.[8] In addition, by the 1870s, ethno-national and religious communities throughout the empire already enjoyed an established school system run by local churches, missionaries and foreign institutions. A European standard of education had been set in these places and was expected by Ottoman subjects.[9] And thus, while the 1869 Educational Act was meant to finally realise the empire's long-conceived educational objectives, during the 1870s and into the 1880s, these were still very hard to achieve.

The 1869 act, nevertheless, opened a new path in this direction. It subjected foreign schools to the empire's authority, setting the condition of their establishment on an imperial *firman* and a state inspection of their operation and curricula.[10] These schools mostly relied on foreign or community funding, often leased land from the state and, in this way, released the empire from a financial burden while supplying Ottoman subjects with modern education. Having these schools acknowledge Ottoman sovereignty by making their operation contingent on a *firman* thus seemed a successful policy. The AIU's request to the Sublime Porte to establish an agricultural school in Palestine was such an instance. Charles Netter presented the initiative to the Sublime Porte in 1869.[11] The goal was to improve living conditions for Jews in Palestine and other places in the empire and to promote Jewish 'national regeneration' through productive farming as an alternative to relying on charity.[12] For the empire, this was an excellent way of imparting professional, advanced European knowledge to some of its subjects with little to no investment on its part. As Emine Evered argues, 'non-Muslim schools were not only sources of concern for a security-driven state but also became a source of inspiration and the preferred models'.[13]

According to the 1869 Education Act, representing the spirit of equal rights for Muslims and non-Muslims alike, post-primary schools were open to all Ottoman subjects.[14] The 1870 *firman* for Mikveh Israel thus decreed: 'Although the school will be established for the children of the Jewish *millet*, students from other *millets* and religious sects shall be accepted as well'.[15] As evident, the *firman* did not determine whether the school was *obligated* to accept non-Jewish students and on what conditions, leaving enough room for the school's personnel and Palestinian applicants to debate the matter. Such was the heated exchange that appeared upon the pages of *Filastin* in the summer of 1912.

On 10 August 1912, *Filastin* informed its readers about a recent visit by the Jerusalem *mutasarrıf* (governor) to the Jewish colonies around Jaffa.[16] The *mutasarrıf* wanted to learn about the new agricultural technologies employed by the Zionists, so the paper argued, in order to establish a modern agricultural school for the general public. Given previous experience with state initiatives, however, *Filastin* was worried that this important project would be forgotten once 'the Honourable *Mutasarrif* is promoted, or heaven forbid, removed from office'. The paper thus proposed its own solution. Only 4 km from Jaffa, as everyone knew, stood the Jewish agricultural school known locally in Arabic as 'Neiter' – after the founder Charles Netter – and to Jews as Mikveh Israel. By then, the school was more than four decades old, a long-standing feature of the local scenery. It therefore seemed only natural to the journalist that the indigenous people of the land should also be able to benefit from its services.[17] Elsewhere in the empire, Abdulhamid II had established a network of agricultural schools, including the 1892 Halkli Ziraat Mekteb-i Alisi in Istanbul, where Ottoman subjects could enjoy the most advanced agricultural instruction by foreign-trained Ottoman officials.[18] Yet, for some reason, this was not the case in Palestine. *Filastin* claimed:[19]

> The school's *firman* clearly orders it to accept a number of local students [*wataniyyin*] that are non-Jewish. We do not know why our government has neglected this matter and failed to demand its application. Why do the residents not cling to this order and repeatedly ask the government to see to it? It is their right granted by the Sultan's *firman*.

This critique might have been lost in the plethora of issues occupying the local newspapers' pages during those years, had it not caught the watchful eye of Jewish journalist Nissim Malul. Born in 1892 to a Jewish-Tunisian family in Safed, he was trained in Islamic Studies and Arabic at the university in Cairo, where he later also taught Hebrew and became a Zionist. As part of his work to disseminate Zionism in Arab newspapers in Egypt and Syria, Malul paid a visit to Palestine in 1911. Supported by the Zionist Organisation's Palestine Office, he decided to settle in Jaffa, where he established connections with Arab newspapers.[20]

Within days of the article about 'Neiter', Malul published a response in the Beirut newspaper *al-Nasir*, accusing *Filastin* of supplying false information about Mikveh Israel.[21] In a subsequent issue, he presented a list of eleven Muslim students who had attended the school in previous years and claimed that they were all well-known to Jaffa folk and that *Filastin* unjustly misled its readers to tarnish the reputation of the Jewish school.[22] *Filastin* seized this opportunity to prove its deep acquaintance with the matter, but not less important, to expose the hidden interests of its articulate Jewish interlocutor. 'Everyone in Jaffa knows who Nissim Malul is, or Dr Malul as he refers to himself', *Filastin* wrote, . . .

> [He] came from Egypt to Jaffa to make a living and repeatedly asked the Zionists to employ him as a teacher in their school, but they did not believe he was adequately knowledgeable or educated. Since he found no other way of earning an income,

he approached newspapers and began writing for them, and some blindly sur-
rendered because of a number of copies he sold for them in the Jaffa markets [. . .]
[T]he majority of his articles on Jaffa defend the Zionists and Zionism [. . .] Little
by little, he began interacting with *Filastin* for no reason except to prove to the
Zionists that he is tirelessly protecting their interests and their rights. But the
Zionists know that Malul is like an ignorant defence lawyer [*al-muhami al-jahil*]
who loses the client's case in court because he does not know the law.

This was more than a political attack against a Zionist propagandist. Exposing
Malul enhanced *Filastin*'s broader critique of Mikveh Israel's discrimination and
Ottoman acquiescence to it. The newspaper identified the school and the Arab-
born Malul as part of the local, Ottoman, Arab and Palestinian culture. Yet, Malul's
clear orientation towards European Zionism and Mikveh Israel's selective body
of students, pointed in a different direction. The Jewish school, so *Filastin* argued,
does not admit 'even their own Sephardic Jewish kin (*Aw'lad abna' jinsiha min
al-Yahud al-Sefardim*)'.[23] Such a deviation from the Ottoman order blurred the
assumed distinction between Zionism – clearly a European colonialist endeavour
in the eyes of Palestinians – and the people and institutions anchored in the land
and its society. Hillel Cohen suggested that the 1929 riots were a key event in
Palestinian identification of all Jews in Palestine, no matter their origin or faction,
as potential Zionists.[24] *Filastin*'s remarks here might attest to an early notion that
Zionism would gradually sweep away even those Jews and institutions accepted
as 'natives of this land'.[25] Importantly, throughout this exchange, *Filastin* did not
identify Mikveh Israel as a Zionist institution. Indeed, the AIU in general and the
school in particular had uneasy relations with Zionism and with students coming from Zionist-affiliated colonies.[26] But the newspaper's remarks do suggest the
fear that 'Neiter' would become Zionist eventually.

Proving this point, *Filastin* exemplified how each of the eleven cases that Malul
mentioned demonstrated the school's discriminatory policy.[27] To begin with, five
of the students were sons of senior Ottoman officials with whom the school sought
to curry favour. None of them, *Filastin* claimed, acquired education in agriculture:
Mustafa Basyuni and Ahmad Sharaf al-Din were not natives of Palestine, but children of 'officials defending the colonialists and their interests' from Antakya and
Kastamonu; Hilmi Ahmad al-Sa'id, son of Hafiz al-Sa'id, who directed the state
orphanage in Jaffa, 'visited' the school for just two months;[28] Fayiz bin Mahmud
Effendi, son of the Jaffa subdistrict secretary, went on to become a scribe for the
Jerusalem Court of Appeals; and Ihsan Rif'at, son of the director of the Ottoman
Public Debt Administration, attended the school as a Turkish language instruc-
tor.[29] The students whom Malul mentioned from the adjacent village of Yazur,
Filastin claimed, were in fact the children of Arab staff at the school.[30]

Concluding the discussion, *Filastin* published an Arabic translation of the
school's *firman*.[31] Slightly altering the original text, *Filastin* quoted that the school

was dedicated 'in the name of (*'ala ism*)' the children of the Jewish community, rather than 'for' them (*min ajli*), as it appeared in the original.[32] This modification allowed *Filastin* to portray Mikveh Israel as operating, like other foreign institutions in the country, *on behalf of* a religious community or foreign country but still under the patronage of the Ottoman state. This was not merely for the sake of criticism: after publishing the *firman*, *Filastin* called on youths aged thirteen to sixteen to contact local government officials and apply for this 'purely Ottoman school (*madrasa 'Uthmaniyyah bahta*)'.[33]

It is unknown whether *Filastin*'s call did, in fact, encourage new students to apply to the school, but its extended attention to the matter definitely awakened some former students who described their harrowing experiences in letters. Mohammad 'Ali Tahir of Jaffa, for instance, wrote that he had applied to the school in 1907 when he was thirteen.[34] Accompanied by his father, he went to see the principal, who claimed he was unable to accept non-Jewish students. Tahir's father insisted, mentioning the school's *firman*. 'The principal debated his response', Mohammad Tahir writes, . . .

> . . . and after looking at me, said – 'How old are you?' I am thirteen years old, I answered. He debated once more what to say and then asked, 'Do you speak Hebrew?' I said – no. He looked at my father and repeated that he could not accept me because I did not know Hebrew. My father got angry and swore on his soul he would never enrol me in a foreign school.

Fayiz Haddad also saw his name on Malul's list and decided to share his experiences.[35] He fared better when it came to admission, but once enrolled, the school refused to teach him agriculture before he had learned French. But even after studying the language, the principal dismissed his request for agricultural training, claiming that he was destined to become 'an office clerk, not a farmer'.[36] School regulations also forbade Palestinian students from conversing in Arabic. 'I'd ask myself, insofar as I was able to then, embarrassed and astonished, why is Arabic so neglected and despised although we are in an Arab country?' Haddad wrote. Muted and distanced from the main curricular activity, Haddad suffered socially from the students' 'barely contained hatred, bitterness and degrading treatment'. He recalled how Jewish students distanced themselves from him 'without me knowing why'.[37] Two other Arab students of his cohort agreed that they did not gain much. One, the son of a labourer at the school, was treated with special contempt because of his rural background.[38]

School correspondence with the AIU's administration in Paris and with Ottoman officials validate the Palestinian perspective. Mikveh Israel walked the line between its commitment to comply with the *firman*'s condition and its desire to serve Jews only. For example, in 1905, after two Muslim students left, Principal Shmuel Loupo replaced them with two children from the village of

Yazur, 'in order to prove to the authorities that Muslims also attend the school'.[39] At the same time, the prestige that the Ottoman authorities ascribed to Mikveh Israel gave it considerable leverage. In September 1906, the *kaymakam* of Jaffa, Mehmed Riza Bey, implored Loupo to admit the two sons of 'Abd al-Rahman Effendi, Director of the Ottoman Public Debt Administration Office in Jerusalem.[40] The students, Basim and Sharaf al-Din, were brought to the school gates by the director of the Public Debt Administration office in Jaffa, an official subordinate to the boys' father. Yet, Loupo agreed to admit only the elder son, who could also serve as a Turkish instructor. The younger boy, a 'beginner in French and [a boy who] knows nothing', was rejected.[41] Underscoring the finality of his decision, the principal wrote to the *kaymakam* that the matter had already been discussed directly with his superior, the *mutasarrif* of Jerusalem.[42] In May 1914, shortly after the next principal, Eliahu Krause, had been appointed, the *mutasarrif* of Jerusalem demanded that the number of Muslim students in the school be increased to four or five each year. The principal's response to the AIU administration reflects the school's approach:[43]

> If Muslim students are recruited as the *Mutasarrif* wishes, in four years, we will have 16–20 Muslim students at the school. This is the maximum we can approve, and I plan on selecting the students from the best families in the country so that under their auspices, I may have some peace and quiet, which the authorities frequently undermine.

Krause's preferences notwithstanding, soon the school was left with no choice. As World War I broke out, the AIU informed the principal that Paris could no longer support the school and was instructed to reduce the institution's personnel to the bare minimum.[44] When the Ottoman Empire joined the war in November 1914, matters worsened. French nationals became enemy subjects, and the fate of the institution was uncertain. When the Ottoman military governor of greater Syria, Cemal Pasha, arrived in January 1915, most Zionist institutions in the country were closed on his order. In the few months under Krause's administration, Mikveh Israel became much more Zionist-affiliated than ever before, yet Krause insisted on continuing the school's work.[45] Recognising that the balance of power had shifted, he made every effort to give the impression that the school was a genuinely loyal Ottoman institution. As a first step, the entire school staff was Ottomanised. Then, Krause made the school Cemal Pasha's conference centre of sorts, a site where he could present officers and visitors with the modern agricultural advances of the Ottoman Empire. The principal quickly became one of Cemal's advisors on agronomy and was even sent on his behalf to research southern Palestine's agricultural potential in preparation for the Ottoman attack on the Suez Canal.[46] It was during the war that an imperial stone plaque bearing the sultanic *tuğra* was placed on the school's façade for the first time.

However, the most important element in forging the school's Ottoman identity was probably admitting local Arab students. In September 1915, advertisements were placed in the official Ottoman gazette *Kudüs-i Şerif*, announcing that the school would reserve ten places for Muslim students.[47] Fifteen Arab students eventually boarded at the school, in addition to thirty Jewish students and labourers. According to visitors, Arabic became the institution's spoken language along with Hebrew.[48] A bundle of *vesika* documents, official exemptions from military recruitment kept in the school's archive, points to the identity of these wartime students. Most came from elite families, including al-Shawwa, Bseiso and al-Nakhal from Gaza; Bani Baytar, Zaytuni and al-Dabbagh from Jaffa; and Tajir from Haifa.[49] The mixed Jewish-Arab group of some forty-five people held the school together during the war years, performing tasks assigned by Cemal Pasha, including planting trees on the new Jaffa boulevard named after him (now Jerusalem Boulevard). This group remained together until the British took over Palestine in 1917. On the eve of the Ottoman collapse, the order of the Ottoman *firman* finally was sincerely fulfilled.

'For the Sake of Peaceable Conduct': Where Zionist Supporters are Made

After World War I had ended, Principal Eliahu Krause led the school back to regular operations according to a clear national ideology. The school integrated naturally into the Zionist education system: classes were held in Hebrew only, and the school admitted mostly students from the Zionist *yishuv* rather than Middle Eastern Jews. And yet, Palestinian students continued to attend the school until the Arab Revolt of 1936–39. With the Ottoman Empire gone, accepting Palestinian students turned from a formal obligation into a voluntary policy designed to foster political ties with prominent Palestinian families. These, on their part, saw the school as a high-quality educational institution capable of offering its students access to economic and employment opportunities.[50]

Admitting sons of Palestinian notables started as part of the Zionist effort to cultivate an Arab alternative to the Muslim-Christian Associations, the Supreme Muslim Council and the Arab Executive. Backed by the Zionist Executive (*Hahanhala Hatziyonit*), the 'Muslim National Association' advocated joint Jewish-Arab development of the country and the continuation of the British Mandate.[51] Members of the Muslim National Association received Zionist financial support, assistance in securing employment in the British government and benefits such as enrolling their children in Jewish schools.[52] Indeed, most Arab students enrolled in Mikveh Israel under the Mandate were from families that were identified as *mu'arada* (opposition) or that could be swayed in that direction.

Consider, for instance, the relationship between members of the Jewish National Council (*Hava'ad Hale'umi*, hereafter JNC) and the Nablus notable Haidar

Bey Tuqan, former mayor of Nablus and member of the Chamber of Deputies in the Ottoman Parliament. Tuqan led the opposition against the Arab Executive Committee from its establishment in 1920, championing the activity of the National Muslim Association in the Nablus area.[53] Besides regular payment, his service won him the acceptance of his young relative Ahmad Tuqan, and later his own son, to Mikveh Israel.[54] Haidar Bey also served as a middleman for other potential supporters of Zionism based on a similar reward. One of these was Nablus Mufti Rashid Hashim, whom Tuqan introduced to the members of the JNC and the Zionist Executive. In a meeting held in September 1922, JNC member Yaakov Tahon promised the mufti that his fifteen-year-old son, Burhan al-Din Effendi, would be admitted to the school. When this promise remained unfulfilled, Tuqan contacted the JNC Secretary for Arab Affairs – none other than Nissim Malul. 'Accepting the sheikh's son at the school is a vital interest', Tuqan wrote. 'His father is a good man, whose words are heeded by the masses [*masmu' al-kilma bayn al-a'wam*] in the Nablus mosques'.[55] True to his long-standing cause of promoting Zionism among Palestinians, Malul took it upon himself to resolve the matter. He sent Burhan al-Din's details to Mikveh Israel and added a list of other Arab students to enrol, stressing how this would contribute to good relations with Arab notables.[56] A response from the school stipulated that the students would need to know Hebrew. Realising the obstacle, Malul attempted to convince the school otherwise:[57]

> I imagine this [would be] difficult and may also [interfere] in the relationship with our friends, the Arabs, whom we seek to bring closer to us and train as much as possible to participate in our national work, meaning, building this country in keeping with our spirit. These Arab students, who would not understand Hebrew upon their admission, could receive lessons in Hebrew from their Jewish peers so that in a short time, they would be able to study in the same class. The school administration should, of course, consider this demand, which is warranted by the situation.

The same issue appeared in the addresses of other mediators to Palestinian notables. In 1925, Sephardi publicist and political leader Avraham Elmaliach attempted to facilitate the admission of the son of Haidar Bey, whom he described in a letter to Mikveh Israel as 'one of the most respected Muslims in Nablus, who has done many favours for the Jews and will continue working for the benefit of good relationships among all parties in the country'.[58] The child, according to Elmaliach, 'knows Arabic and some English; he does not know Hebrew, but he will learn [. . .]'[59]

The school saw things differently. While willing to welcome 'one or two Arab students', recognising the gesture's importance, Principal Krause claimed that basic knowledge of Hebrew was a justified requirement. He suggested that the mufti's son learn the language 'at least to the level of understanding what he is being told'. However, he then added that 'we shall not be stringent regarding the rest of [his] studies and exams'.[60] This note is telling. Providing agricultural or educational training to Arab students was not the goal of accepting them and, therefore, one could 'not be stringent' about academic achievements in order to keep them at school. In contrast, knowledge of the Hebrew language was non-negotiable for basic communication and for exposing them to Zionist education. While the JNC and Zionist Executive saw these students' admission as merely a boon for Palestinian associates, the school sought to infuse the arrangement with educational value: turning these students into pro-Zionist ambassadors like their parents.

It is evident that the school exercised more than a modicum of independence in deciding which students to accept, when and on what terms. In another instance, in 1924, Haim Margaliot Kalvarisky, Head of the Zionist Executive Department of Arab Affairs, asked Krause to accept several sons of his close contacts.[61] 'As you know', the principal responded,

> . . . our school is barely able to provide for the needs of children from our own colonies, and every year many are left out due to lack of room. However, for the sake of peaceable conduct, we accept a small number of Arab students annually, and this year, I have already promised a certain Arab, a distinguished member of the Nimr family, to accept his son. We may accept one or two more.

The school's insistence on sifting applicants led Malul to change course and try placing Mufti Rashid Hashim's son, Burhan al-Din Effendi, and other students in the AIU's vocational school in Jerusalem instead.[62] His previous efforts did lead to several students from the families of 'our Arab friends' studying mechanics at the school.[63] But Mufti Rashid Hashim was not willing to sell his friendship for any price and insisted on enrolling his son in Mikveh Israel.[64] The school's reputation for professionalism in agricultural training eclipsed its recognition, by then widely accepted, as a Zionist institution. Burhan al-Din Effendi was sent to take Hebrew lessons with David Miller, a Zionist Hebrew teacher in Nablus' Samaritan community.[65] The school agreed to admit him at the start of the second semester in April 1923.[66] In November of that year, Haidar Bey's relative, Ahmad Tuqan, graduated from the school in a lavish ceremony. Being the only Arab among the fifty-six graduates of that cohort, the Hebrew press reported, he was applauded with 'special enthusiasm' by the crowd.[67]

During the second half of the 1920s and into the 1930s, Arab students also approached Mikveh Israel without Zionist wooing. These applicants mostly addressed the school directly in Arabic, presenting their social profiles. Mohammad 'Isa Ibrahim from the village of Jimzu, for instance, applied after completing two years at the well-regarded al-Madrasa al-Rashidiyyah in Jerusalem, one of the only secondary schools in the government education system during the Mandate.[68] Reaching out to Mikveh Israel testifies that some Palestinian families positioned the school at or near the top of the pyramid in terms of the country's higher education institutions. Yusuf Salim, a known landowner from Beisan, applied for his son, who had graduated from the city's government school 'top of his class in agriculture'.[69] He wanted his son to be trained in agriculture, Salim wrote, so he might someday oversee the family's lands. Responses to both applicants were positive and mentioned that the students must know Hebrew, have at least eight years of schooling and pay the school's tuition. Salih Jarallah, son of a renowned Jerusalemite family, applied twice in 1936–37, after receiving his entire education in Jewish institutions: the AIU school and the Hebrew Gymnasium in Jerusalem (*Gymnasia Ha'ivrit*). On his entrance examination, Jarallah proved knowledge of Hebrew and English and even had a letter of recommendation from acclaimed Jewish pedagogue and politician David Yellin. Krause also discovered that the student had family relations to a Jarallah branch that had sold land to Jews in the Ramla area. Despite the impressive resume, his acceptance was reversed in August 1937, for reasons that were never put in writing.[70] It would not be too far-fetched to assume that contemporary Arab responses to the Peel Commission Plan (exposed in July 1937) and fear of a renewal of the revolt influenced the decision.

Palestinian students in the school indeed suffered quite explicit discriminatory policies in periods when political tension was high. In one of the school's first historical accounts, Shlomo Hillels, who taught there from 1925 to 1935, described a very peaceful daily routine:

> Every year, a few Arab students also enter, primarily students from the most respected families in the country; they quickly learn the Hebrew language, live in fraternity and amity with the rest of the students, and it is impossible to tell the Arabs from the Jews. When they leave school, they continue to respect the institution and their peers.[71]

The lack of sources about the daily lives of Arab students among the Jewish majority makes it difficult to challenge this account. We do not know, for instance, if their religious rights were respected, how they perceived their peers or whether they truly identified with the institution. Yet, periods of unrest did leave an archival paper trail that offers a glimpse into these students' feelings and experiences. A complex picture appears of general admiration for the school, combined with uncertainty, disappointment, even despair.

Khalil Yunis of the village of 'Ar'ara began studying at Mikveh Israel in late 1928. His admission was supported by warm recommendations from his neighbours, members of the Zikhron Ya'akov colony committee.[72] The country-wide riots of August 1929 caught Yunis at the end of his first year at school while he and his friends were writing their final exams. But as violent clashes started around Jaffa, school activity was halted; Haganah forces took command of the facility, and some Jewish students were even drafted to guard isolated settlement points.[73] The Arab students, caught up in an awkward (and rather dangerous) situation, were sent home temporarily. Yet, once calm ensued and the school reopened, Khalil Yunis was not summoned back to conclude the school year. His report card was sent to him via a student of the Aaronsohn family when he returned home to Zikhron Ya'akov for the summer break.[74]

Mikveh Israel did not call back Khalil, even when the new school year opened. His benefactors in Zikhron Ya'akov seem to have understood what was behind this and wrote to the principal once again.[75] Thanks to the influence of the Yunis family, they argued, the village of 'Ar'ara refrained from taking part in the recent violence. Its residents even prevented neighbouring villages from attacking other Jewish colonies. The Zikhronis thus requested that the student Khalil be treated 'sympathetically, as the son of our friends', and that the administration inform other students of the matter 'in order to put him in good and friendly relations with his peers'.[76]

The school's failure to respond brought Khalil's family to approach the administration directly. His older brother, As'ad Yunis, saw to the matter. He was a student at the Arab College of Jerusalem (al-Kuliyyah al-'Arabiyyah), the most prestigious governmental institution of higher education in Palestine, but more importantly, a known bastion of Arab national education. On 8 November 1929, As'ad wrote to Mikveh Israel in neat hand-writing and ornate language, asking whether the school year had begun, and if so, why his brother had not been informed. Without mentioning the recent violent clashes explicitly, he manifested his awareness that this was behind the school's poor treatment of Khalil:

> My brother aspires to complete his studies at your school, which instilled a love of labour and agriculture deep in his heart. [However,] if you seek to deny it of him, and I do not think this is so [wa-la azun], then you would be betraying the [value] of knowledge and of imparting it to humanity. Nevertheless, I do not doubt your good intentions and your service to mankind and to individuals. I shall request from your honour a positive response that will give me joy and encourage me to place my brother's neck between your hands and his mind [to learn] from your teaching, advice, and instruction.[77]

Stressing education and knowledge as values in their own right, divorced from national affiliation, As'ad could transcend the unbridgeable political gap between the Zionist ideals of Mikveh Israel and those of the Arab College, from where he sent his letter. The Yunis family, having a son in each of these institutions, showed that some combination of the two worlds was not unimaginable. Interestingly, the Mikveh Israel administration was convinced by As'ad Yunis' letter, replying immediately that Khalil was welcome to return to school. According to his file in Mikveh Israel's archive, Khalil attended the school until his graduation in 1931.[78]

Student Sidqi 'Abd al-Raziq of Taybah (in the subdistrict of Tulkarm) experienced an even more arduous trial. He was admitted to Mikveh Israel in November 1934, after his older brother 'Abd al-Ra'uf, a former graduate of the school, had lobbied on his behalf.[79] 'Abd al-Ra'uf wrote heartfelt letters in Hebrew to Principal Krause in which he described his gratitude to the institution and faculty.[80] 'Because I studied at Mikveh Israel and was satisfied in every possible way', he wrote, 'Now I have a great job and good reputation among the people'.[81] Following lengthy negotiations over the school's tuition and once the prospective student was examined, Sidqi 'Abd al-Raziq joined the school.[82]

The Arab Revolt broke out in April 1936, halfway through his second year, and Sidqi was sent home for an unknown period. In a telephone call, Principal Krause told him that he would be sent a letter once the school decided that he should return.[83] But the letter did not come, and after four idle months at home Sidqi decided to check where matters stood. In a slightly clumsy hand, written in Hebrew translated from Arabic rather associatively, Sidqi expressed his desire to return to school:[84]

> I am writing you this letter and am very sorry it has been a long time since I have seen you, and I hope my letter here will describe to you how eager I am to see you and be at the school. I would have liked to write to you before and what delayed me was waiting to receive a letter from you . . . and I waited all the time, and there was no response! Now I ask you to send me an explanation about school and what I can do if the strike does not conclude by the end of the school year. And second, if you could send me my copy books and textbooks from my cabinet although there is some difficulty. Maybe I could come back for a little while. I am free all the time [and] have nothing to do. I have lost the key to the cabinet, and because of this, you may cut the lock. And that is what I wished to say, and finally, goodbye to you and my regards to all the teachers and all my classmates and everyone at Mikveh Israel.

At the bottom of the letter, next to his signature, Sidqi added the phrase 'writing is mine' to prove to the principal that the school's efforts to teach him Hebrew had been successful. While he was show-casing his knowledge of Hebrew, however, his classmates were taking their final exams, which he was denied. In an address somewhat more sensitive than to other Palestinian students, calling Sidqi 'my dear student', Krause notified him in a letter that his belongings would be sent to him, and when developments were clearer, he would have to contact the school.[85] By October 1936, the country-wide general strike had temporarily ceased, and the school debated what to do about students who had been forced to suspend their studies. Besides the Arab students, Jewish students drafted to serve in the Haganah also had to make up for the missed time. The school's administration finally decided that all such students would resume their studies at the point where they had halted them. Sidqi was called to return in April 1937.[86] In the meantime, Krause arranged for him to work at the government agricultural experiment station in Acre.[87] It is reasonable to assume that the principal, who seems to have truly cared about his student, sought not only to strengthen his professional experience in agriculture, but to remove him from his home village of Taybah, where Palestinian rebels were highly active. Indeed, Sidqi's own brothers, 'Abd al-Ra'uf and 'Arif Abd al-Raziq, were among the leaders of the revolt in the Tulkarm and Nablus areas.[88]

In December 1936, Sidqi began working in Acre and awaited the call to return to school, but again it failed to come. In May 1937, he sent another letter to Krause: 'While I am happy with work at the station and with life', he wrote, 'I am a little bit tired of this, and I now wait every day to be able to come to Mikveh Israel and carry on with my studies'.[89] The school did not respond, but in July, the Peel Commission published its partition proposal. Violence ensued, and Sidqi was sent home from Acre. In August, he sent his final letter to the school, wondering about the classes and despairing at what the future seemed to hold:[90] 'By now, I have been idle at home for more than three months, waiting for what will be done with me'. With youthful sensitivity for seeing into the future, he added: 'I see that the matter between the Arabs and the Jews will not be ending soon'. Later that month, Sidqi was sent a parcel of textbooks for independent study; it included a book on raising fowl, growing vegetables, animal husbandry and dairy production.[91] This was probably the school's last pedagogical action concerning an Arab student in the British mandate period.

Conclusion

In the eyes of its founders, Mikveh Israel was a means for weaning Middle Eastern Jews off charity and turning them into productive, active farmers. This goal guided the work of its administration and staff from the school's inception in 1870 until World War I. Despite the school's focus on the Jewish community, the local Arab population did not regard Mikveh Israel as a European ex-territory. In the spirit of the changes that the country experienced under late Ottoman rule, Mikveh Israel was viewed as the last word in modern education and professional training and reflected the spirit of progress that swept through the Ottoman domains. Ottoman subjects in Palestine, as elsewhere across the empire, used many European-run services that operated with Ottoman authorisation. Yet, as exactly such an institution, Mikveh Israel also became one of the first sites where Palestinians began wondering about the essence of Jewish activity in the country. During the British Mandate, Mikveh Israel took on a clear Zionist orientation and sought to educate its students in Zionist values, even if they were Arabs. Arab students were admitted to the school as part of Zionist efforts to put down roots in Palestine by establishing relationships with its native inhabitants. But at least until the Arab Revolt, Palestinians saw beyond this image, taking Mikveh Israel as a legitimate vehicle for social mobility, a status symbol and a path to government posts. In between these contending perspectives were the Palestinian children who navigated the escalating social and political tension in Palestine through their experiences of embarrassment, shame, boredom and fear, side by side with love, longing and faith in a better future. This chapter has attempted to expose something of their worlds.

Notes

1. An earlier version of this chapter was published in Hebrew as 'Kegerim Ba'aretz: Beit Hasefer Hahakla'i Mikveh Israel ve Talmidav Ha'arvim', *Zmanim* 135 (2016): 82–99. We thank the *Zmanim* journal editorial board for agreeing to the publication of this revised version. Thanks also to Tsameret Levi-Dafni, Giordano Bottecchia and Maya Johnston for their assistance.
2. Gelvin, *Modern Middle East*, pp. 71–86.
3. Ali Yıldırım, 'Osmanlı'da İlk Çağdaş', pp. 224–25; Williams, 'Cultivating Empires', p. 29.
4. Quataert, 'Dilemma of Development', p. 212.
5. Evered, *Empire and Education*, pp. 2–3.
6. Somel, *Modernization of Public Education*, p. 8.
7. Williams, 'Cultivating Empires', pp. 31–37. The first experiment in establishing an agricultural school was in the Vidin region on the banks of the Danube in 1847. The same year saw the establishment of the Ziraat Talimhanesi under the nascent agricultural council of the Sublime Porte in Yeşilköy. See 'Halkalı Ziraat Mektebi'nin Tarihçesi', p. 295.
8. Evered, *Empire and Education*, pp. 17, 31. Agricultural schools that had opened in the 1840s closed within several years of their foundations; see Yıldırım, 'Osmanlı'da İlk Çağdaş', pp. 234–36.
9. Evered, *Empire and Education*, p. 3.
10. Evered, *Empire and Education*, p. 18.
11. Krause, 'Hevle Haleda (According to the Letters of Netter)', pp. 107–8.
12. Rodrigue, *French Jews, Turkish Jews*, p. 56; on the AIU's broader initiatives in agricultural education, see ibid., pp. 110–11.
13. Evered, *Empire and Education*, p. 23.
14. Evered, *Empire and Education*, p. 21.
15. '*Bu mekteb her nekadar millet-i musaviye atfali için yapılacak ise de, milel ve mezahib saireden daha şagird kabul olacak*'. The Ottoman *Firman* for the Establishment of Mikveh Israel School, 1869.
16. 'Mulahazat', *Filastin,* 10 August 1912, p. 3.
17. Ibid.

18. Kadıoğlu, 'Halkalı Ziraat Mekteb-i Alisi (Halkalı Agricultural Academy)', https://istanbultarihi.ist/662-halkali-ziraat-mekteb-i-alisi-halkali-agricultural-academy-18921928. The 1880s was the decade in which Ottoman educational goals as a whole started to materialise. See Evered, *Empire and Education*, p. 2.

19. Ibid.

20. On Malul's biography and work, see Jacobson, 'Jewish Writing in Arabic', pp. 165–82.

21. 'Nisim Malul wa-Jaridat al-Nasir', *Filastin*, 21 August 1912, p. 3.

22. 'Madrasat Neiter al-Zira'iyyah', *Filastin*, 4 September 1912, p. 1.

23. Ibid. This claim was unsubstantiated. Sephardi students were certainly not excluded from the school. Yet, the message that the paper was trying to convey is clear.

24. Cohen, *1929: Year Zero*, p. 53.

25. Jacobson and Naor, *Oriental Neighbors*, pp. 8, 19–21.

26. Benbassa, 'Zionism in the Ottoman Empire', pp. 127–40; Rodrigue, *French Jews*, pp. 129–38. Mikveh Israel graduate Musa Goldenberg noted in his memoir that there were only three Hebrew-speaking students from the Zionist colonies in his 1910 class. The rest were 'distanced from Zionism and Hebrew and did not want to learn this language at all'. Goldenberg, *Vehakeren 'Odena Kayemet'*, p. 17.

27. 'Madrasat Neiter al-Zira'iyyah', *Filastin*, 4 September 1912, p. 1.

28. This student's acceptance to the school is also registered in Mehmed Riza Bey Jaffa Kaymakam to Mikveh Israel Principal Shmuel Loupo 518, 25 September 1906, CZA, J41/423.

29. 'Madrasat Neiter al-Zira'iyyah', *Filastin*, 4 September 1912, p. 1; on the Ottoman obligation to teach Turkish in all foreign schools, see Rodrigue, *French Jews*, p. 87.

30. The land for the school was appropriated by the Ottoman state from the villagers of Yazur with the school's foundation. The school and the village saw periods of tense relations throughout the decades up to 1948. See Levi-Dafni, Bottecchia and Halevy, 'Mikveh Israel', pp. 12–20, http://www.mikveisrael.org.il/upload/mi.pdf

31. 'Madrasat Neiter: Surat al-Firman al-Sultani', *Filastin*, 2 October 1912, p. 1.

32. 1870 Ottoman Firman for the Establishment of Mikveh Israel School, Mikveh Israel School Archive; see also a different phrasing of the *firman* given by al-Wa'ari, *Mawqif al-Walah*, pp. 89–90.

33. 'Madrasat Neiter al-Zira'iyyah', *Filastin*, 5 October 1912, p. 3.

34. 'Ghayirna Yatakalam', *Filastin*, 25 September 1912, pp. 2–3.

35. 'Ghayirna Yatakalam', *Filastin*, 11 September 1912, p. 2.

36. Ibid.

37. Ibid.

38. Ibid.

39. Shmuel Loupo to President of AIU, March 1905, AIU Archives, Israel XLIV E 127 Loupo [1905].
40. Correspondence between Jaffa Kaymakam Mehmed Riza Bey and Mikveh Israel Principal Shmuel Loupo, September 1906, J41\423, Central Zionist Archive (CZA).
41. Ibid.
42. Ibid.
43. Mikveh Israel Principal Eliahu Krause to the president of the AIU, 3 May 1914, AIU Archive, Israel XLI E 123 Krause (1914–17). Krause himself was a graduate of Mikveh Israel, former principal of the AIU agricultural school Or Yehuda in Izmir and a former manager of Sejera colony of the Jewish Colonisation Association.
44. President of AIU to Mikveh Israel Principal Eliahu Krause, September 1914?, AIU Archive, Israel XLI E 123 Krause (1914–17).
45. Shapira, *Me'a Shana Mikveh Israel*, pp. 211–17.
46. Rubinstein, *Tatzkir Eliyahu Krause Le-Djamal Pasha.*
47. 'Muslemim bemikveh Israel', *Haherut*, 14 September 1915; 'Bebet Hasefer Hahakla'i Mem Yod', *Haherut*, 29 October 1915.
48. M. Segev to Rahel Yana'it, 5 June 1962, CZA, J41/410.
49. Mikveh Israel School Archive, File 1317.
50. On the separation between Jewish and Arab education in Palestine, see Furas, *Educating Palestine*, pp. 39–69.
51. On the Muslim National Association, see Cohen, *Army of Shadows*, pp. 18–20.
52. The Jewish National Council Files, CZA, J25/4380; Cohen, *Army of Shadows*, p. 67.
53. Ibid.
54. 'Mikveh Israel's Celebration', *Do'ar Hayom*, 6 September 1923; Avraham Elmaliach to Mikveh Israel School, 26 September 1925, CZA, J41/384.
55. Haidar Bey Tuqan to Nissim Malul, 18 September 1922, CZA, J1/289.
56. (Mikveh Israel Acting Principle) S. Buskilah to Nissim Malul, 1 October 1922, J1/289, CZA.
57. Nissim Malul to S. Buskilah, 5 October 1922, CZA, J1/289.
58. Avraham Elmaliach to Mikveh Israel School, 26 September 1925, CZA, J41/384.
59. Ibid.
60. Eliahu Krause to Nissim Malul, 19 December 1922, CZA, J41/328.
61. Eliahu Krause to Haim Margaliot Kalvarisky at the Zionist Executive, 22 July 1924, CZA, J41/317
62. Nissim Malul to (AIU Vocational School in Jerusalem's Principal) Shmuel Loupo, 5 October 1922, CZA, J1/289.
63. Shmuel Loupo to Nissim Malul, 17 October 1922, CZA, J1/289.
64. Haidar Bey Tuqan to Nissim Malul, 25 October 1922, CZA, J1/289.
65. Haidar Bey Tuqan to Nissim Malul, 28 December 1922, CZA, J1/289.

66. Haidar Bey Tuqan to Nissim Malul, 19 April 1923, CZA, J1/289.

67. 'Mikveh Israel 's Celebration', *Do'ar Hayom*, 6 September 1923.

68. Mohammad 'Isa Ibrahim to Eliahu Krause, 25 August 1932, Mikveh Israel School Archive, File 854.

69. Yusuf Salim to Mikveh Israel School, 12 December 1935, Mikveh Israel School Archive, File 896.

70. Eliahu Krause to Salih Jarallah, 1 August 1937 and 23 June 1937; Eliahu Krause to Yitzhak Ben Zvi (Deputy Director of the JNC), 13 September 1936, Mikveh Israel School Archive, File 1333.

71. Hillels, *Toldot Hanisayon Harishon*, p. 76.

72. Mikveh Israel School to Zikhron Ya'akov Colony Council, 1 November 1928, Mikveh Israel Archive, Khalil Yunis Student File (no. 27).

73. Shapira, *Me'a Shana Mikveh Israel*, pp. 338–41.

74. Mikve Israel to As'ad Yunis, 13 November 1929, Mikveh Israel Archive, Khalil Yunis Student File (no. 27).

75. Zikhron Ya'kov Colony Council to Mikve Israel, 29 October 1929, Mikveh Israel Archive, Khalil Yunis Student File (no. 27).

76. Ibid.

77. As'ad Younis to the Eliahu Krause, 8 November 1929, Mikveh Israel Archive, Khalil Yunis File.

78. Mikve Israel to As'ad Yunis, 13 November 1929, Mikveh Israel School Archive, Khalil Yunis Student File (no. 27).

79. On 'Abd al-Ra'uf's colourful biography, see Cohen, *Good Arabs*, pp. 11–12.

80. 'Abd al-Ra'uf abd al-Raziq to Eliyahu Krause, 1 April 1934, Mikveh Israel School Archive, Sidqi 'Abd al-Raziq Student File (no. 102).

81. Ibid.

82. Correspondence between 'Abd al-Ra'uf abd al-Raziq and Eliyahu Krasue, 1 April 1934–15 November 1934, Mikveh Israel School Archive, Sidqi 'Abd al-Raziq Student File (no. 102).

83. Sidqi 'Abd al-Raziq to Eliyahu Krause, 18 August 1936, Mikveh Israel School Archive, Sidqi 'Abd al-Raziq Student File (no. 102).

84. Ibid. The excerpt has been translated into English with a view to remaining true to the original language as much as possible.

85. Eliyahu Krause to Sidqi 'Abd al-Raziq, 27 August 1936, Mikveh Israel School Archive, Sidqi 'Abd al-Raziq Student File (no. 102).

86. Eliyahu Krause to Sidqi 'Abd al-Raziq, 25 October 1936, Sidqi 'Abd al-Raziq Student File (no. 102).

87. Eliyahu Krause to the Government Agricultural Experiments Station, 1 December 1936, Sidqi 'Abd al-Raziq Student File (no. 102).

88. Cohen, *Good Arabs*, p. 11.

89. Sidqi 'Abd al-Raziq to Eliyahu Krause, 3 May 1937, Mikveh Israel School Archive, Sidqi 'Abd al-Raziq Student File (no. 102).

90. Sidqi Abd al-Raziq to Eliyahu Krause, 2 August 1937, Mikveh Israel School Archive, Sidqi Abd al-Raziq Student File (no. 102).
91. M. Vinik, Acting Principal of Mikveh Israel, to Sidqi Abd al-Raziq, 23 August 1937, Sidqi Abd al-Raziq Student File (no. 102).

Bibliography

Al-Wa'ari, Naela. *Mawqif al-Walah wa-al-'Ulama wa-al-A'yan wa-al-Ikta'yyin fi Filastin min al-Mashru' al-Sahayuni (1856-1914)*. Beirut: Al-Mu'assasa al-'Arabiyyah li-al-Dirasar wa-al-Nashr, 2012.

Benbassa, Esther. 'Zionism in the Ottoman Empire at the End of the 19th and the beginning of the 20th Century'. *Studies in Zionism* 11, 2 (1990): pp. 127–140.

Cohen, Hillel. *1929: Year Zero of the Arab-Israeli Conflict*. Waltham Brandeis University Press, 2015.

Cohen, Hillel. *Army of Shadows: Palestinian Collaboration with Zionism, 1917-1948*. Berkeley: University of California Press, 2008.

Cohen, Hillel. *Good Arabs: The Israeli Security Agencies and the Israeli Arabs, 1948-1967*. Berkeley: University of California Press, 2010.

Evered, Emine Ö. *Empire and Education under the Ottomans: Politics, Reform, and Resistance from the Tanzimat to the Young Turks*. London: I. B. Tauris, 2012.

Furas, Yoni. *Educating Palestine: Teaching and Learning History under the Mandate*. Oxford: Oxford University Press, 2020.

Gelvin, James L. *The Modern Middle East: A History*. New York: Oxford University Press, 2011.

Goldenberg, Musa. *Vehakeren 'Odena Kayemet: Pirke Zihronot*. Merhavya: Sifriyyat Hapo'alim, 1965.

Halevy, Dotan and Amin Khalaf. 'Kegerim Ba'aretz: Beit Hasefer Hahakla'i Mikveh Israel ve Talmidav Ha'arvim'. *Zmanim* 135 (2016): pp. 82–99.

Hillels, Shlomo. *Toldot Hanisayon Harishon Lehakla'ut Yehudit Be'eretz Yisrael*. Tel Aviv: Omanut, 1940.

Jacobson, Abigail and Moshe Naor. *Oriental Neighbors: Middle Eastern Jews and Arabs in Mandatory Palestine*. Waltham: Brandeis University Press, 2016.

Jacobson, Abigail. 'Jewish Writing in Arabic: Shimon Moyal, Nissim Malul and the Mixed Palestinian/Eretz Yisraeli Locale'. In *Late Ottoman Palestine: The Period of the Young Turk Rule*, edited by Yuval Ben-Bassat and Eyal Ginio, pp. 165–82. New York: I. B. Tauris, 2011.

Kadıoğlu, Sevtap. 'Halkalı Ziraat Mekteb-i Alisi, 1892–1928'. *History of Istanbul from Antiquity to 21st Century*, vol. 8. https://istanbultarihi.ist/662-halkali-ziraat-mekteb-i-alisi-halkali-agricultural-academy-18921928.

Krause, Eliyahu. 'Hevle Haleda shel Mikveh Israel'. *Zion* 2, 7 (1942): pp. 104–8.

Levi-Dafni, Tsameret, Giordano Bottecchia, and Dotan Halevy. 'Mikveh Israel: Historiya Hevratit'. *Hasadna le-Historiya Hevratit*, 2014, http://www.mikveisrael.org.il/upload/mi.pdf

Quataert, Donald. 'Dilemma of Development: The Agricultural Bank and Agricultural Reform in Ottoman Turkey, 1888–1908'. *International Journal of Middle East Studies* 6, 2 (1975): pp. 210–27.

Rodrigue, Aron. *French Jews, Turkish Jews: The Alliance Israélite Universelle and the Politics of Jewish Schooling in Turkey, 1860–1925*. Bloomington: Indiana University Press, 1990.

Rubinstein, Shimon. *Tatzkir Eliyahu Krause Le-Djamal Pasha*. Jerusalem: Independent Publisher, 1985.

Shapira, Yosef. *Me'a Shana Mikveh Israel: 1870–1970*. Tel-Aviv: Tarbut ve-Hinuch, 1970.

Somel, Selçuk Akşin. *The Modernization of Public Education in the Ottoman Empire, 1839–1908: Islamization, Autocracy, and Discipline*. Boston: Brill, 2001.

Williams, Elizabeth Rachel. 'Cultivating Empires: Environment, Expertise, and Scientific Agriculture in Late Ottoman and French Mandate Syria'. Unpubl. PhD Dissertation. Georgetown University, 2015.

Yıldırım, Mehmet Ali. 'Osmanlı'da İlk Çağdaş Zirai Eğitim Kurumu: Ziraat Mektebi (1847–1851)'. *Osmanlı Tarihi Araştırma ve Uygulama Merkezi Dergisi* 47 (2018): pp. 223–40.

Yıldız, Özgür. 'Halkalı Ziraat Mektebi'nin Tarihçesi'. *The Journal of Academic Social Science Studies* 5, 4 (2012): pp. 293–306.

CHAPTER 4

Costumes and the Image: Authenticity, Identity and Photography in Palestine

Sary Zananiri

From microhistories tracing the lives of individuals to the broader currents that shaped the collective lives of those in the region, over many decades Salim Tamari's work has given us an important understanding of late Ottoman and Mandate Palestinian society. The agile shift between society and individual is a hallmark of Tamari's work, as is the use of Palestinian sources to explicate the way in which transnational politics affected the minutiae of Palestinian social life, particularly through the lens of diaries, memoirs and photography.

In light of this tension between the social world and the individuals who occupied it, this chapter looks at the social, cultural and political dimensions of the traditions surrounding clothing and costuming, particularly what has been termed 'cultural cross-dressing'. Ideas of cultural cross-dressing have primarily been advanced in relation to Orientalist touristic practices that came to be adopted by local communities in Palestine and elsewhere. However, untangling the practice by analysing period photographs shows a significantly more complicated social history surrounding the genre in Palestinian communities, particularly when read in combination with questions of fashion, class, nationalism and the modern tourism and souvenir market.

One of the earliest examples of foreigners in cultural cross-dress is Francis Frith's self-portrait *Frontispiece: Portrait in Turkish Summer Costume* (1858).[1] Another early instance, two images of Princess Nazli Hanim, of Khedival Egypt, one in a subversive cultural and gendered cross-dress, the other in European clothing, were likely taken at the same time, in the late 1870s or 1880s.[2] From a western perspective it has been argued that this was a strategy for empowering aristocratic women;[3] a queered Orientalist cultural appropriation;[4] or an adventurous insertion of the Western self into the Orientalist and Biblical imaginary in Palestine specifically.[5]

Evidence from the analysis of family albums and other archival sources from Palestine and Lebanon suggests that the peak of activity for Arab portraits in cultural cross-dress by the aspirant bourgeois classes of the Levant was the 1920s;[6] nonetheless, the practice continued to persist to the Nakba and beyond.[7]

From a technological perspective, in the 1920s photography, including vernacular photography, became much more accessible.[8] More importantly, this decade and those on either side of it hold local cultural and political significance with respect to identity formation processes that were shifting dramatically in Palestine. Arab nationalism, the Nahda and shifts from more confessional communal towards nationalist identities were creating a context of cultural metamorphosis, alongside the establishment of colonial rule via the British and French Mandates of the Levant. In Palestine, this can be seen in rising nationalist sentiment, culminating in the strike and revolt of 1936–9.

The 1920s appear to have been a 'golden age' for photo postcards and *cartes de visite* of Arabs in cultural cross-dress. Scholarly opinion, however, is divided on what this Arab adoption meant. It has variously been argued that this was an emulation of European practices that helped to distance the middle and upper classes from rural *fellahin*;[9] that it was an instatement of cosmopolitanism;[10] that it was the modern fashion of the moment;[11] that there were resonances of a satirical indigenous cultural reply to Orientalist assumptions about Arabs;[12] and, in relation to gender cross-dressing, as a mode of self-expression with respect to Arab vernacular photography in the broader region.[13] Untangling these various arguments and scholarly opinions requires much contextualisation. It is, however, worth noting that photographic studios appear to have serviced a local clientele as much as visitors and expatriates in the cosmopolitan cities of the region.[14]

In analysing Palestinian family photographic collections – and those of the region more broadly – images of cultural cross-dressing are common, although the efficacy of the term as applied to Arabs might be debated, given the proximity of those adopting 'cross-dress' to those for whom it was a simply a daily reality. These images of men and women in 'traditional' costume are often accompanied by props such as amphorae and baskets for women, guns for men, as well as tree stumps, stools or ottomans.[15] These images are generally taken against painted backgrounds, with scenes often involving idealised nature such as foliage or landscapes. This 'costuming' stands in contrast to the everyday wear of the people being photographed, which would in most cases have included suits or dresses fairly similar to their western, middle-class counterparts.

This chapter asks what these photographic portraits can tell us and how we can read the social, cultural and political dynamics of commissioning them in late Ottoman and British Mandate Palestine. What can the content of an image tell us about middle-class Palestinians, their self-perceptions and the ways in which they related to broader Palestinian society? And, most importantly, how did modern notions of fashion affect changes in the ways in which 'traditional' Palestinian clothing was mobilised?

Performing Self, Performing Other

Constructing Biblical Authenticity

'Cultural cross-dressing' – that is, the practice of donning the clothing of the 'Orient', or an imagined approximation of it – and having one's photo taken by a studio photographer appears to have been a relatively common practice, and certainly a service that was actively advertised by photographic studios in Palestine. In Jerusalem, photographers such as Garabed Krikorian (1847–1918), Khalil Raad (1869–1957) and Hanna Toumayan (dates unknown, active in the early twentieth century)[16] advertised photos in 'Bedouin' costumes, generally those of towns such as Ramallah and Bethlehem.[17]

While the practice was far from unique to Palestine,[18] the conditions of cultural cross-dressing in Palestine were significantly augmented by a parallel photographic industry – sometimes involving the same photographers – oriented towards the souvenir market and coloured by notions of Biblical authenticity. In analysing photos of cultural cross-dress, I ground them in broader vocabularies of photography, including vernacular photography (which by the 1920s was becoming commonplace for middle classes globally)[19] and biblified photography for the souvenir market, which had an ever-expanding presence since the birth of the medium.[20]

Photographers' advertisements aimed at customers who might want their portraits taken in cultural cross-dress seemingly made little distinction between Bedouin clothing and that of the *fellahin* (rural dwellers, villagers, peasants), with the strong tradition of regionalism in clothing such as *thobs* (traditional embroidered dresses) bearing localised *tatreez* (embroidered cross stitch) patterns. The collapsing of the two socially distinct categories of *fellah* and Bedouin in advertisements to foreign markets indicates an amorphous spectrum of exotic otherness positioned in relation to the modern (western), middle-class subject centred in the photograph. However, it also putatively constructs the authenticity of *fellah* and Bedouin identities in line with the broader photographic trends of biblification in the region.[21]

Biblified photography claimed to reconstruct the Biblical past through the imaging of its contemporary 'traces', while eschewing Palestinian modernity. This is now a well-documented phenomenon in the photography of Palestine,[22] which began with the birth of photography in 1839, continued through the British Mandate period, arguably continuing to have impacts into the present.[23] In a cultural context where the space between the urban world of the merchants and intelligentsia and the rural sphere of peasants and agricultural industry was formative of different lived experiences,[24] there is a significant class subtext to biblified photography, which focused on the 'ancient' subjects of the *fellah* world.

Biblification projected images of rural Palestinian life (conflated with an imagined Biblical past), through photographic studios that were almost entirely based in cities where there was a density of clientele. Biblified photography often featured rustic tropes such as fishermen, shepherds, peasants sowing and reaping harvests or other archetypal religious figures as evidence of continuity with the ancient past. In a photographic market geared towards Western consumption, people were generally excised from the framing of the 'Holy Land' if they did not appear in traditional costume.[25] This formalised a vocabulary of Biblical aesthetics that had far-reaching effects, equating traditional Palestinian clothing of the early twentieth century with Biblical costume, a trend that has continued in post-World War II western cinema and beyond.[26]

Even in scholarly circles, early-twentieth-century *fellah* culture was coloured by Biblical perceptions, with anthropologists such as Tawfik Canaan arguing in his work on agriculture that he depended on the Old Testament to compare past and present practices. He shared with Gustav Dalman the idea that the Old Testament could not be understood without understanding contemporary Palestinian folk practices.[27] In this regard, *fellah* authenticity, and by extension the clothing/costuming worn by those communities, was presumed central – even on a scholarly level – by urban middle-class Palestinians.

The putative Biblical authenticity denoted by costuming in the myriad biblified photographs – produced by both local and visiting photographers of Palestine – is fundamental to understanding the emergence and valency of cultural cross-dressing in Palestine. Indeed, the role of fashion as the signifier of an originary Biblical past is underscored by the photographing of 'pilgrim groups' in 'traditional costumes of the natives',[28] offering opportunities for tourists to temporarily inhabit and perform the space constructed by the Western Biblical imaginary before returning to their modern selves.[29]

The conflation of Biblical narrative with *fellah* identity through costuming can also be seen elsewhere in the tourist industry. The market for souvenirs and antiquities, for instance, which featured photography and a plethora of religious goods, often sold Palestinian clothing described as 'Oriental costume' or 'Eastern embroidery' (Figure 4.1), particularly in high-profile establishments such as the Boulos Meo store and the American Colony's Vester & Co, both located in the prestigious Grand New Hotel at Jaffa Gate (Figure 4.2).

The incorporation of rural styles of clothing into the realm of souvenirs indirectly relied on the assumed sanctity of the Palestinian landscape. *Thobs* and *tatreez* joined a plethora of souvenirs such as carved mother-of-pearl and olive-wood items, prayer books in olive wood bindings, local pressed flowers arranged in botanical displays and vials with water from the River Jordan or samples of earth from the 'Holy Land'.[30]

The sale of Palestinian clothing alongside other such materials tacitly draws a link between the 'holy landscape' and the people that inhabited it, mediated *through* the garments that they wore. Indeed, the clothes that were increasingly available in the souvenir market might be seen as a disembodied, performative extension of the 'Holy Land' for tourists who purchased them. This in turn was

Figure 4.1 Advertising on the back of a Jerusalem map produced by the American Colony (1904). Image courtesy of Chadbourne Antiques.

Figure 4.2 American Colony store, Jerusalem, with Frederick Vester standing out front (1905–13), American Colony Photo Dept, LOT 13845. Image courtesy of the Library of Congress.

supported by the vast bodies of biblified photography produced by foreign and Palestinian photographers, addressed to a primarily western popular consumer market hungry for Biblical content.

The question of authenticity seems to have extended beyond the sale of such costumes into the realms of performance for the tourist market. Yazan Kopty's cross-analysis of photos from the National Geographic Society (NGS) archive related to an article by Edward Keith-Roach (1885–1954, a colonial administrator and governor of Jerusalem) is highly informative of such performances. The first image, titled *A Christian Girl of Jerusalem in Bethlehem Costume*, shows a young woman wearing a Bethlehem dress and *shaṭwa* (head dress). A second image in the same article is captioned with the following: 'Many American visitors to Jerusalem will recognize this girl: A young Christian student in a handicrafts class at the American Colony is here wearing the Bethlehem costume'.[31]

This demonstrates a performance of authenticity through costume for both the readership of *National Geographic* and visitors to the American Colony. More importantly, it also hints at networks of garment production for the tourist market, given the American Colony's interests in the industry through the Vester & Co store at Jaffa Gate, as well as their involvement in charitable institutions. It gives us some insight into the ways in which Western humanitarian ventures may have influenced the popularisation of clothing styles from Ramallah and Bethlehem through Christian charity networks. Training in embroidery, sewing and handicrafts was given to many girls, from Armenian orphans in the wake of the Genocide and World War I,[32] to orphans at the American Colony Christian Herald Orphanage,[33] both of which operated until the early 1920s. Handicrafts had become not only an industry, but also a tool for fundraising, as evidenced by the efforts of staff at the Swedish School, which was also in Jerusalem.[34]

The costume from Keith-Roach's article also matches several unpublished portraits in the NGS archive of another woman, a servant at the American Colony. Although in the style of Bethlehem, the costume in each of these images has been identified as of low quality and for the tourist market. The fact that both girls are shown wearing it suggests that they may have been asked to pose in it,[35] or that it may have even been a uniform of sorts. This acts as a very different marker of class than the *cartes de visite* and photo postcards commissioned by middle-class sitters in cultural cross-dress. It also draws a sartorial correlation between urban and rural working people.

While these commercial underpinnings of costuming have a basis different from middle-class adoptions of 'traditional' clothing, they demonstrate some of the classed intra-Palestinian intersections of involvement with the garment production industry and the entrenchment of ideas of authenticity and belonging through clothing and costume. Indeed, the market for Biblical content, in this case, is mediated by the enaction of biblification through the performance of costume. This is in stark contrast to more straightforward biblified images.

A prime example of the latter material is Khalil Raad's photo of a peasant girl holding a sickle and a sheaf of wheat, titled *Ruth the Gleaner* (Figure 4.3). The Biblical reference to Ruth transforms an image of rustic peasantry into one that not only transcends time, but also collapses the divide between the earthly and ethereal planes. The photographic subject here transgresses time in the creation of the image, collapsing Biblical past with modern present.

While the context of popular imaging addressed the lucrative market for biblified photography, there are parallel dynamics in scholarly imaging. *Fellahin* workers – particularly those on archaeological sites and surveys – are treated as endemic to the landscape, effectively constructed as an indigenous vestige in which the 'ancient' body is an extension of the 'ancient' land.[36]

However problematic these biblified tropes might be, they point towards a perceived acknowledgement of authenticity that is conferred through these sartorial signifiers. This authenticity might be problematised by questioning the terms costume and clothing. That is, costume as an ethnographic marker denoting a distance between the wearer and the garment, as opposed to those for whom the same garments represent a daily life experience – clothing. This changing signification from clothing to costume reinforces the classed subtext of photography, with notable impacts on the ways in which we might understand the practice of cultural cross-dressing and the performativity of wearing such clothing. The shift from the clothing of daily life to a mode of costuming performatively adopted by

Figure 4.3   *Ruth the Gleaner*, by Khalil Raad. Image courtesy of Wikimedia.

those from outside its typical sphere thus denotes a confluence of biblified markers, class and culture in which a mode of transgression is implicit.

With studio photographers providing a range of costumes for portraits in cultural cross dress and souvenir purveyors selling similar clothing to the tourist market, rural fashions came to be popularly understood as a site of authenticity, whether Biblical, nationalist, or a mixture of the two.

A key question in navigating the Palestinian adoption of cultural cross-dress is the garments themselves, in particular the *thob*, typically worn by women. Analysis of costumes gives a sense of some of the broader networks involved in producing this genre of images. While Bethlehem costume appears to have been advertised – and certainly features in imaging – the significant bulk of photographic portraits of women show them dressed in the Ramallah style. This can be seen in the image of the Sahhar family (Figure 4.4), the portrait of Julia Luci and her sister-in-law,[37] the various images of the Ramallah-based Friends Girls School (Figure 4.8) and the majority of images thus far unearthed in other archives.

The Joseph Malikian collection of studio photographs dealing with cultural cross-dressing presents an extremely useful sample of thirty images;[38] it is one of

Figure 4.4 Image of Ajia (back left), Ellen (front) and Yousra (back right) Sahhar, c. 1932. Studio photograph, studio unknown. Image courtesy of Micaela Sahhar and the Sahhar Family.

the few collections actively addressing this genre. The images contain a mixture of male and female, local and foreign subjects. Of these photographs, twenty contain images of women either on their own, in groups, or in groups with men.

While there is sometimes a mix of costumes in the same image, thirteen photos show Ramallah dress, eight Bethlehem costume and six Bedouin attire, with three that are undefinable or the product of fantasy. The collection ranges from images taken between 1890 and 1930, with two peaks: the 1900s (twelve images) and the 1920s (eleven). There is just a handful for the 1910s, which might be explained by the dire economic and political situation during World War I. The collection also includes various studio photographers' family members in cultural cross-dress. Examples include portraits of Najla Nijim Krikorian (c. 1910) and Sara Raad Nijim (c. 1915), although many of the Krikorian family members had such portraits taken.[39]

There may be several reasons for the over-representation of Ramallah – and to a lesser degree Bethlehem – dress in these photos. They are both larger regional cities, and both are located close to Jerusalem and to a lesser degree Jaffa, the main economic hub. They were also predominantly Christian cities, so their over-representation in such portraits may also have been impacted by the patterns of mercantile networks, given that the majority of studio photographers came from Christian denominations, both Arab and Armenian.

Performing Class

Photography, including images of cultural cross-dressing, was fashionable among the growing mercantile classes that emerged in the nineteenth century and represented a performance of class status,[40] but more broadly demonstrated participation in the practices of modern life with accoutrements of technology and taste.[41]

An article in the Arabic press, dated 1904, instructed those sitting for portraits 'not [to] wear anything that is not worn naturally or that is a contrivance "such as tarboosh, 'ammah, hats, and seductive clothing"'.[42] These questions of *dhawq* (taste) were central to the construction of modern Nahda aesthetics and, as Stephen Sheehi argues, were 'integral to a process of *embourgeoisement*' in urban centres.[43] Indeed, the act of commissioning more typical studio portraits was to engage in the personification of modern ideals, effectively putting one's best self forward. It was to enter into a formal visual language that embodied questions of *dhawq*, class and aspiration with props that often replicated idealised domestic interiors, such as books, desks and other accoutrements.[44]

While such an article railed against portraiture aesthetics that upset notional good taste, the evidence in photographic archives suggests different social attitudes. The culture of *cartes de visite* and portrait photo postcards, of which images of cultural cross-dressing are but a sub-category, saw the spread of studio portraits through social networks as a mode of exchange, particularly among the bourgeois and *nouveaux riches* classes.[45] The reformulation of taste vis-à-vis cultural cross-dressing in local communities hints at shifting attitudes to a matrix of class and modernity in how they saw themselves and how they related to other communities to which they were in proximity.

Read against more typical portraits, photographs in cultural cross-dress begin to hint at cultural fracture lines in Palestinian society. This cultural fracture can be seen as operating on two levels: firstly, and more obviously, around delineations of class and the cultural differences between urban and rural populations. Portraits in cultural cross-dress show a very different relationship between the photographic subject and the camera lens. The commissioning of a studio portrait from a professional photographer is a process very different from either the documentation of rural communities or the staging of images with models for the biblified photographic market, by photographers who were either middle-class compatriots of the objects or foreigners visiting the region.

Secondly, it demonstrates a deviation of different middle-class attitudes and fashions. The Mandate-era journal *Iqtisadiyyat* is discussed at length by Sherene Seikaly in her seminal work *Men of Capital*. She outlines the journal's profiling of the figure of *al-adib al-za'if* (the false intellectual) 'who was "excessive in imagination" [and part of] an "army"' of 'unprofessional poets and writers who wander aimlessly [. . .] that emphasized "trivial" and "useless" "theoretical knowledge"'.[46] This figure is contrasted against *al-adib al-haqiqi* (the true intellectual) who . . .

> . . . was the 'man of the nation' [. . .] successful businessmen [. . .] such men exhibited the 'judicious and prudent work' of 'authentic nationalism' [. . .] In addition to their material achievements, these men provided a moral compass. Distant and scientific, they were above 'arrogance, pageantry, and ostentation'.[47]

This examination of differing middle-class attitudes shows the definitive role of social respectability – and implicitly moral panic – in shaping taste, particularly where youth was concerned in the context of the nationalist ambitions of the period. On the one hand, such a comparison lauds the building of business, industry and even political structures, which are redolent of the nationalism associated with the period. On the other hand, it hints at a playful, bohemian, cosmopolitan cultural paradigm, in which the urban intelligentsia and those in proximity to the cultural trendsetters of the day sought to redefine themselves at a time of great social, cultural and political change.

The latter attitude might be best exemplified by the figure of Wasif Jawhariyyeh, now well documented with the publication of his memoirs *The Storyteller of Jerusalem* by Salim Tamari and Issam Nassar and the release of a second book, *Camera Palaestina*, by Tamari, Nassar and Stephen Sheehi, examining his photographic collection.[48] Tamari described an image of Jawhariyyeh 'taken in the late fifties show[ing] the man on his sixtieth birthday, lying on a garden lawn in a silk abbayeh near the Beirut corniche with a mixed look of boredom and nostalgia. An aging dandy and traumatized flaneur'.[49]

The image of a post-Nakba Jawhariyyeh in cultural cross-dress, pining for the Jerusalem of his youth, gives us an inkling of the social and cultural loss, not just of the land, but also of a particular site of urban bohemian identity at a time formative for the region. Indeed, the vivid social life engendered by his photographic albums and memoirs paints a picture of a Jerusalem different from its often-dour subtext in Biblical imaging.[50] What emerges from this is a youth culture marked by drinking, cannabis and even cocaine at private parties in the mansions and *oda* (bachelor apartments) of Jerusalem, while nightlife in the form of cafés and bars mushroomed in the years after World War I.[51]

To contextualise the Palestinian adoption of cultural cross-dressing in this context is to consider it as a generational trend in sartorial experimentation during a formative period in Arab nationalism. The act of class transgression in adopting *fellahin* clothing by urban Palestinians, even if only for the moments needed to produce a studio photograph, tells us much about processes of identity formation in urban youth culture and how they may have related to their compatriots in rural communities, albeit through the lens of class transgression.

As much as these transgressions of class upset notions of *dhawq* within the upper- and middle-class strata of Palestinian society, the impacts of this transgression came through a re-identification with the rural sphere of the *fellahin*, whether real or imagined. If we consider the act of cultural cross-dressing as a site of class transgression, how can we begin to understand the ways in which those engaged with such practices related to their rural compatriots? What can other aspects of identity present in the genre tell us about the relationship of urbanites to the rural 'periphery'? How does class transgression intersect with other transgressions of identity as the practice developed during the late Ottoman and British Mandate period? And how did such transgressions operate in shaping urban identities?

Performing Gender

While the context of a class analysis of cultural cross-dress yields an argument around a transgression of urban–rural divides and a shift in identification with rural compatriots, analysis of gender in such images beckons other questions. Indeed, in thinking through questions of gender relations and transgression, a matrix develops in which the aspect of culture in cross-dress might be reread in a more nuanced light.

In a world where modern gender norms were becoming increasingly formalised and regulated, particularly within the context of Arab nationalist ambitions, the humour of gendered cultural cross-dress at once delineated gender roles, while at the same moment undermining them by transgressing gender performativity. While there is less evidence of gendered cultural cross-dress in comparison to the broader genre, it appears to have operated on several levels: firstly, there are images of two men in studio photographs, with one dressed as a *fellaha* (rural woman); secondly, women dressing in urban men's attire, with a suit and *tarboosh*, in both vernacular and studio photographs; and thirdly, contexts of fancy dress parties, with androgynous people whimsically dressed in men's and women's costumes that are amorphously, but fashionably, 'Oriental'.

Özge Calafato's recently released *The Making of the Modern Turkish Citizen: Vernacular Photography in the Early Republican Era* is a landmark study about the reproduction and regulation of gender in modern Turkish photography.[52] While the geographic terrain dealt with is Turkey, the production of gender tropes in portraiture points to parallel nationalist projects in the Arab Levant. This study of vernacular photography points to the radical restructuring of post-Ottoman Turkish society, concerned with reformulating unity in the production of the new secular Republican state, particularly in the 1920s.[53] While gender cross-dressing rarely appears in this seminal study of portraiture,[54] the importance of new modes of representation around gender in photographic tropes shows the ways in which the image was a significant mediator for reshaping the gendered, national identity of the new Turkish state created after World War I. In contemplating this, Calafato points to the . . .

> . . . sometimes contradictory relationship between photography and gender roles in the early Republican era, since these images urge us to probe the visibility of gender and rethink the normative forms of masculinity and femininity that the Turkish modernization project worked so hard to establish, impose and propagate.[55]

Comparing the Turkish case to *Iqtisadiyyat* is instructive. While men may have been contrasted as *al-adib al-za'if* and *al-adib al-haqiqi*, women's behaviours and roles were also subject to nationalist comparison. Women were categorised as either *musrifa* (spendthrift) or *hasifa* (judicious). The *musrifa* was the archetypal elegant urban woman, driven by the spendthrift consumption of fashion and jewellery. In contrast, the *hasifa* was frugal and resourceful, yet still fashionable. She would make her own clothes based on the latest fashions in a display of domesticity but might also be engaged in professional life as 'a doctor, a lawyer, a teacher, a writer, a journalist, and an engineer'.[56] In both cases, it would appear that gender was regulated by modernity and modes of consumption and pre-figured upon an urban or semi-urban identity.

While the genre of cultural cross-dressing clearly had a significant element of class transgression in crossing urban–rural divides, the element of gender cross-dress embodies a double transgression: first, that of class through breaching urban–rural divides in the assumption of *fellah* and Bedouin clothing; and secondly, a transgression that toyed with gender norms.

Figure 4.5   Unknown (left) and Salim Zananiri (right), c. 1927. Photo postcard,
photographer unknown, Jerusalem. Image courtesy of the author and
the Zananiri family.

Images such as Figure 4.5 typify male-to-female cross-dressing. Similar images,
while not common, can be found elsewhere. For instance, an image of two men
dressed in village costume, one as a woman, appears in artist Qais Assali's new
video work on the subject of Khalil Sakakini.[57]

The temptation to read these images of same-sex couples as evidence of homosexual or trans identity is strong to the contemporary eye, although there is no
textual evidence to support this, but future research may reveal other narratives.
Questions of these more recent gender and sexual identities aside,[58] these images do
display a level of intimacy that is queerly homosocial, if not homosexual,[59] from our
position today. In other geographies, such as North America, similar photos, albeit
without the dimensions of cross-dressing – either gendered or cultural – have been
explored under changing rubrics of male friendship in the nineteenth and early
twentieth centuries.[60] This has been described as *romantic friendship*, a term applied
to deeply emotionally intimate – though generally non-sexual – friendships that
were typically formed in the late teens or early twenties.[61]

In reading these images of male cultural and gendered cross-dressing, notions
of romantic friendship both upset and uphold familial relations and the familial
unit. On the one hand, they embody an idealised vision of gender which operates
on normativity that espouses the frugal industry of the *hasifa*, with her industri-
ous nature, holding an amphora to fetch water. On the other hand, the gender

transgression mocks notions of class both in its idealised production of middle-class virtue and through a classist humour that breaches the urban–rural divide in embodying *fellaha* femininity. While these images hold a humorous intent, they also portray earnest, if bourgeois, intimacies between the sitters, despite highly gendered photographic props such as the masculine rifle and feminine amphora that uphold gender divides.[62]

The question of intimacy in these photos becomes even deeper if we consider them from the perspective of their circulation. The majority of these images were *cartes de visite*, cabinet cards or portrait postcards. They thus represented a form of social currency exchanged between peers of a certain social class.[63] The exchange of such images through private networks of friends and acquaintances or inclusion in family photo albums reflects another mode of intimacy through the limitation of access to such images. This is a mode of circulation very different from and more private than the public access of the enormous catalogues of biblified images available for purchase in photograph or souvenir stores or turned into postcards or photo books for purchase on the tourist market. In this regard, the context of gender cross-dress, while humorous, must be read as part of a private joke between intimates.

The question of humour intersects between the consequences of gender play and the realm of class and culture. While the tradition of cultural cross-dressing as an Orientalist touristic practice clearly predates Arab adoption of the practice – at least in Palestine – the complexities of intra-Arab class relations clearly inform the humorous subtext.

Mary Roberts, in discussing the two images of Princess Nazli described above, suggests that humour was fundamental to understanding the exchange of *cartes de visite* with her European interlocutors:

> The power of the joke is premised on that gap between the stereotype and its knowing performance by the indigenous subject [. . .] What better demonstration of mastery of another culture than to parody that culture's stereotypes of one's own?[64]

In the case of Nazli, photographed in both European dress and in the masculine guise of an Ottoman *effendi* (gentleman, or high-ranking official), the subversion of both cultural and gender expectation treads a careful line between two differing visions of modern selfhood, western and Ottoman. It must be noted that, dating to the early part of the last quarter of the nineteenth century, there were different cultural and political contexts in which the Ottoman Empire still held great sway, in contrast to images of the post-Ottoman context of the 1920s.

The genre of images of women dressed as men operates quite differently from those of men dressed as women and often accompanied by a friend. Looking at a number of vernacular photographs, such as the portrait of Adeline Abiad (c. 1920, Haifa) or Marie al-Khazen's *Two Women Dressed as Men* (1927, Lebanon)[65] in which she and her sister pose, gender play becomes a means of disrupting patriarchal social power. In both images, women are dressed in *tarbooshes*, with male attire such as suits, ties and pocket squares. Describing these images as a culturally syncretic form of dandyism – echoing Tamari's reading of Jawhariyyeh – Yasmine Nachabe Taan suggests that the phenomenon is more than simply a fashion trend, but a form of 'power dressing' that destabilises gender and was part of producing the modern cosmopolitan figure.[66]

In the cases of Princess Nazli, Adeline Abiad and the al-Khazen sisters – all from different degrees of elite background – assuming the figure of the *effendi* was not a transgression of class, but of gender. While humour plays a part in the construction of identity in these images, they still embody the same contradictions of men dressing as women in that they simultaneously reify and disrupt gender norms. Where these images of women dressed as men differ from men dressed as women is in maintaining or extending, rather than relinquishing, class and gender privilege.

Outside of elite female-to-male cross-dressing, a curious case documented in a letter by Helen Bentwich, dated 24 February 1919, describes the motivations of a woman of significantly fewer means to don men's clothing:

> She is a woman from Jaffa, an Orthodox Christian, who, during the [First World] War, was starving. Her husband went away to fight, and she was left with her child alone. So she put on men's clothes, and went out as a porter. But the Turks took her for a man, and conscripted her, & for 9 months she fought in the Turkish army, up Beersheba way, right in all the fighting. After we [the British] came, she came to Jerusalem, & her husband died. The Syrian & Palestine Relief ladies gave her work as their door-keeper, but she would wear her soldier's trousers and tarboosh, as she is very proud of having been a soldier. So these dear ladies were horrified & turned her away. Since then, she has been cleaning boots outside the Jaffa Gate. Her child is in a convent. She looks full of life & interest & is willing to do any sort of work – from washing or scrubbing to carpentering or driving a car.[67]

The unnamed woman's story is clearly grounded in the economics of gender during the financial crises accompanying the war. Cross-dressing, in this case, came with an economic prerogative. Her approach ironically mirrors the visions of gender, economy and nationalism put forward by *Iqtisadiyyat* some fifteen years later. Yet, it is clear that the woman's actions were seen as transgressive and culturally at odds with social values, at least for the well-to-do ladies of the Syrian and Palestine Relief Fund, and likely to many others.

Her motivations for such gender play were clearly very different from her upper- and middle-class counterparts. This was not a playful engagement with bohemian or dandyist youth culture or the fashion of the day. However, as a member of the urban poor, she may have been in proximity to those groups. Yet, to continue wearing her Ottoman army uniform in the years after the war was also a decision. Whether through processes of self-identification, for economic reasons, or both, the incident demonstrates a confluence with Taan's ideas of power-dressing in more elite women's photos.

These questions of class shift again with photographs of costume parties. Alfred Roch, an Arab Nationalist businessman and 'politician with a bohemian panache' held a series of Easter costume parties in the 1920s. The image of one such party, dated 1924, with those in attendance dressed as Pierrot clowns, is immortalised as the last of its kind in the video work A Sketch of Manners by Jumana Manna, with the date inverted to 1942.[68] The re-appropriation of Commedia dell'arte costumes has a resonance of the humorous cultural replies to Princess Nazli's photographs decades earlier. However, another one of Roch's costume parties demonstrated some of the implications of gender play. At this party, likely in the 1920s,[69] a different constellation of gender and culture in cross-dress was visible.

Another photo clearly is of the same party at Roch's home in Jaffa, cited as 1924 and ascribed to Rachman,[70] a Jewish photographer who was apprenticed to Issa Sawabini in Jaffa.[71] The date 1924, however, conflicts with the photo used by Manna. This image of apparent self-orientalisation revels in the fantastical. A group of five androgenous people are dressed as women, in costumes that included feathered turbans and the draped lines of loose-cut dresses and 'harem pants' that had become the staple of European fashion designers such as Jeanne Paquin and Paul Poiret and the costuming of the Ballet Russe in the years before and after World War I. The influences of the east had affected the fashions of the colonial centres and the accompanying trend of androgyny in a period that toyed with gender as much as with the identity of exotic others. Behind them stand a further three men, one in costume akin to a maharaja and two as attendants, with ties and suit sleeves peeping out from beneath their plain robes.

The element of gender cross-dress reflects a significant disruption to this vision of European high-end fashion which is purported to mirror – at least in some semblance – the sorts of things that 'Oriental' elites may have worn in day-to-day reality. Indeed, the frivolity and fashion-forward design of the costumes sits at a threshold of the global taste of the times. This makes the event a subversion through gender of western sophistication, but it also enacts and embodies that taste at the same time.

This contradiction is all the more interesting given the yearly political timing of the event, not just with Easter, but also with the Nabi Musa (Prophet Moses) festival. As Nisa Ari points out, the Nabi Musa festival was in the process of being remade into a nationalist, rather than a Muslim, holiday, moving in reference to the Christian Easter. This was particularly so after the Nabi Musa riot in 1920, which left several people dead. Given Roch's Melkite background and his centrality to the Arab nationalist cause, which would see him become a member of the

Arab Higher Committee by 1936, the political timing of a party in such a season is a statement unto itself.[72] It shows a commitment to bridging historical communal divides by ritualising new and modern entertainments at a time of year that was increasingly marked by the assertion of Palestinian nationalist identity. The image is documentation of an event *in situ*, rather than a studio photograph taken with costumes expressly prepared for the purposes. In this regard, the fine clothing, details of jewellery and even the use of make-up takes on a particular significance within the social context of a masquerade party.

Indeed, this cultural duel between urban sophisticates east and west, demonstrating their broad horizons in the world through costume, says as much about the global interconnections of class that modernity brought with it as it did about the brewing nationalist debates. In considering the gender dimensions from a more local perspective, however, these paradigms and parodies of the *musrifa* weaponise her figure as a mark of both their own urbane sophistication and a tacit rebuke of the new colonial regimes establishing themselves throughout the region.

This makes the group very interesting to analyse, considering the political and economic significance of a man like Roch, an Arab nationalist figure as well as a successful orange-grower and -exporter. This made him not only one of *Iqtisadiyyat*'s revered *adib al-haqiqi*, but clearly also a bohemian dreamer, the reviled *adab al-za'if*. A memoir relays a story of Hajj Amin al-Husayni – with whose family Roch enjoyed good relations – attending Purim parties in Tel Aviv surreptitiously dressed as a blond woman, complete with make-up.[73] It would seem that even within the innermost social circles of Arab nationalism, gender transgression had at least some degree of permissibility, even if just in moments of social jest carved out of cultural rituals.

The nationalism that pervades studio portraits of Arabs in cultural cross-dress – laying claim to Palestinian authenticity by embodying the figure of the *fellah* – features a confluence with the nationalism of elites such as Roch. However, the guests at his Easter party appear to be less interested in claiming a historicised authenticity, more in mobilising the authenticity of their own cultural capital through their knowledge of the contemporary fashions of the day. Nationalist trajectories appear to have been an underlying cultural path of cross-dressing, as practiced in studio photographs and in real-life events. While these practices relate to a colonial reply, the aspect of women dressing as men also engaged with, undermined and sought patriarchal power in an agenda that was slightly different from images of men dressed as women.

How did the performance of nationalism that is present in various forms of gender and cultural cross-dress manifest in notions of belonging? How did notions of belonging and the revisionism of the past create expressions of nationalism? And what can cultural cross-dressing tell us about identity formation processes and their porosity in the 1920s?

Performing Nation

The positioning of a linear narrative of progress was an ideologically forma-tive cultural factor around the globe. If Arab cultural cross-dressing is viewed from this perspective, the performance of Arab authenticity in these photos is as much about distancing the modern subject from an originary, yet-to-be mod-ern position, as it is about claiming a nationalist historical lineage in a period where nationalism was reshaping identity and reconstructing it in reference to the past.

If we are to consider the interaction of modern subjectivity and auto-orientalisation, where does that place the local subjects of such photos? In questions of humour, implicit classism aside, part of the answer lies in the very modern redefinition of heritage, particularly by the 1920s in Palestine. A parallel can be seen not only in urban policies that limited modern construc-tion materials in Jerusalem's Old City and a programme of demolishing mod-ern architecture in pursuing its historical preservation by the Pro-Jerusalem Society,[74] thereby prioritising a biblified architectural heritage, but also in the establishment of modern archaeological institutes concerned with the study, research and historical preservation of the past.[75] Viewed from such a per-spective, the modernising project, begun in the late Ottoman era and continu-ing under the British Mandate after the war, marks a departure point which was concerned with shaping and preserving the past as much as with future nationalist aspirations.

Looking at a number of Palestinian cross-dressing images from the interwar period, Christian Palestinian individuals and families – both Arab and Armenian – are over-represented. This points to the shifting prioritisation of national iden-tity by the beginning of the British Mandate over the communal identities that had shaped the civic culture of Palestine in the late Ottoman period, reflecting the changing political realities from the turn of the century to the 1930s. Despite this, however, a very real gap existed between those who had come to form the 'embourgeoised' modern middle classes and those *fellah* and Bedouins who were subjects of biblified photography. This classed division in the photography of Palestine again informs questions of nationalism where clothing and costuming meet in the imaging of Palestine.

Evidence from family albums such as the engagement photo of Hanna Bastoli depict a spectrum of clothing (Figure 4.6). While Bastoli and her fiancé are dressed in the latest modern fashions, her mother-in-law Hilwa Al-Douiri wears a *thob*, while the figure to the right, presumably her brother or brother-in-law, wears a *dishdash* and suit jacket. This is not so much an image of cultural cross-dress, but one that gives us a sense of the immense cultural shifts taking place in the early 1920s in wealthy regional centres such as Bethlehem, which were connected to major urban centres. It shows the proximity of the younger generations to the fashions of their parents or grandparents, as much as it demonstrates new modes of identification.

Figure 4.6   Hanna Bastoli and family members on her engagement day, 1924
(Hanna Bastoli, George Ayyoub and her mother-in-law, Hilwa Al-Douiri). From
Maha as-Saqqa's photo album, 0027.01.0054, https://palarchive.org/index.php/
Detail/objects/81449/lang/en_US. Image courtesy of the Palestinian
Museum and Maha as-Saqqa.

It is interesting to note, however, that Al-Douiri's dress does not have the distinctive traditional *tahriri* stitch of Bethlehem, but a form of cross-stitch, terminating
on the bodice with a chevron, reminiscent of the Ramallah style.

Nevertheless, images such as the photo of the 1924 graduating class of the
Friends Girls School (Figure 4.7) attest to the importance of clothing as an
instatement of national identity. The decision to picture a graduating class in
matching *thob*s highlights the coalescence of an authentically Palestinian subject position within a framework that prioritised modern educational models.
The photo contrasts with other school photos dating from as early as 1901 to
the interwar period, which show the pupils dressed in pinafores and typical
middle-class clothes of the day.[76] The 1924 image also demonstrates a confluence of transnational attitudes to authenticity, from a localised nationalist
response on the one hand to a religious-run Quaker school, with its mixture
of Arab and foreign staff, on the other. A similar photo of Ermina Totah, wife
of the school's headmaster Khalil Totah,[77] taken as a photo postcard in cultural
cross-dress, demonstrates that the school's administration was also culturally
invested in performing Palestinian authenticity and indigeneity through such
photographs.

Figure 4.7   The Friends Girls School Graduates in 1924, 0097.01.0465. Image courtesy of the Palestinian Museum digital archive.

This Arab performance of indigeneity has valence for considering the cultural conditions under which Palestine and Palestinians were seen abroad in both photography and cinema.[78] If this is the case, it makes such performances part of a localised – albeit ideologically modern – redefinition of the past, again underscoring the transnational attitude toward Palestinian indigeneity born of biblified photographic tropes.

A different insight into the significant context of cultural and political change of the 1920s comes from the Frank Scholten photograph collection, shot between 1921 and 1923 for his two-volume book *Palestine Illustrated*.[79] A handful of the many unpublished photos within the significantly larger corpus deals with a recently migrated Jewish woman, part of the Third Aliyah which primarily came from Russia and Eastern Europe (Figure 4.8). Many of the images show her in a *thob* derived from the Ramallah style, as well as in other contexts, including as a nurse working at a Jewish-run quarantine station. Most of these photos are marked Tel Aviv – barely a decade old at the time – and the caption on one suggests that this image was part of an engagement celebration.[80]

The adoption of the *thob* by a Jewish immigrant to Palestine poses a number of questions, especially in light of present-day debates about cultural appropriation surrounding *tatreez*.[81] Notwithstanding these very real questions, the cultural context of the early 1920s demands a more detailed analysis of this series of images.

Figure 4.8   *Untitled* [marked Tel Aviv], 1921–3, photographed by Frank
Scholten, UBL_NINO_F_Scholten_Fotos_Doos_15_0355.
Image courtesy of NINO and UBL.

The image, and the broader context of the series, raises interesting questions
about the approach of Zionist immigrants in Palestine towards authenticity and
how such authenticity was acculturated across confessional spheres. It is notable
that this particular photograph was taken in the context of the Third Aliyah. This
wave of Zionist immigration was notable for labour organisation (particularly in
fields such as agriculture) and the purchase of land, and is widely regarded as
having played a 'pioneering' Zionist role.[82]

Given that the *thob*, as already argued, was seen as a Biblical continuity of the
land, the migrant's choice of costume here is telling. As the new wave of immigrants built colonial connections to the land through purchase and labour, the
act of wearing the *thob* indicates a process that is significantly more politicised
than an Orientalist touristic practice of cultural cross-dress. Its adoption is recast
as a signifier of indigeneity to the landscape. The sartorial assumption of the
thob becomes conflated with an assumption of indigeneity, part of the process
of Zionist re-periodisation of Zion/exile/return that had other cultural parallels
designed to signify a putative resumption of indigeneity.[83]

Yael Zerubavel discusses the concept of the 'Hebrew Bedouin', the Palestinian-
born children of Zionist immigrants of the Second Aliyah (1904–14). She describes
the identity formation process in which they embraced 'native' identity and distanced themselves from European notions of the exilic Jew:

The *kafiya*, especially the white variety (also known as the *hatta*) popular among the local *fellahin* and Bedouins, and the *abbaya* (the Arab overcoat), resembled the portrayals of the ancient Hebrews' dress. During the first decades of the Yishuv, putting on the *kafiya* (and to a lesser degree the *abbaya*) became an act of displaying a local identity by drawing on ancient and contemporary features of a native culture.[84]

This positions the performance of Zionist cultural cross-dress as a process of indigenisation that bridged the space between the colonial project and the colonial body *through* costume. This question of indigeneity, as noted by Jonathan Gribetz, was supported by Zionist historiography of the time, including the ideas of Yitzhak Ben-Zvi and David Ben Gurion, in which the *fellahin* were assumed to be the descendants of ancient Jews and Samaritans who had converted first to Christianity and later Islam.[85]

What is unaccounted for in Zerubavel's analysis is the role of popular biblified imaging, projected out of Palestine through photography, in shaping the aesthetics of Biblical authenticity in the period. A more detailed account of the role of biblified popular culture – and the link between Christian and Jewish European perceptions of such material – in shaping the identity of the 'New Hebrew' deserves future study.

Figure 4.9 *Untitled* [marked Tel Aviv], 1921–3, photographed by Frank Scholten, UBL_NINO_F_Scholten_Fotos_Doos_13_0079.
Image courtesy of NINO and UBL.

A number of other photos shot in Tel Aviv by Scholten show children dressed up for Purim, a Jewish holiday that involved donning costumes, sometimes likened to Halloween (Figure 4.9). The photographs depict children wearing iterations of *fellah* and Bedouin costume. This is less an assumption of indigeneity as in the image of the woman above, but it still indicates the location of a Biblical Jewish identity in the contemporary clothing of rural Palestinians, a parallel to those of Christian European touristic practices. In the Ashkenazi case, cultural cross-dress thus became a means of bridging the gap in their liminal position in Europe where such populations were viewed as 'Oriental'.[86] Such a context demonstrates that the adoption of traditional Palestinian clothing had a culturally nationalist subtext in the production of a new Zionist identity.

Conclusion

In considering these images of Zionists and their comparison to studio portraits of middle-class Palestinians in cultural cross-dress, it is apparent that there was a broad cross-cultural consensus about the authenticity of *fellah* and Bedouin identity, and the material signifiers of such identities, for those outside the communities being emulated. What is even more interesting are the ways in which middle-class Palestinians and Zionists alike utilised such costuming as a marker of cultural identity and a means of situating themselves within the context of growing nationalist agendas. Although the same cannot be explicitly said of tourists, arguably a tacit claim is still made through the fleeting performance of the 'Holy Land' in connecting with a putative Christian past. It is evident that, in each of these cases, modern subjectivity is transmogrified through costume. Such images, while they depict a putative ancient authenticity, are indeed very modern in their attempt to reconstruct a relationship to the past.

In the Palestinian case, we might consider this performance more of a bohemian transgression of class supported by gender play, rather than cultural boundaries, which makes the term cultural cross-dress less appropriate than an idea of class or urban-rural cross-dress. This hints at the changing modes of identification between urban middle-class Palestinians and their *fellahin* and Bedouin compatriots in generating the definition of a new nationalist identity. These new porosities can be seen as part of the nationalist romanticisation of folk culture that constituted the global hallmark of much nationalist cultural production in the early twentieth century and might be usefully compared to composer and ethno-musicologist Béla Bartók's approach to documenting and reinventing folk music in constructing new nationalist cultural paradigms.[87]

In each aspect of the examples of cross-dress cited above, reinventions of identity are mobilised individually and collectively. In contextualising them across communal, cultural and class divides through the prism of gender, this chapter has demonstrated the politicised subtext of the cultural practices of photography which may or may not have been evident or intended by those imaged at the time of their production. It also raises the question of how we evaluate Palestinian social history through photography when the classed relationship to popular imaging means that *fellahin* and Bedouins are predominantly recorded photographically for a western market by photographers. This is in stark contrast to studio portraits of cultural cross-dress, where control over representation is a negotiation between those commissioning the portrait and those producing it, and where control of the dissemination of the image lies with those who commissioned it.

The question of humour in local adoptions of cultural cross-dress is another factor. While gender cross-dress contradictorily upsets and reifies contemporary notions of gender, its implications for cultural cross-dressing also hint at a subtext of class and power more broadly in the genre. This again supports a transnational cultural attitude to class that in some ways supersedes nationalist divides. It also demonstrates that the performance of Palestinian middle-classness was certainly not immune to biblified and Orientalist tropes. Questions concerning the intent of those individuals who commissioned portraits aside, imaging systems overlapped, with moments of confluence as well as collision, which certainly makes sense given that local photographers catered to locals and foreigners alike. Rather, what is pertinent are the ways in which such imaging systems were impacted, disrupted, or re-appropriated through those who took part in the practice.

Cross-dressing also speaks to the centrality of clothing and costume in constructing personal identification and authenticity. This returns us to Tamari's nimble contextualisation of personal microhistories within the macro-level context of politics that shaped daily life. In the classed context of shifts towards modern clothing and the distance between such attire and 'traditional' dress, there was clearly a modern notion of linear progress, one that constructed those who continued to wear such costume as part of an originary authenticity, but an authenticity that constructed those who did not as the vanguard of modernity. Despite this, the act of local upper- and middle-class engagement in cross-dressing must also be seen as a reification of the performance of Palestinian-ness in the period, which connected people to the land itself. Despite this classed agency, however, such nationalist demonstrations left little autonomy in photographic oeuvres for the articulation of *fellahin* and Bedouin identity by those communities themselves.

Acknowledgements

The author would like to acknowledge the assistance of a number of people who have contributed information, images and feedback to this paper: Qais Assali,

Sarah Irving, Karim Kattan, Joseph Malikian, Jumana Manna, Rami Meo, Micaela Sahhar, Yair Wallach and Eddie Zananiri, as well as the Palestinian Museum Digital Archive, The Netherlands Institute for the Near East and Leiden University Library's Special Collections department, the Matson Collection at the Library of Congress, the American Colony Archive, Jerusalem and Chadbourne Antiques.

Notes

1. Nassar, 'Bearers of Memory', p. 169.
2. Roberts 'Cultural Crossings', p. 84.
3. Sachko McLeod, 'Cross-Cultural Cross-Dressing', pp. 63–86.
4. Garber, 'Selections from the *Chic of Araby*', pp. 304–74.
5. Bair, 'The American Colony Photography Department', p. 32.
6. Figures 4.4, 4.5 and 4.7 in this chapter, as well as the image of Julia Luci in Nassar, 'Bearers of Memory', Figure 5.6, p. 170.
7. Karim Kattan's family has family photographs of cultural cross-dress dating to the early 1950s in Bethlehem, showing that the practice continued in the immediate aftermath of 1948. Likewise, the author has visited tourist ventures such as Khan Zaman in Jordan, where a photographic studio still catered to a similar market for images taken in Bedouin dress in 2015.
8. Coe and Gates, *The Snapshot Photograph*, pp. 22, 36.
9. Nassar, *Bearers of Memory*, p. 169.
10. Taan, 'Negotiating an Entry', p. 107.
11. Nassar, 'Photographs as Source Material', p. 145.
12. Roberts, 'Sartorial Adventures', pp. 89–90.
13. For instance, Taan, *Reading Marie Al-Khazen's Photographs*, pp. 86–89.
14. Sheehi, *The Arab Imago*, p. 58.
15. Zananiri, *Indigeneity, Transgression and the Body*, p. 721.
16. An advertisement from Hanna Toumayan's studio is featured in Nassar, 'Photography as Source Material', p. 144.
17. Nassar, 'Photography as Source Material', pp. 143–44.
18. For examples of the practice in Egypt we might look to Mary Roberts' *Sartorial Adventures*; as for a social history approach to the practice, Yasmine Nachabe Taan has documented the practice in Lebanon through the work of Marie Al Khazen; see Taan, *Reading Marie Al-Khazen's Photographs*, pp. 93–116.
19. Coe and Gates, *The Snapshot Photograph*, p. 36.
20. See, for instance, Nasser, 'Biblification in the Service of Colonialism', pp. 317–26.
21. For a full account of the extent of this, see Zananiri, 'Indigeneity, Transgression and the Body', pp. 717–37.
22. See, for instance, Nassar, *European Portrayals of Jerusalem*; Nassar, 'Biblification in Service of Colonialism'; Sanchez Summerer and Zananiri, *Imaging and Imagining*

Palestine; Zananiri, 'From Still to Moving Images'; Zananiri, 'Indigeneity, Transgression and the Body'.

23. Zananiri, 'Indigeneity, Transgression and the Body', pp. 731–34.

24. Indeed, this division is one of the significant and underlying themes of Tamari's *Mountain against the Sea*.

25. Behdad, *Camera Orientalis*, p. 57.

26. Zananiri, 'From Still to Moving Image', pp. 75–79.

27. Nashhef, 'Tawfik Canaan', p. 16.

28. Advertisement by J. Toumayan, 1907, in Nassar, 'Photography as Source Material', p. 144.

29. Bair, 'The American Colony Photo Department', p. 32.

30. Zananiri, *Orthodox Aesthetics*.

31. Kopty, 'Edward Keith-Roach's Favourite Things', pp. 327–28.

32. Kevorkian, 'From a Monastery to a Neighbourhood', pp. 152.

33. Jacobson, 'Little Orphans of Jerusalem', p. 40.

34. Okkenhaug, 'A "Significant Swedish Outpost"', p. 396.

35. Kopty, 'Keith-Roach's Favourite Things', p. 329

36. Zananiri, 'Indigeneity Transgression and the Body', p. 9.

37. Nassar, *Bearers of Memory*, p. 170.

38. *Cultural Cross-Dressing in Studios*, online exhibition, Malikian Photography Collection. http://malikianphotography.com/studios/tourism-and-cultural-cross-dressing-in-palestine/

39. I would like to thank Joseph Malikian for this very interesting insight into the Krikorian family and with much excitement look forward to his forthcoming volume on the topic.

40. Nassar, 'Bearers of Memory', pp. 169–71.

41. Watenpaugh, *Being Modern in the Middle East*, pp. 2–4.

42. Sheehi, *The Arab Imago*, p. 124.

43. Sheehi, *The Arab Imago*, p. 122.

44. Sheehi, *The Arab Imago*, pp. 121–22.

45. Sheehi, *The Arab Imago*, p. 55.

46. Seikaly, *Men of Capital*, p. 36.

47. Ibid.

48. Tamari and Nassar, *Storyteller of Jerusalem*; Tamari, Nassar and Sheehi, *Camera Palaestina*.

49. Tamari, 'Flanneurism, Spectacle and Modernity'.

50. Tamari and Nassar, *The Storyteller of Jerusalem*, p. 44.

51. Ibid., pp. 41–44.

52. Calafato, *Making the Modern Turkish Citizen*, p. 21, and Chapters 1 and 2.

53. Ibid., p. 6.

54. Ibid., pp. 93–95.

55. Ibid., p. 34.

56. Seikaly, *Men of Capital*, pp. 37–38.

57. This work is still in production. I thank Qais Assali for taking the time to discuss the work with me and introduce me to some of the materials and sources with which he is working.

58. There exist controversial arguments proposing that identity categories such as homosexual, gay, lesbian and trans are products of Western identity from a later period, and as such had little valence in the region until later colonial interventions in the second half of the twentieth century; see Massad, 'Re-Orienting Desire', pp. 361–85.

59. Akram Zaatari points to social restrictions around mixed-gender kissing, pointing to historical social contexts in analysing the 'queer' appearance to the contemporary eye in an interview. See Venema, 'Zaatari and Madan'.

60. Deitcher, *Dear Friends*.

61. Rotundo, 'Romantic Friendship', pp. 1–25.

62. This question of gender is raised again in later studio photographs of the post-1967 period, particularly in images by Hashem el Madani. These photographs focus on men performing the image of *fedayee*; see Venema, 'Zaatari and Madani'.

63. Sheehi, *The Arab Imago*, p. 73.

64. Roberts, *Cultural Crossings*, p. 89.

65. These images are shown in Taan, *Reading Marie al-Khazen's Photographs*, figs 36 and 1, respectively.

66. Taan, *Reading Marie al-Khazen's Photographs*, pp. 86–87.

67. Glynn, *Tidings from Zion*. I thank Sarah Irving for drawing my attention to her blog post on the subject: 'For 9 Months She Fought'.

68. Manna, 'A Sketch of Manners'; Ari, 'Orientalism Repeated', pp. 7–8.

69. The photo appears in Nassar's *Different Snapshots, 1850-1948* (Figure 134, p. 161), dated 1935. However, a similar image is included by Sanbar in *The Palestinians*, which dates the event to 1924. This is unlikely given that the Pierrot image used by Manna was taken in 1924. This is further complicated by another image that Nassar in *Different Snapshots* references (Figure 24, p. 53), taken at the same event and ascribed an early-twentieth-century date. This makes dating the photograph difficult, although it may have been a product of the 1920s, rather than of the 1930s.

70. Sanbar, *The Palestinians*.

71. Nassar, 'Familial Snapshots Representing Palestine', p. 146.

72. Ari, 'Orientalism Repeated', pp. 9–11.

73. I thank Dr Yair Wallach for leading me to this reference in the memoirs of Totakly, *My Life Path*.

74. Zananiri, *Imaging and Imaging Palestine*, Introduction, p. 12.

75. These included the Russian Imperial Orthodox Palestine Society (1882), the École biblique et archéologique français de Jérusalem (1890), the American

School of Oriental Study and Research in Palestine (1900), the Deutsches Evangelisches Institut für Altertumswissenschaft des Heiligen Lands (1902) and the British School of Archaeology in Jerusalem (1919).

76. See, for instance, 'Third Graders at the Friends Girls School' (December 1901) 0097.01.0004 https://palarchive.org/index.php/Detail/objects/100023/lang/en_US; 'Second Graders at the Friends Girls School' (December 1901) 0097.01.0005, https://palarchive.org/index.php/Detail/objects/100024/lang/en_US and 'The Elementary Students at the Friends School' (November 1918–May 1919) 0097.01.0009, https://palarchive.org/index.php/Detail/objects/100028/lang/en_US [accessed 18 March 2022].

77. There are two photo postcards of the same image. An original postcard dated 1928 has a hand-written inscription on the back, reading '1928, first wife of Khalil Totah, cottage at FGS named in her memory'. However, a more recent reproduction of the image suggests that it is of Eva Rae Totah, his second wife. It is unclear which is correct, yet the inscription on the original is more likely to have been recorded first. 'Arminah Tutah' 0097.01.0160, https://palarchive.org/index.php/Detail/objects/100179/lang/en_US, and 'Eva Rae Totah' 0097.01.1278, https://palarchive.org/index.php/Detail/objects/109332/lang/en_US [accessed 18 March 2022].

78. Zananiri, 'From Still to Moving Image', pp. 64–81.

79. Scholten's *Palestine Illustrated* was produced in English (1931), French (1929), German (1930) and only the first of the two volumes in Dutch (1935).

80. Zananiri, 'Documenting the Social', pp. 290–91.

81. Najjar, 'Bedouin Women "Misled"'; Farah, 'Heritage is to Art'.

82. Gorni, 'Zionist Socialism and the Arab Question', pp. 51–52.

83. Bardenstein, 'Tree, Forests and the Shaping of Palestinian and Israeli Collective Memory', pp. 157–65.

84. Zerubavel, 'Memory, the Rebirth of the Native', pp. 322–23.

85. Gribetz, *Defining Neighbors*, pp. 123–24.

86. Grosmann, 'Negotiating Presences', p. 138.

87. Bennett, 'Béla Bartók's Evolutionary Model of Folk Music', pp. 219–95.

Bibliography

Primary Sources

Tourism and Cultural Cross-Dressing in Studios, curated by Joseph Malikian, Malikian Collection, http://malikianphotography.com/studios/tourism-and-cultural-cross-dressing-in-palestine/

Matson Collection, Library of Congress.

Palestinian Museum Digital Archive (PDMA).

Sahhar Family Collection.

Scholten Collection.
Zananiri Family Collection.

Secondary Sources

Ari, Nisa. 'Orientalism Repeated: Shifting in Time in Jumana Manna's *A Sketch of Manners* and the Politics of Photography in Palestine'. *Third Text* 30, 5–6 (2017): pp. 331–45.

Assali, Qais. [artwork title] (still in production)

Barbara, Bair. 'The American Colony Photography Department: Western Consumption and "Insider" Commercial Photography'. *Jerusalem Quarterly* 44 (2010): pp. 28–38.

Bardenstein, Carol. 'Tree, Forests and the Shaping of Palestinian and Israeli Collective Memory'. In *Acts of Memory: Cultural Recall in the Present*, edited by Mieke Bal et al., pp. 157–65. Hanover: University Press of New England, 1999.

Behdad, Ali. *Camera Orientalis: Reflections on Photography of the Middle East*. Chicago: University of Chicago Press, 2016.

Bennett, James. 'Béla Bartók's Evolutionary Model of Folk Music'. *Twentieth-Century Music* 1, 2 (2016): pp. 219–95. doi: 10.1017/S1478572216000062

Calafato, Özge Baykan. *Making the Modern Turkish Citizen in Vernacular Photographs from the 1920s and 1930s*. London: I. B. Tauris, 2022.

Coe, Brian and Paul Gates. *The Snapshot Photograph: The Rise of Popular Photography 1888–1939*. London: Ash & Grant, 1977.

Deitcher, David. *Dear Friends: American Photographs of Men Together 1840–1918*. New York: Harry N. Abrams, 2005.

Reem, Farah. 'Heritage is to Art as the Medium is to the Message: The Responsibility to Palestinian Tatreez'. *Third Text*, 26 January 2021, http://www.thirdtext.org/farah-tatreez

Garber, Marjorie. 'Selections from the *Chic of Araby*: Transvestitism and the Erotics of Cultural Appropriation'. In *The Transgender Studies Reader*, edited by Susan Stryker and Stephen Whittle, pp. 635–55. Hoboken: Taylor and Francis, 2013.

Glynn, Jenifer, ed. *Tidings from Zion: Helen Bentwich's Letters from Jerusalem, 1919–31*. London: I. B. Tauris, 2000.

Gorni, Yosef. 'Zionist Socialism and the Arab Question'. *Middle Eastern Studies* 13, 1 (1977): pp. 51–55.

Gribetz, Jonathan Marc. *Defining Neighbors: Religion, Race, and the Early Zionist-Arab Encounter*. Princeton: Princeton University Press, 2014.

Grosmann, Rebekka 'Negotiating Presences: Palestine and the Weimar German Gaze'. *Jewish Social Studies: History, Culture, Society* 23, 2 (2018): pp. 137–72.

Irving, Sarah. 'For 9 Months She Fought in the Turkish Army up Beersheba Way'. Blog post, 25 August 2014, https://sarahirving.wordpress.com/2014/08/25/for-9-months-she-fought-in-the-turkish-army-up-beersheba-way/

Jacobson, Abigail. "'Little Orphans of Jerusalem": The American Colony's Christian Herald Orphanage in Photographs and Negatives'. In *Imaging and Imagining Palestine*, edited by Karène Sanchez Summerer and Sary Zananiri, pp. 31–65. Leiden: Brill, 2021.

Kevorkian, Raymond. 'From a Monastery to a Neighbourhood: Orphan and Armenian Refugees in the Armenian Quarter of Jerusalem (1916–1926), Reflexions Towards an Armenian Museum in Jerusalem'. *Contemporary Levant* 6, 2 (2021): pp. 141–57.

Kopty, Yazan. 'Edward Keith-Roach's Favourite Things: Indigenising National Geographic's Images of Mandatory Palestine'. In *Imaging and Imagining Palestine*, edited by Karène Sanchez Summerer and Sary Zananiri, pp. 309–39. Leiden: Brill, 2021.

Manna, Jumana. 'A Sketch of Manners (Alfred Roch's Last Masquerade)'. 13 minutes, HD video, 2013, https://www.jumanamanna.com/A-Sketch-of-Manners-Alfred-Roch-s-Last-Masquerade

Massad, Joseph. 'Re-Orienting Desire: The Gay International and the Arab World'. *Public Culture* 14, 2 (2002): pp. 361–85.

Najjar, Farrah. 'Bedouin Women "Misled" into Embroidering Gown for NYFW'. *Al Jazeera*, 13 September 2017, https://www.aljazeera.com/features/2017/9/13/bedouin-women-misled-into-embroidering-gown-for-nyfw

Nashhef, Khaled. 'Tawfik Canaan: His Life and Works'. *Jerusalem Quarterly* 16 (2002): pp. 12–26.

Nassar, Issam. 'Bearers of Memory: Photo Albums as Sources of Historical Study'. In *Imaging and Imagining Palestine*, edited by Karène Sanchez Summerer and Sary Zananiri, pp. 157–84. Leiden: Brill, 2021.

Nassar, Issam. 'Photography as Source Material for Jerusalem's Social History'. In *Transformed Landscapes: Essays on Palestine and the Middle East in Honour of Walid Khalidi*, edited by Camille Mansour and Leila Tarazi Fawaz, pp. 137–58. Cairo: American University in Cairo Press, 2009.

Nassar, Issam. 'Biblification in the Service of Colonialism: Jerusalem in Nineteenth-Century Photography'. *Third Text* 20 (2006): pp. 317–26.

Nassar, Issam. *European Portrayals of Jerusalem: Religious Fascinations and Colonialist Imaginations*. Lewiston: Edwin Mellen Press, 2006.

Nassar, Issam. *Laqatat Mughayira: al-taswir al-mahalli al-mubakkir fi Filastin, 1850–1948* [Different Snapshots: Early Local Photography in Palestine, 1850–1948]. London: Qattan Foundation, 2005.

Nassar, Issam. 'Familial Snapshots Representing Palestine in the Work of the First Local Photographers'. *History and Memory* 18, 2 (2006): pp. 139–55.

Okkenhaug, Inger Marie. 'A "Significant Swedish Outpost": The Swedish School and Arab Christians in Jerusalem, 1920–1930'. In *European Cultural Diplomacy and Arab Christians in Palestine, 1918-1948: Between Contention and Connection*, edited by Karène Sanchez Summerer and Sary Zananiri, pp. 381–410. Basingstoke: Palgrave Macmillan, 2021.

Roberts, Mary. 'Sartorial Adventures, Satiric Narratives, and the Question of Indigenous Agency in Nineteenth-Century Europe and the Near East'. In *Edges of Empire: Orientalism and Visual Culture*, edited by Jocelyn Hackforth-Jones and Mary Roberts, pp. 70–94. Oxford: Blackwell Publishing, 2008.

Rotundo, Anthony. 'Romantic Friendship: Male Intimacy and Middle-Class Youth in the Northern United States, 1800–1900'. *Journal of Social History* 23, 1 (1989): pp. 1–25.

Sachko McLeod, Dianne. 'Cross-Cultural Cross-Dressing: Class, Gender and Modernist Sexual Identity'. In *Orientalism Transposed: The Impact of the Colonies on British Culture*, edited by Julie F. Codell and Dianne Sachko Macleod, pp. 63–86. Abingdon: Routledge, 2018.

Sanbar, Elias. *The Palestinians: Photographs of a Land and Its People from 1839 to the Present Day*. New Haven: Yale University Press, 2015.

Sanchez-Summerer, Karène, and Sary Zananiri. *Imaging and Imagining Palestine: Photography, Modernity and the Biblical Lens, 1918-1948*. Leiden: Brill, 2021.

Scholten, Frank, *Palestine Illustrated* [English] (1931), also published in French (1929), German (1930) and one of the two volumes in Dutch (1935). London: Longmans, 1931.

Seikaly, Sherene. *Men of Capital: Scarcity and Economy in Mandate Palestine*. Palo Alto: Stanford University Press, 2016.

Sheehi, Stephen. *The Arab Imago: A Social History of Portrait Photography 1860-1910*. Princeton: Princeton University Press, 2016.

Taan, Yasmine Nachabe. *Reading Marie Al-Khazen's Photographs: Gender, Photography, Mandate Lebanon*. London: Bloomsbury Visual Art, 2021.

Taan, Yasmine Nachabe. 'Negotiating an Entry to Modernity through Marie al-Khazen's Photographs (1920–30)'. In *Cultural Entanglement in the Pre-Independence Arab World: Arts, Thought and Literature*, edited by Anthony Gorman and Sarah Irving, pp. 93–116. London: I. B. Tauris, 2021.

Tamari, Salim. *Mountain against the Sea: Essays on Palestinian Society and Culture*. Berkley: University of California Press, 2009.

Tamari, Salim. 'Flanneurism, Spectacle and Modernity in the Photographic Albums of Wasif Jawhariyyeh'. Keynote address at the conference *Imaging and Imagining Palestine*, Leiden University, 16 October 2019, https://www.universiteitleiden.nl/en/events/2019/10/flanneurism-spectacle-and-modernity-in-the-photographic-albums-of-wasif-jawhariyyeh

Tamari, Salim and Issam Nassar. *The Storyteller of Jerusalem: The Life and Times of Waasif Jawhariyyeh*. Northampton: Olive Branch Press, 2014.

Tamari, Salim, Issam Nassar and Stephen Sheehi. *Camera Palaestina: Photography and Displaced Histories of Palestine*. Oakland: University of California Press, forthcoming 2022.

Totakly, Yehudah. *My Life Path: Memories, Activities, Events*. Tel Aviv: [self-published by the author], 1967.

Venema, Vibeke. 'Zaatari and Madani: Guns, Flared Trousers and Same-Sex Kisses'. *BBC World Service*, 17 February 2014, https://www.bbc.com/news/magazine-26146004

Watenpaugh, Keith David. *Being Modern in the Middle East: Revolution, Nationalism, Colonialism, and the Arab Middle Class*. Princeton: Princeton University Press, 2014.

Zananiri, Sary. 'Indigeneity, Transgression and the Body: Orientalism and Biblification in the Popular Imaging of Palestinians'. *Journal of Intercultural Studies* 42, 6 (2021): pp. 717–37.

Zananiri, Sary. 'From Still to Moving Image: The Shifting Representation of Jerusalem and Palestinians in the Western Biblical Imaginary'. *Jerusalem Quarterly* 67 (2016): pp. 64–81.

Zananiri, Sary. *Orthodox Aesthetics: Christianity, Solidarity and the Secularisation of Religious Aesthetics* [forthcoming 2023].

Zananiri, Sary. 'Imaging and Imaging Palestine: An Introduction'. In *Imaging and Imagining Palestine*, edited by Karène Sanchez Summerer and Sary Zananiri, pp. 1–28. Leiden: Brill, 2021.

Zananiri, Sary. 'Documenting the Social: Frank Scholten Taxonomising Identity in British Mandate Palestine'. In *Imaging and Imagining Palestine*, edited by Karène Sanchez Summerer and Sary Zananiri, pp. 266–306. Leiden: Brill, 2021.

Zerubavel, Yael. 'Memory, the Rebirth of the Native, and the "Hebrew Bedouin" Identity'. *Social Research* 75, 1 (2008): pp. 315–52.

CHAPTER 5

'The Reconstruction of Palestine': Geographical Imaginaries after World War I

Nadi Abusaada

The Great War accelerated material transformations that had been underway in Palestine since the nineteenth century; these were repurposed to serve as war-effort innovations in infrastructure, architecture and urban planning that had changed the face of the country parallel to the Ottoman Tanzimat.[1] Palestine's significance within this effort derived from its geographical and strategic position as the main frontier between Ottoman Bilad al-Sham and British-controlled Egypt.[2] This critical position, coupled with new advances in warfare technology, especially aerial photography and cartography, influenced and mirrored the shifts in imperial conceptions of the country's geography.[3] But the war and the developments it brought about also left a profound impact on the local populations and their daily lives. It was no coincidence that Khalil Totah and Omar Salih al-Barghouti's book *Tarikh Filastin* ('The History of Palestine'), produced in the war's aftermath, thoroughly discussed the 'major changes brought about by the technological exigencies of war'.[4] As Salim Tamari has explained, 'within Palestine and in the Syrian provinces, a new intelligentsia was looking with enchantment at the pace of social change brought about by this modernity, invigorated by the preparations for the Great War'.[5] Crucially, as Tamari further notes, these figures debated these modernities not only in the wartime moment, but 'with an anticipation of the great changes to come'.[6]

If the Great War itself was what altered Palestine's geography in physical and tangible terms, it was in the post-war moment that the conceptual questions and uncertainties regarding Palestine's future geography fully crystallised. The mutual optimism and apprehension that accompanied the beginning of British colonial rule in Palestine were soon accompanied by a pressing question regarding the country's fate: where were the future geographical boundaries of Palestine to be drawn? It did not take long following the start of the British occupation for it to become clear that the continuity of the regional interdependencies and interconnections that linked Palestine with the broader geography of the

Ottoman Syrian provinces would be threatened. While the demise of Ottoman despotism was commonly viewed among the Palestinian intelligentsia as a precondition for social and political reform, schemes for the geographical partitioning of the Arab East into spheres of British and French influence in the war's aftermath were perceived as a grave step backwards. Unsurprisingly, uncertainty regarding the question of Palestine's geographical future, including its relationship to the broader Syrian and Arab regions, emerged as a pressing concern within the Palestinian public sphere and as a key arena for political debate and mobilisation in the interwar era.

This chapter aims to trace and scrutinise some of the main directions of the geographical thought and imaginaries regarding the future of Palestine after the Great War, particularly the nature of Palestine's relationship to its broader regional context. Drawing on understudied textual and visual sources, mostly in Arabic, it focuses on how Palestinians conceived of these relationships amid the turbulences brought about by the termination of Ottoman rule and the beginning of the British occupation after the Great War. It is divided into two main sections. The first section focuses on geographical thinking within Palestine in the initial years of the British military occupation. It specifically traces the logics and explanations underpinning the Palestinians' conception of their country throughout this period as 'Southern Syria', as an inseparable part of a Greater Syria region. While it did not disappear, this idea gradually faded in the face of geopolitical shifts in the years that followed, especially with the introduction of the British civil administration in Palestine in 1920. The second section examines how Palestinians reconciled their geographical imagination of Palestine and its relationship to Greater Syria and the wider Arab region with the exceptionalisms that characterised their political, economic and social realities during the Mandate years.

'A New Spirit in the Syrian Lands': Palestine as Southern Syria

An unprecedented attention to geography accompanied the seismic shifts following the Great War in the Middle East. At a time when political subjectivities were in flux and when the future of the region was uncertain, an opportunity was presented to rethink and reimagine geographical relationships. Of the different possible iterations for Palestine's future in this era, one arrangement was particularly popular among the Arab inhabitants of Palestine: Palestine's unity with the Greater Syria region. It did not take long after the war for Palestine to become commonly referred to as Southern Syria. In his formative work on the emergence of modern national consciousness in Palestine, Rashid Khalidi examines the idea of Palestine as Southern Syria through the lens of identity formation. He argues that the idea was 'entirely new' and that 'its emergence was as rapid as that of

Palestine as a focus of identity'.[7] 'Like Palestinian identity', Khalidi further explains, 'it overlapped with Arabism, albeit to an even greater degree during the two brief years when Syria was the location of the Arab state that seemed the incarnation of Arab nationalist aspirations'.[8]

Indeed, the shifting Arab political landscape of the post-war era had a great influence over geographical imaginations, including the quest for Greater Syria's unity. The 1919 Pan-Syrian Congress held in Damascus was particularly effective in this regard. Attended by delegates from Palestine, Lebanon and Syria, the congress set the tone and vocabulary that moulded the political and geographical imaginaries of the region's inhabitants in the years that followed. Its final report, which was to be presented to the delegates of the King-Crane Commission, demanded that 'there be no separation of the southern part of Syria, known as Palestine, nor of the littoral western zone, which includes Lebanon, from the Syrian country'.[9] On 8 March 1920, the Arab Kingdom of Syria, headed by King Faysal, proclaimed its independence. A map produced to commemorate the event included the entire Greater Syria region within the boundaries of the new kingdom. The Ottoman-era Hijaz Railway appears on the map as the connecting tissue that binds these geographies. Damascus, the declared capital of this short-lived kingdom, is marked with the tri-colour flag of the Arab Revolt.

In Palestine, Jerusalem was a main centre for political activity and mobilisation towards Greater Syrian nationalism. In September 1919, the lawyer Muhammad Hasan al-Budayri and 'Aref al-'Aref published the newspaper *Suriyya al-Janubiyya* ('Southern Syria'). This was the first Arabic periodical published after the Great War and the mouthpiece of the newly founded Arab Club in Jerusalem, headed by Hajj Amin al-Husayni. The newspaper viewed Palestinian nationalism and anti-Zionist advocacy as complementary, and not contradictory to Greater Syrian nationalism. Crucially, it also took a clear stance against the British colonial authorities who, in turn, suspended its publication multiple times throughout 1919 and 1920. This distinguished it from its main competitor at the time, *Mirat al-Sharq*, which maintained an elusive stance towards the British colonial authorities and remained in operation throughout this period.

Rashid Khalidi, who briefly mentions *Mirat al-Sharq*, suggests that the newspaper was more 'Palestinian in focus' than *Janub Suriyya*.[10] However, a closer examination of its initial issues reveals that, like *Janub Suriyya*, *Mirat al-Sharq* also referred to Palestine as Southern Syria in its early years of publication. What distinguished *Mirat al-Sharq*'s coverage, besides its vague stance towards the British authorities, was that it viewed the significance of Palestine's unity with Syria not as a political priority, but as a necessary condition for meeting the social and economic challenges of the post-war moment. This was an explicit position declared in the newspaper's opening statement, published in September 1919, where it distanced itself from the 'world of politics' and declared its prioritisation of 'social concerns' and the 'recovery of economic interests' after the Great

War.[11] This separation between the political and socio-economic spheres, which the publication advocated throughout its initial issues, presented an argument for Greater Syria's unity that was more focused on the material realities of the region's populations than the question of identity.

Mirat al-Sharq emphasised economic development as the initial step towards eventual national independence. 'Economic progress', so the newspaper's first issue pronounced, 'is evidence for the renaissance and attentiveness of the nation'.[12] 'Money, money, our newspaper will continue to cry, as it is the true means for maintaining our nation from deterioration and leading it towards glory, dignity, and independence'.[13] Indeed, over the next issues, the newspaper granted considerable space to economic matters. A special column on 'Syrian commerce', including Palestine, appeared regularly throughout 1919.[14] It addressed several issues pertaining to the future of economic life in the Syrian provinces, including natural resources, prices and markets.[15] Of particular importance was the growing inflation after the Great War, especially with the scarcity of imported essential goods such as gasoline, sugar, coffee and rice.[16]

Despite its promise to distance itself from political affairs, *Mirat al-Sharq* could not but address some of the key political developments taking place in the following months. Although its stance towards the British government remained obscure, it held a clearly anti-Zionist position, dedicating numerous articles to the question of Jewish colonisation in Palestine. It also reported on the multiple demonstrations taking place throughout the Syrian provinces, including in Damascus and Jerusalem, rejecting the partition of Greater Syria.[17] These took place in tandem with the growing popular support for the new Arab Kingdom in Syria ruled by Amir Faysal, which remained unrecognised by Great Britain and echoed the demands of the pan-Syrian Congress of 1919.[18] On 10 March 1920, *Mirat al-Sharq* dedicated its entire first page to Faysal's coronation as the King of Syria, with Damascus as his capital.[19] Referring to the parallel mass demonstrations in Jerusalem, the newspaper proclaimed: 'Syria, the unpartitioned, protests. Cities and villages reject Zionist immigration. Thousands participate in a peaceful demonstration in Jerusalem'.[20]

A week later, anticipating the imminent San Remo conference, *Mirat al-Sharq* published an article making the case for 'Syrian unity'.[21] 'We never read in history', so the article claimed before running through a *longue-durée* of Palestine's administrative boundaries since Roman times and throughout successive periods of Arab-Islamic rule, 'that Palestine was ever separated from Syria except for a few years'.[22] 'There is also no doubt that the country has natural boundaries and geographical markers', it elaborated, referring to the Taurus Mountains, the Mediterranean and the Arabian desert, demarcating what it considered Greater Syria's natural boundaries.[23] The newspaper concluded, referring to the imminent plans for Greater Syria's partition: 'We remain unconvinced as to how the Allies wish to disintegrate lands which are not divided by nature itself'.[24]

Although it was not suspended, as was the case with *Janub Suriyya*, this clear and critical stance placed *Mirat al-Sharq* in more explicitly adversarial terms with the British than its more elusive position during the first months of its publication.

The momentum for rejecting Greater Syria's partition reverberated well beyond the region's boundaries. Arab intellectuals in the diaspora understood that they had a role to play, too. Amid the failed efforts in Paris and London, the United States seemed like fertile ground for mobilisation. The King-Crane Commission was underway, and the Syrian and Palestinian intelligentsia certainly hoped that the petitions and opinions they raised to the American commissioners upon their arrival in Greater Syria could make a difference.[25] At the same time, a substantial Arab diasporic community, many from Greater Syria, resided in the United States. Crucially, many figures within this community took it upon themselves to mobilise their individual and collective capacities towards imagining an alternative future for their homeland.

Already in 1918, a group of New York-based Arabs and Palestinians established the Palestine Anti-Zionist Society to influence popular opinion within the United States against Jewish colonial settlement in Palestine. In 1919, the same society published an edited volume in Arabic, titled *Filastin wa tajdid hayatuha* ('Reconstruction of Palestine').[26] This volume, which is largely overlooked in historical writings on this period, was edited by Hanna Suleiman Salah. Salah, a Palestinian from Ramallah, had studied mechanical engineering at Harvard and the Massachusetts Institute of Technology, before heading the Palestine Anti-Zionist Society in 1919. The volume he edited brought together well-known Arab academics and professionals, including figures such as Philip Hitti, Khalil Totah and Najib Katibah, to reflect upon the future of Palestine, with particular focus on its relationship to Zionism and to the Greater Syria region. This early effort at anti-Zionist action within the United States was the seed for later organisational initiatives. Both Hitti and Totah later served as the heads of the similarly aimed Institute of Arab American Affairs in the 1940s.[27]

The Reconstruction of Palestine was closely in touch with the pressing concerns in Palestine and Greater Syria after the Great War. As with the Jerusalem-based *Mirat al-Sharq*, it saw the Great War, despite its devastating legacies in Syria and Palestine, as an opportunity to enter a new epoch. Addressing topics such as the economy, health, education, women's rights and politics, it delineated the scope for the political, economic and social reconstruction of Palestine after the Great War. 'The war', Rushdi Taqi al-Din writes in his chapter, 'has transpired a new spirit in Syrian lands: the spirit of *wataniyya* (patriotism)'.[28] This spirit of *wataniyya*, Taqi al-Din explains, is the precondition for a *nahda haditha* ('modern renaissance').[29] These ideals had been familiar since the nineteenth century but were viewed as more realistic in the war's aftermath. Importantly, for Taqi al-Din, as well as for the other authors in the book, this spirit of *wataniyya* necessarily engulfed Palestine and Syria within the same national geography. Taqi al-Din explains that, historically and geographically, 'Palestine is a part of Syria and Syria is a part of Palestine'.[30]

The future-oriented and optimistic nature of the book echoed the articles on the pages of *Mirat al-Sharq*, which similarly saw the Great War as an opportunity for social change, despite the dark legacies of the war years. In fact, following its publication, the Palestine Anti-Zionist Society in New York sent a copy of the book to the editors of *Mirat al-Sharq*. In turn, *Mirat al-Sharq* published an article praising the volume's 'richness', asserting that it was 'a must-read for every Palestinian'.[31] Indeed, the edited volume's format allowed for a more extensive and thorough elaboration on issues that were only briefly addressed in Greater Syria's Arabic newspapers. As with articles in local Arabic newspapers, however, the book was written with a clear sense of urgency and anticipation for the near future. 'Will the [Syrian] lands be divided? Is it just to separate Syria from Palestine and Lebanon from Syria?' Taqi al-Din asks rhetorically.[32] He adds: 'It is without a doubt that this division would be as harmful to Syria as it would be to the countries of influence [France and Britain]'.[33]

Reconstruction of Palestine was primarily directed towards an Arabic-speaking audience and the population of Greater Syria. This was reflected in its extensive focus on internal and autogenetic possibilities for change from within, not only relying on external actors. This is most evident in Philip Hitti's chapter: 'Are we a nation? How do we become one?'[34] In it, he suggests that the ascent of nations 'depends on two main tenets: a material one – the geographical nation; and a moral one – the desire for a collective life based on common qualities'.[35] He elaborates that 'any disarray to the geographical unity of Syria is an unforgivable crime, whether it is committed by the English, the French, the Arabs or the League of Nations because it would mean a blow to one of the two tenets of nation-building'.[36] Hitti's argument for the geographical unity of Syria and Palestine was not solely based on their shared history and language, as was frequently emphasised on the pages of Arabic newspapers in Palestine. Rather, it was primarily framed around the shared interests for Syria and Palestine in the present. He understood the moral basis of modern national identity not as an inherent connection by blood, religion or language, despite the importance of these elements, but as a cultivated common desire among populations to live a shared futurity.[37]

Through its future-focused orientation, academic approach and geographical distance, the *Reconstruction of Palestine* opened up a space to address material concerns that received cursory attention in the Pan-Syrian congress and in Arabic newspapers within the region. The future of the health sector, women's participation in social and political life, regional industries, agriculture and morality were all dealt with extensively and thoroughly. The physical infrastructures and commercial links connecting the different parts of Greater Syria received equal attention. A map included with the book, titled 'Southern Syria or Palestine', highlights existing maritime and land routes connecting Palestine to its wider Syrian geography, including major inter-city roads and railway lines. In his chapter, Taqi al-Din suggested that maintaining Greater Syria's unity after the war is contingent upon the unification and extension of these lines.[38] He specifically proposed constructing new bridges and railway lines connecting Amman with Jerusalem and Nablus as well as a line linking the coastal cities of Sidon and Tyre with the Hijaz railway.[39]

In 1920, the geographical imaginaries of a united Greater Syria in the region and the diaspora were shattered by the unsolicited outcomes of the San Remo Conference, resulting in their geopolitical division into territories of British and French influence. The disillusionment was compounded by the formal British endorsement of a Jewish national home in Palestine, driving a greater wedge between Palestine and other mandated territories. Khalidi suggests that this moment virtually brought an end to the idea of Palestine as Southern Syria. However, as more recent studies of Palestinian national politics during the British Mandate have shown, the idea of Southern Syria witnessed a resurgence in later years, especially in the 1930s. Unlike the relative consensus surrounding the idea in the post-war interim, this later resurgence was cast in factional moulds. Its advocates were mainly affiliated with the Hizb al-Istiqlal (Independence Party) established in 1932.[40] Founded by Arab nationalist Muhammad Izzat Darwaza, the party formally endorsed the idea of Palestine as Southern Syria.[41] However, the idea was not favoured by other political factions and figures within Palestine, especially the Majlisi faction led by Hajj Amin Husayni.[42]

The Mandate Years: Foreclosures and Possibilities

Although the idea of Southern Syria did not fully disappear, the new administrative, social and economic landscape that paralleled the establishment of the British civil administration in Palestine in 1923 had an undeniable effect on local Arab perceptions of the country's geography. A gradual, but effective, shift was underway. Palestine's imagined geography was being more strictly defined as a national entity distinct from the rest of Greater Syria. The British played a significant role in this redefinition, but it would be inaccurate to assume that this was merely an imposed notion. Palestinian urban elites, too, were increasingly participating in this same process. While some still held on to the Southern Syria idea during the Mandate, especially in the context of rural popular mobilisation during the 1936–39 Palestinian Revolt, others were progressively coming to terms with Palestine's political and geographical distinctiveness.[43] National interests were increasingly viewed in primarily Palestinian terms. 'Now, after the recent events in Damascus', Musa al-Husayni reportedly proclaimed after the fall of Faysal's government in Damascus, 'we have to effect a complete change in our plans here. Southern Syria no longer exists. We must defend Palestine'.[44]

One arena where the dynamics underlying Palestine's geographical redefinition were noticeably visible was Arabic educational publications. Already by 1923, Arabic geography textbooks had been commissioned for elementary and secondary school levels in Palestine. These textbooks were all published under the aegis of the British administration, with reports of active censorship of potentially 'subversive' content.[45] At the same time, as Rashid Khalidi demonstrates, they had a significant influence on Palestinian national consciousness and the conception of Palestine as a distinctive political and geographical entity.[46] The extent to which different publications oscillated towards British colonial visions or Palestinian national aspirations was evident in their framing of the country's history and geography.

Two publications from the Mandate's early days demonstrate this schism: *Jughrafiyat filastin* ('Geography of Palestine') by Khalil Totah and Habib Khoury, and *al-Mukhtasar fi jughrafiyat filastin* ('A Summary of Palestine's Geography') by Husayn Ruhi, both published in 1923.[47] Both were elementary-level geography textbooks. Nonetheless, given the distinct political positions and backgrounds of their authors, the two books reflected some of the anxieties underlying Palestine's national geography in different ways. This was particularly the case with the two books' position on Palestine's relationship to Greater Syria as well as the growth of Jewish colonial settlement in Palestine.

Totah and Khoury, the authors of *Geography of Palestine*, were leading figures in Palestine's Arabic educational movement during the British Mandate. Totah in particular played a leading role as the head of the Government Arab College in Jerusalem and later as principal of the Friends School in Ramallah.[48] His passion for education matched his political commitment to anti-Zionism both in Palestine and abroad, having contributed to the above-mentioned 1919 volume *Reconstruction of Palestine* and later heading the American Institute for Arab Affairs. The same year that he co-published the *Geography of Palestine*, he also co-authored another book, *Tarikh filastin* ('History of Palestine'), with Omar Salih al-Barghouti. The history book was later banned by the British authorities because it described the British commissioner's inability to convince Arab Palestinians of the validity of Zionist colonial settlement in Palestine.[49] The *Geography of Palestine* was intended to fill a serious gap in knowledge production on the country's geography. 'It is not an exaggeration to say that since the foundations of the scientific movement in Palestine have been laid, its brethren have not studied the geography of their country in their language', Totah and Khoury wrote in their preface, referring to the numerous foreign-language geography books of Palestine and the lack of similar Arabic-language geographical publications.[50]

The geography of Palestine, as conceived in Totah and Khoury's book, departed considerably from the 1919 book *Reconstruction of Palestine* to which Totah himself had contributed. Unlike *Reconstruction of Palestine*'s explicit and unwavering depiction of Palestine's geography as embedded within and inseparable from

Syria, *Geography of Palestine* depicts Palestine as a self-contained entity separate from the rest of Syria. Palestine's international connections to the Mediterranean Sea are prioritised over its interior regional geography:

> While the Mediterranean Sea links Palestine with Europe and facilitates its interconnectivity, the desert separates Palestine from the Arabian Peninsula and Iraq. Thus, the sea constitutes an open gateway for Palestine and the desert a closed one.[51]

The text turns more hesitant as the two authors describe Palestine's northern relationship to Syria:

> The northern border is hard to define. There is the natural border created by God and nature since the dawn of history and there are the everchanging political borders shifting with wars and political conditions.[52]

The authors further explain that, whereas Palestine's natural northern border extends all the way to northern Syria, its political border 'as decided by the 1920 borders committee extends from Ras al-Naqqura [. . .] to Banyas'.[53] This distinction between natural and political borders can be understood as a form of pragmatism to avoid British censorship without maintaining a clear stance on Palestine's geopolitical separation from Syria in 1920.

The same year that Totah and Khoury published their book on Palestine's geography, another textbook on the same topic was published by Husayn Ruhi. Ruhi, an Egyptian of Persian origin who had served as spy and translator for Britain during the war, joined the Department of Education in Palestine in 1920.[54] As with Totah and Khoury's book, Ruhi's was written with an understanding of Palestine's national geography as confined to the country's mandatory boundaries. However, unlike Totah and Khoury's relative elusiveness on the certainty of geopolitical boundaries, Ruhi's book leaves no room to question Palestine's mandatory borders and its separation from Syria. Adopting the gaze of a military strategist, he takes the reader on an imagined aerial journey, narrating the country's natural topography as it is viewed from above and from a distance. Most strikingly, when compared to other Arabic-language publications, Ruhi's *Summary of Palestine's Geography* includes an extensive section presenting Jewish colonial settlements in Palestine in a positive and progressive light, detailing names, locations and years of establishment.[55] His book more clearly exemplified Palestine's distinctiveness from the wider regional environment and, in line with British colonial imaginaries, included Jewish colonies as a natural element in the social and physical landscape.

Although Palestinians remained connected to their broader regional environments throughout the Mandate, and although the idea of Greater Syria did not fully fade, publications from the 1930s reflect a certain shift in how Palestinians conceived of their national and regional geographies compared to the Greater Syrianism of the post-war moment. These changes did not take place in isolation. They were part of a broader shift in Palestinian political and economic thinking that had been underway for decades but crystallised with the regional developments of the late 1920s and 1930s. Particularly significant were the rising independence movements, in Palestine and neighbouring Arab countries, that increasingly formulated national independence in country-specific terms.[56] The distinctive preoccupations that had emerged in each country since the Great War set them onto different social, political and economic trajectories. In Palestine, these fears were reflected in the sense of urgency with which local Arabic publications emphasised the need for pan-Arab national *istiqlal* ('independence') and *wihda* ('unity').

Throughout the 1930s, Palestinian-run Arabic publications – including newspapers, magazines and guidebooks – were at the fore of constructing a new geography of Palestine that positioned it as an inseparable part of the Arab world. On the one hand, this image contested the region's colonial fragmentation following the Great War. On the other hand, it also imagined Palestine's regional affinities in geographical terms broader than the earlier emphasis on a natural connection to Greater Syria. Pan-Arab nationalism overtook the pan-Syrian quest, not only as an ideological project, but also as a framework for thinking about geography and physical space. In August 1932, Ajaj Nuwayhid, the renowned Arab nationalist historian, inaugurated the first issue of the newspaper *al-Arab* in Jerusalem. In his opening letter, Nuwayhid wrote: 'This is *al-Arab*, a newspaper for Arabs, established in this central Arab territory'.[57] He continued: '*Al-Arab* was founded in this rapidly changing era, the sweeping event in Arab countries after the Great War, and its aim is to fight for the ultimate cause: Arab independence'.[58]

The newly established newspaper's visual content asserted and displayed its spatial and geographical imaginaries of Palestine's connection to the broader Arab region. Among the illustrations included in *al-Arab*'s first issue, a map showed the site of the Battle of Hittin.[59] Its caption reads 'Palestine and Syria', a clear departure from the 'Palestine or Southern Syria' that appeared in the *Reconstruction of Palestine* over a decade earlier. A second illustration filled the front page of the newspaper's first issue. At its centre was a large circular map of the Arab region, and under it the two tricolour flags of the Arab Revolt. Importantly, the map has no boundaries except between land and sea. None of the post-war geopolitical divisions are represented. Instead, the Arab region's geography appears as a continuous terrain, extending from the Rif to Aleppo to Aden. Cities are emphasised as the main nodes within this terrain, and the main points of contact and entanglement. Appearing on every cover of *al-Arab* thereafter, the illustration became the newspaper's main emblem, communicating a growing spirit that was popularised through and beyond its pages, that of Arab unity and independence.

The spirit of pan-Arab unity and independence spilled beyond Palestine's Arabic newspapers. In some measure, this drive towards pan-Arab nationalism was more pragmatic than the earlier Greater Syrian nationalism. It saw Palestine in independent terms as a coherent national geography. Still, it realised that this independence could not be achieved without a strong connection to the rest of the Arab region. It sought to challenge the increasingly hard colonial borders that the British and French were creating between these nations through economic and administrative procedures. This proved especially important in a context where the British colonial policy of 'economic separatism' in Palestine was increasingly privileging the Jewish over the local Arab economy.[60] Throughout the 1930s and 1940s, therefore, Palestinians turned to their Arab brethren to strengthen the regional bonds that were tethered in the Great War. Reinvigorating inter-Arab economic exchange was at the heart of this quest, turning the question of Arab unity from the realm of semantic gestures into more tangible commitments, especially for the rising Arab urban bourgeoisie.[61]

One undertaking engendered the economic underpinnings that shaped Palestinian urban elites' understandings of their connection to Arab regional geography during the Mandate years: hosting the 1933 and 1934 Arab National Exhibitions in Jerusalem. The two exhibitions were explicitly framed as attempts to re-forge inter-Arab economic ties that had disintegrated in the Great War.[62] Local newspapers, especially al-Arab, provided elaborate coverage of the two exhibitions from the planning stages to their openings.[63] Upon the inauguration of the Second Arab Exhibition, several reproductions of the exhibition's visual content appeared in al-Arab. One illustration was of the golden medal distributed to the winning exhibitors. The illustration was a map of the Arabian Peninsula and Egypt,[64] featuring lines radiating from Jerusalem to the different Arab capital cities in its vicinity. A second illustration, from the same exhibition, was of a postage stamp used on the exhibition letters. 'The symbolism is obvious', al-Arab wrote, 'he is an Arab with a sure stand, breaking his chains, and raising his hand carrying a ball with the word Jerusalem written at its centre, and from it the light shines to the rest of the Arab World'.[65] Unlike the former illustration's centring of the Arabian Peninsula and Egypt, this one was more inclusive, encompassing the Maghreb, specifically Tripoli, Tunis, Algeria, Marrakesh and al-Rif.

Besides the heavily geographical visual content produced in the form of medals, postage stamps and postcards for the two exhibitions, the organisers also published exhibition guidebooks accompanying the two events.[66] The two guidebooks are significant in revealing the extent to which local understandings of the region's geography, and Palestine's role in it, were still in flux, even if certain waves were more dominant than others. A fleeting, but telling trace of Southern Syrian sentiment appears in the opening statement of the first guidebook:

> A group of businessmen in Southern Syria, which is a part of the larger Arab home-
> land, have taken it upon themselves to create a company for an exhibition of the
> different Arab industries and products to enhance the economic bonds between
> Arab countries.[67]

This was the first and last mention of Southern Syria in either of the guidebooks. One possible explanation is that several individuals on the Arab Exhibition Company's Board of Directors, including its head, Ahmad Hilmi Pasha, were members of the newly formed Independence Party that valorised the Southern Syria idea and reintroduced it to popular discourse in the 1930s.[68] Given that factional politics had already influenced the exhibition throughout its planning process, the terminology could be understood as an expression of internal dynamics within Palestinian local politics inasmuch as it was of a geographical understanding of Palestine's regional affinities.[69]

Besides this single mention of Southern Syria, the rest of the guidebooks leaves no room for mistaking Palestine's conception as an independent geographical and political unit within a broader Arab homeland. Both guidebooks include a large section that focuses on the 'history of the Arab Peninsula'.[70] Within this section are included brief subsections named after 'the modern designations of the Peninsula's parts': Palestine, Lebanon, Inner Syria, Iraq, Najd, Hijaz, Yemen and Egypt.[71] The part on Palestine made no mention of a special connection to Syria and instead asserted Palestine's Arab character. Meanwhile, although the section on Inner Syria explicitly grieved the French colonial division of 'Greater Syria' after the fall of Faysal's government, Palestine's separation from Greater Syria was not what was lamented. Rather, it was the establishment of three separate states in Syria, Alexandretta and Jabal al-Druze.[72] This framing was very different from how Greater Syria was described in a 1919 publication like *Reconstruction of Palestine*, in which the main preoccupation was insisting that Palestine constituted an inseparable part of Greater Syria.

As Laila Parsons demonstrates, the 1936 Palestinian Revolt brought the language of Greater Syria back to Palestine, especially among rural populations, supporters of the Independence Party and Fawzi al-Quwaqji's followers.[73] However, the Palestinian urban bourgeoisie continued to assert an economic geography of the region that saw Palestine as a distinctive entity, albeit with a strong connection to its broader Arab economic sphere. Nowhere was this depiction more pronounced than a map printed on the cover page of the Palestinian economic journal *al-Iqtisadiyyat al-'Arabiyya*,[74] on which lines of infrastructure and transport appear connecting the different Arab capitals, emphasising economic exchanges within the region. At first glance, the map appears similar to *al-Arab*'s cover depicting the bonds connecting Palestine to its broader Arab region. However, upon a closer look, one realises that, in contrast to *al-Arab*'s borderless geography, *al-Iqtisadiyyat al-'Arabiyya*'s map plainly marks these countries as distinctive geopolitical entities. Giving up on the fluidity that marked the geographical expressions of the previous years, it foreshadowed the sternness of the borders that would continue to mark the region for decades to come.

Conclusion: Overlapping Geographies

The twists and turns that Palestine's political, social and economic trajectories undertook following the Great War resulted in multiple and overlapping visions of its conceived and material geography. Most writings on Palestine and Palestinians in this period focus on the identarian and political aspects underpinning the rise of a modern national consciousness. While this chapter builds on these works, it focuses on how these developments overlapped with, and were embedded within, a shift in how Palestine's Arab inhabitants conceived of and imagined their geography and connection to their broader regional setting. Tracing these shifts across two main periods, the interim post-war moment and the post-Mandate years, I traced the shift from the conception of Palestine as Southern Syria to its construction as an independent political unit, distinctive yet connected to a broader Arab regional geography.

In some measure, this chapter reveals that questions of geography were closely tied to questions of identity but were not reducible to them. Other pressing material considerations were equally significant. Economic relations, in particular, took precedence in how Palestinians sought to align themselves within their regional settings. This was the case both as the country exited the Great War and well into the Mandate period, as Palestinian elites sought to establish strong economic bonds with their Arab counterparts. Meanwhile, the variety of different iterations of how Palestinians understood their national and regional geographies revealed the extent to which facts-on-the-ground had hardly translated into a strict and unchallenged Palestinian conception of Palestine's geography. Even at a time when Palestinian national consciousness was very high, Palestinians continued to deploy different depictions of their country's geography to serve different purposes. As the *Reconstruction of Palestine* reveals, representations of Palestine's geography were as much a testament to existing social, economic and political realities as they were vignettes of imagined possibilities for their future.

Notes

1. On architecture and urban planning in the Ottoman Arab provinces, including Palestine, during the Tanzimat, see Çelik, *Empire, Architecture, and the City*. On the utilisation and expansion of these developments during the Great War, see, for example, Rogan, *The Fall of the Ottomans*, p. 327.

2. Ben-Bassat and Ben-Artzi, 'The Collision of Empires', pp. 25–36.
3. Tamari, 'Shifting Ottoman Conceptions of Palestine, Part 1'; Tamari, 'Shifting Ottoman Conceptions of Palestine, Part 2'; Abusaada, 'Combined Action', pp. 20–36.
4. Tamari, *The Great War*, p. 60. See also Totah and Al-Barghouti, *Tarikh Filastin*.
5. Tamari, *The Great War*, p. 60.
6. Ibid.
7. Khalidi, *Palestinian Identity*, p. 165.
8. Ibid.
9. Pipes, *Greater Syria*, p. 26.
10. Khalidi, *Palestinian Identity*, p. 170.
11. 'Introduction', *Mirat Al-Sharq*, 17 September 1919, p. 1.
12. Ibid.
13. Ibid.
14. 'Syrian Commerce', *Mirat Al-Sharq*, 15 October 1919, p. 1.
15. Ibid.
16. Ibid., p. 1. See also Totah and Al-Barghouti, *Tarikh Filastin*, p. 259.
17. Mogannam, *The Arab Woman*, p. 138. On the politics of Arabic banners in late Ottoman and Mandate Jerusalem, see Wallach, *A City in Fragments*.
18. For more on the British position regarding the Arab state in Syria and Amir Faysal, see Khalidi, *Palestinian Identity*, pp. 163–64.
19. 'The Second Large Demonstration', *Mirat al-Sharq*, 10 March 1920, p. 1.
20. Ibid.
21. 'Syrian Unity', *Mirat al-Sharq*, 17 March 1920, p. 1.
22. Ibid.
23. Ibid.
24. Ibid.
25. For a recent critical reading of the King-Crane Commission and its legacy, see Arsan, 'Versailles: Arab Desires, Arab Futures'.
26. Salah, *Filastin Wa Tajdid Hayatuha*.
27. See 'Manifesto of the Institute'; Jenison, 'American Citizens', pp. 35–51; Abusaada, 'Urban Encounters', pp. 366–97, 382–83.
28. Taqi al-Din, 'Between Syria and Palestine', pp. 167–77.
29. Ibid.
30. Ibid.
31. 'Palestine and Its Reconstruction', *Mirat al-Sharq*, 17 December 1919, p. 2
32. Taqi al-Din, 'Between Syria and Palestine'.
33. Ibid.
34. Hitti, 'Are We a Nation?' pp. 178–86.
35. Ibid.
36. Ibid.
37. Ibid.

38. Taqi al-Din, 'Between Syria and Palestine'.
39. Ibid.
40. On the Istiqlal Party in Palestine, see Matthews, *Confronting an Empire*.
41. Ibid.
42. Parsons, 'Rebels Without Borders', pp. 395–408.
43. See, for example, Parsons on Fawzi al-Qawaqji and the 1936 Arab Revolt in Palestine. Ibid.
44. Musa Husseini, quoted in Khalidi, *Palestinian Identity*, p. 165.
45. On British sponsorship of educational content in Mandate Palestine, see Tibawi, *Arab Education*.
46. Khalidi, *Palestinian Identity*, pp. 174–75.
47. Totah and Khoury, *Jughrafiyat Filastin*; Rouhi, *Al-Mukhtasar fi jughrafiyat Filastin*.
48. On Khalil Totah's life, see Totah Hilden, *A Passion for Learning*.
49. Tibawi, *Arab Education*.
50. Totah and Khoury, *Jughrafiyat Filastin*.
51. Ibid.
52. Ibid.
53. Ibid.
54. Kalisman, 'The Little Persian Agent', pp. 65–74.
55. Ruhi, *Al-Mukhtasar fi jughrafiyat Filastin*.
56. On the rising country-specific nationalisms in the Arab region and their relationship to pan-Arab nationalism in this period, see Khalidi, *The Origins of Arab Nationalism*; Khoury, *Syria and the French Mandate*; Cleveland, *The Making of an Arab Nationalist*; Schayegh and Arsan, *The Routledge Handbook of the History of the Middle East Mandates*; Gelvin, 'Was There a Mandates Period?' pp. 420–32.
57. 'Arab Independence', *Al-Arab*, 27 August 1932, p. 1.
58. Ibid., p. 1–2.
59. At which Salah al-Din al-Ayyubi defeated the Crusaders in 1187.
60. Smith, *The Roots of Separatism in Palestine*.
61. On the modern history of the rise of an urban bourgeois class in the Arab region, including in Palestine, distinctive from the landholding elite notables, see Watenpaugh, *Being Modern*; Seikaly, *Men of Capital*.
62. Abusaada, 'Self-Portrait of a Nation', pp. 122–35; Ari, 'Competition in the Cultural Sector', pp. 213–46.
63. Abusaada, 'Self-Portrait of a Nation', p. 132.
64. Ibid.
65. *Al-Arab*, quoted in ibid., p. 132.
66. Arab Exhibition Company, *Dalil al-maʿrad al-ʿarabi al-awwal* (Guidebook for the First Arab Exhibition); Arab Exhibition Company, *Dalil al-maʿrad al-ʿarabi al-thani*.

67. Arab Exhibition Company, *Dalil al-maʿrad al-ʿarabi al-awwal*, p. 1.
68. On the political affiliations of the Board of Directors of the Arab Exhibition Company, see Abusaada, 'Self-Portrait of a Nation'. On the Independence Party and the Southern Syria idea, see Parsons, 'Rebels Without Borders'. On Ahmad Hilmi Pasha, see Seikaly, *Men of Capital*.
69. Most members of the Board of Directors belonged to the Independence Party. However, the exhibition was held at the Palace Hotel, owned by the Supreme Muslim Council. The exhibition was mentioned in both the pro-Independence Party and pro-Majlisi Party press. Abusaada, 'Self-Portrait of a Nation'.
70. Arab Exhibition Company, *Dalil al-maʿrad al-ʿarabi al-awwal*.
71. Ibid., p. 4.
72. Ibid., p. 7.
73. Parsons, 'Rebels Without Borders'.
74. On the history of *al-Iqtisadiyyat al-ʾArabiyya*, see Seikaly, *Men of Capital*.

Bibliography

Newspapers

Al-ʿArab.
Mirat al-Sharq.
Suriyya al-Janubiyya.

Secondary Sources

Abusaada, Nadi. 'Combined Action: Aerial Imagery and the Urban Landscape in Interwar Palestine, 1918–40'. *Jerusalem Quarterly* 81 (2020): pp. 20–36.

Abusaada, Nadi. 'Self-Portrait of a Nation: The Arab Exhibition in Mandate Jerusalem, 1931–1934'. *Jerusalem Quarterly* 77 (2019): pp. 122–35.

Abusaada, Nadi. 'Urban Encounters: Imaging the City in Mandate Palestine'. In *Imaging and Imagining Palestine: Photography, Modernity and the Biblical Lens, 1918–1948*, edited by Karéne Sanchez Summerer and Sary Zananiri, pp. 366–97. Leiden: Brill, 2021.

Arab Exhibition Company. *Dalil al-maʿrad al-ʿarabi al-awwal* (Guidebook for the First Arab Exhibition). Jerusalem: Al-Arab Press, 1933.

Arab Exhibition Company. *Dalil al-maʿrad al-ʿarabi al-thani* ('Guidebook for the Second Arab Exhibition'). Jerusalem: Dar al-ʾAytam al-Islamiyya, 1934.

Ari, Nisa. 'Competition in the Cultural Sector: Handicrafts and the Rise of the Trade Fair in British Mandate Palestine'. In *European Cultural Diplomacy and Arab Christians in Palestine, 1918-1948*, edited by Karène Sanchez Summerer and Sary Zananiri, pp. 213–46. Cham: Palgrave Macmillan, 2021.

Arsan, Andrew. 'Versailles: Arab Desires, Arab Futures'. *Public Books* (blog), 26 January 2021, https://www.publicbooks.org/versailles-arab-desires-arab-futures/.

Ben-Bassat, Yuval and Yossi Ben-Artzi. 'The Collision of Empires as Seen from Istanbul: The Border of British-Controlled Egypt and Ottoman Palestine as Reflected in Ottoman Maps'. *Journal of Historical Geography* 50 (2015): pp. 25–36, https://doi.org/10.1016/j.jhg.2015.04.022.

Çelik, Zeynep. *Empire, Architecture, and the City: French-Ottoman Encounters, 1830-1914.* Seattle: University of Washington Press, 2008.

Cleveland, William L. *The Making of an Arab Nationalist: Ottomanism and Arabism in the Life and Thought of Sati' Al-Husri.* Princeton: Princeton University Press, 2015.

Gelvin, James. 'Was There a Mandates Period? Some Concluding Thoughts'. In *The Routledge Handbook of the History of the Middle East Mandates*, edited by Cyrus Schayegh and Andrew Arsan, pp. 420–32. Abingdon: Routledge, 2015.

Hilden, Joy Totah. *A Passion for Learning: The Life Journey of Khalil Totah, a Palestinian Quaker Educator and Activist.* Bloomington: Xlibris Corporation, 2016.

Hitti, Phillip. 'Are We a Nation? How Do We Become One?' In *Filastin Wa Tajdid Hayatuha* ('Reconstruction of Palestine'), edited by Hannah Salah, pp. 178–86. New York: The Syrian-American Press, 1919.

Jenison, Denise Laszewski. '"American Citizens of Arabic-Speaking Stock": The Institute of Arab American Affairs and Questions of Identity in the Debate over Palestine'. In *New Horizons of Muslim Diaspora in North America and Europe*, edited by Moha Ennaji, pp. 35–51. New York: Palgrave Macmillan US, 2016.

Kalisman, Hilary Falb. 'The Little Persian Agent in Palestine: Husayn Ruhi, British Intelligence, and World War I'. *Jerusalem Quarterly* 66 (2016): pp. 65–74.

Khalidi, Rashid. *Palestinian Identity: The Construction of Modern National Consciousness.* New York: Columbia University Press, 2010.

Khalidi, Rashid, ed. *The Origins of Arab Nationalism.* New York: Columbia University Press, 1991.

Khoury, Philip S. *Syria and the French Mandate: The Politics of Arab Nationalism, 1920-1945.* Princeton: Princeton University Press, 2014.

'Manifesto of the Institute of Arab American Affairs on Palestine'. New York: Institute of Arab American Affairs, 1945.

Matthews, Weldon. *Confronting an Empire, Constructing a Nation: Arab Nationalists and Popular Politics in Mandate Palestine.* London: I. B. Tauris, 2006.

Matthews, Weldon C. 'The Arab Istiqlal Party in Palestine, 1927–34'. Unpubl. PhD dissertation. University of Chicago, 1998.

Mogannam, Matiel E. T. *The Arab Woman and the Palestine Problem.* London: Herbert Joseph, 1942.

Parsons, Laila. 'Rebels Without Borders: Southern Syria and Palestine, 1919–1936'. In *The Routledge Handbook of the History of the Middle East Mandates*, edited by Cyrus Schayegh and Andrew Arsan, pp. 395–408. Abingdon: Routledge, 2015.

Pipes, Daniel. *Greater Syria: The History of an Ambition*. Oxford: Oxford University Press, 1992.

Rogan, Eugene. *The Fall of the Ottomans: The Great War in the Middle East, 1914–1920*. London: Penguin, 2015.

Ruhi, Husayn. *Al-Mukhtasar Fi Jughrafiyat Filastin* ('A Summary of Palestine's Geography'). Jerusalem: L. J. S. Printing Press, 1923.

Salah, Hannah, ed. *Filastin Wa Tajdid Hayatuha* (Reconstruction of Palestine). New York: The Syrian-American Press, 1919.

Schayegh, Cyrus and Andrew Arsan, eds. *The Routledge Handbook of the History of the Middle East Mandates*. Abingdon: Routledge, 2015.

Seikaly, Sherene. *Men of Capital: Scarcity and Economy in Mandate Palestine*. Palo Alto: Stanford University Press, 2015.

Smith, Barbara Jean. *The Roots of Separatism in Palestine: British Economic Policy, 1920–1929*. Syracuse: Syracuse University Press, 1993.

Tamari, Salim. 'Shifting Ottoman Conceptions of Palestine, Part 1: *Filistin Risalesi* and the Two Jamals'. *Jerusalem Quarterly* 47 (2011), https://www.palestine-studies.org/en/node/78436.

Tamari, Salim. 'Shifting Ottoman Conceptions of Palestine, Part 2: Ethnography and Cartography'. *Jerusalem Quarterly* 48 (2011), https://www.palestine-studies.org/en/node/78453.

Tamari, Salim. *The Great War and the Remaking of Palestine*. Oakland: University of California Press, 2017.

Taqi al-Din, Rushdi. 'Between Syria and Palestine'. In *Filastin Wa Tajdid Hayatuha* (Reconstruction of Palestine), edited by Hannah Salah, pp. 167–77. New York: The Syrian-American Press, 1919.

Tibawi, Abdul Latif. *Arab Education in Mandatory Palestine: A Study of Three Decades of British Administration*. London: Luzac, 1956.

Totah, Khalil and Omar Al-Barghouti. *Tarikh Filastin* (History of Palestine). Jerusalem: Maktabat al-thaqafa al-diniyya, 1923.

Totah, Khalil, and Habib Khoury. *Jughrafiyat Filastin* ('Geography of Palestine'). Jerusalem: Matba'at Bayt al-Maqdes, 1923.

Wallach, Yair. *A City in Fragments: Urban Text in Modern Jerusalem*. Palo Alto: Stanford University Press, 2020.

Watenpaugh, Keith David. *Being Modern in the Middle East: Revolution, Nationalism, Colonialism, and the Arab Middle Class*. Princeton: Princeton University Press, 2014.

CHAPTER 6

Decolonising the Social History of Rural Palestinian Women: The Economic Activity of Rural Women in Galilee during the British Mandate

Rawda Morkus-Makhoul

Writing about the economic role of Palestinian rural women during the British Mandate resembles trying to see through an opaque screen of piled-up history volumes, in Arabic, Hebrew, English, or other European languages, all describing the major historic events of Ottoman and Mandatory Palestine. Through this curtain, you hear the roar of marching armies, the rhetorical speeches of the male leaders of the Arab Higher Committee, the clacking boots of the male revolutionaries on the hills of the Galilee, or the folkloric chanting of the *fellaheen*. But where are the *fellahat*?

Fellahat-free historisation of mandatory Palestine (and reluctance to engage in a feminist rural research of Palestine) ruled until the mid-1980s, when Palestinian oral history started to bloom and calls to write the social and economic history of the Palestinians started to spread within and outside academia. This is especially hard to explain if we consider that major historic works on Palestine describe its population as mostly rural and agricultural, and the urban community, constituting no more than twenty-five to thirty per cent of the population, as dependent on the rural economy. A non-critical reading of a *fellahat*-free research on Palestine is thus a reading that misses a major section of the population. It seems that, amidst the havoc that arose from the battles over the history of Palestine, the history of Palestinian working women, as a separate field of study or as part of the working class, has often been lost.

I use the word *fellahat* – that is, female peasants – as a general word to denote all the jobs and roles which Palestinian women have always performed, but received little scholarly attention. As a result, both academically and generally, we have failed to create or establish a solid body of gendered research on the Palestinian rural economy. Broadly, this is a sub-field that falls under the umbrella of researching the historic past while using gender as a category of historical analysis; when taking into account the time frame of this specific research, we must add colonialism as a global phenomenon, with its 'civilising mission' and its subaltern subject. As Jane Humphries and Carmen Sarasúa state, through this challenge, 'feminist readings rescue the history of women's work from its marginal, "off the record" status'.[1] Likewise, devoting the core of historiographic discussion to non-elites is vital, because of the need to democratise the discipline, allowing 'silenced voices' to speak.[2]

Theoretically speaking, I argue that the process of conveying the story of forgotten persons is an act of *placing* as the opposite of the violent act of *displacing*, both physically and symbolically, in research, from the land and in contemporary consciousness, intellectual awareness and attention. Placing rural women where they belong in the social sciences, not only Palestinian rural women, but also those of other societies, means expanding our knowledge of the scale of their share in social life, their economic activity, including for basic subsistence, and for other goals as set by them, in their own eyes and through their own words. I look here at *place* not only as a geographic location, but also as a symbolic term. *Placing* the experience of rural women is thus a legitimisation of their knowledge and of their narrative. As Salim Tamari puts it, describing the uniqueness of Beshara Doumani's work on Ottoman Palestine, this research adds to previous work in Palestinian Studies that '[shifts] the focus' towards 'the political economy of the interior; inserting the voices of subaltern elements such as peasants, craftsmen, and rural women in the historical account; systematically using local records as legitimate sources of historical knowledge'.[3]

Writing and Decolonising Women's History: The Missing Half of Palestinian History

Palestinian historiography has been characterised by its focus on political leadership and elites.[4] It has left out 'the life of common people and their experiences in its different forms; as fellaheen in rural areas, the working class in the cities, poor women'.[5] Using oral history, as in works by Rosemary Sayigh,[6] Nur Masalha and Nahla Abdo, falls into the category of feminist research methodologies that return power to 'simple' people who are usually deprived of it, allowing them to convey their experiences, when usually their stories are neglected while the narratives of the powerful stand out.[7]

Some light is cast on the life of these groups by the genre of village books, as Na'ama Ben Ze'ev describes. However, although village books offer surveys of rural families and local functionaries such as teachers and midwives, wedding and holiday customs, and local agricultural lifestyle, they lack the context of broader historical processes.[8] The work-life histories I present in this chapter instead reveal the strategies that rural women workers used to gain autonomy and agency amidst complex interactions of patriarchy, on the one hand, and ways to adapt gender norms to their working conditions and goals, on the other. Women pedlars, for example, learned to travel in couples or groups from their villages to nearby towns as a strategy to escape the traditional social pressures on women.[9]

Colonialist discourse and historiography have blurred and obscured memory and knowledge about the significant economic role of rural women. Native people's wisdom and practical agricultural knowledge have been ignored and under-researched. The mission of decolonising the work history of rural women in pre-1948 Palestine is therefore necessary, and particularly crucial is the task of collecting oral histories from those who witnessed the Mandate period. The material in this chapter is drawn from the oral narratives that I collected from thirty-five senior women and men from Upper and Western Galilee between 2008 and 2017. The interviews focused on the economic activity of Palestinian women in the area and the significance of the cities of Safad, Acre and Haifa for these women. It also explored their anti-colonial resistance, their survival strategies, how they coped with different challenges, individual and collective, as women and as Palestinians under British occupation and in the shadow of Zionist colonialism, with loss of land and dispossession, being uprooted from their villages and familiar environments and becoming waged workers, pedlars, service providers, or other types of workers. The oral narrators also related the role of educated women in their villages, of missionary schools in their lives, and how the British education system influenced them, their work chances and their social status.

This research found that oral narratives of Palestinian Galilean women and men who lived and worked at all stages of the British occupation are an indispensable source for a bottom-up historiography of the rural economy. Standing alone, or used with archival and other primary resources, oral narratives can help consolidate a base for gendered rural labour studies on Palestine. The narratives show that Palestinian women saw themselves as active economic subjects, locally and within their districts, and that their work, paid or unpaid, documented or not, was of major importance to their families and communities. Male interviewees, who described the work of their mothers, wives, sisters, or other village women, expressed the same view of women's work.

All the narrators who shared their life stories and testimonies for this chapter were born and lived most or all of their lives in the Western and Upper Galilee. They have lived and experienced a rural lifestyle, as did their parents before them. They told the stories of their working lives as women and their mothers' experiences. My questions aimed only to invite elaboration, along with assurances such as 'yes', 'of course', 'I understand', or 'I can imagine'. The purpose of the questions was to motivate longer answers or to encourage continuation of the narrative, especially with informants who spoke in less detail, or to elicit information such as the names of workplaces, tools, materials, plants and so on. These kinds of details were important to me, especially from those persons who had intensive working lives during the second half of the British Mandate. I also inserted questions or asked for clarification to cross-reference the oral narrative with significant events in the history of the region and to obtain more knowledge about working women's role in them, as well as the social and economic changes with which they had to deal as a result. Being the daughter and granddaughter of an agricultural family, women's work in the fields was an easy subject for me to broach, discussing topics with which both the interviewee and I were familiar, such as seasons, work procedures and stages. However, I also bore in mind the useful methodology of the 'hermeneutics of suspicion' as developed by Josselson and Spector-Mersel.[10]

As interviewees I chose older Palestinian women, as well as men who could talk about women, and I mainly asked about the economy, stopping at some crossroads in the narrative to come back to the main story of their work. On the crossroads they met themselves as schoolchildren of five or six, sitting on a straw rug, with a piece of cold, solid white board made of earth on which they wrote what the teacher or the shaykh from the mosque taught them. They met themselves as teenage girls being courted by a young man who would spill the jar that they had filled from the village well in order to keep them one more minute by the well, to insert a love letter or a flower into her hand. On the fields and down the hill slopes, and while gathering firewood, the sixth grader Nayef would follow his eleven-year-old neighbour, Najibi, walking with some older women, to read her his new love poem. In the interview, Nayef would show me his seventy-year-old poem notebook and Najibi, now eighty years old, would smile, confirm the event and turn her face in shyness.

Mapping the scale of the work that Palestinian women did and their share in the rural economy is not an easy task. Several elements contribute to this difficulty, especially in measuring the work done in the villages and rural women's work in towns such as Safad, Acre and Haifa. Unlike quantitative research, research that draws on oral history and archival material is by nature amorphous. In my research I did not decide on the number of the persons I would speak to until I had interviewed the first fifteen. Then, by studying the quality and usefulness of the interviews, I decided that I would need at least double that number of people from different villages, from the two Galilees, from the three religious communities, educated and uneducated women, women who continued to work after marriage and those who remained single, women who worked in towns in education, services, domestic labour, as pedlars, and so on.

I live in the Western Galilee and have personal connections with people in most of its villages. Upper Galilee is geographically joined to the Western Galilee, and the Palestinian community in both areas is socially networked by familial, work and community relations. I used key informant sampling to choose suitable persons for the interviews. I made telephone calls to my acquaintances, explained the goals of my research and asked about women, aged in their late seventies to nineties, from all religious affiliations, whose physical condition and mental health allowed them to tell their work-life stories and their role in their families' well-being during the British Mandate. In each village I tried to reach two or three women. In villages where internal refugees (displaced Palestinians) live, I interviewed more women so that they could tell me about those villages that no longer exist. For example, in Tarshiha I asked about women who were originally from nearby Suhmata, destroyed during the Nakba, and in Abu Snan I interviewed a woman who told the story of her original home, Kuwaykat.

In the Palestinian case, there is widespread agreement that oral history is one of the most important tools for the re-narration of the Nakba, its preceding years and its aftermaths.[11] In this research, I argue that in the case of writing rural Palestinian women into Palestinian history, oral history derived from the elder community about women's roles in the social, economic and political fields is vital. Having been marginalised by patriarchal social structures and as labourers in the Palestinian, Jewish and colonial economies, the narratives that a researcher can collect from women in particular are indispensable.[12] Palestinian researchers have contrasting attitudes to written and oral testimonies: some adhere to classical conceptions of historical research, its documentary evidence and methods of adjudicating accuracy; others may approach oral history with a bias toward a certain narrative and are on the lookout for supporting testimonies, while yet other researchers deploy multiple methodologies.[13]

Academic writing using oral history as a research method for Palestinian history began in doctoral and master's theses in the 1970s. For example, Bayan Nuwayhid al-Hout wrote her doctoral thesis on the Palestinian political leadership during the Mandate period; Nafez Nazzal collected oral interviews with Palestinian refugees in Lebanon to write his doctoral thesis on Palestinian refugees from Galilee; and Rosemary Sayigh and Julie Peteet used oral history narratives to understand the conditions of refugees in Lebanon.[14] Sayigh's work especially had a significant impact on the interest in memory as a source for historical writing, while both Sayigh and Peteet drew attention to the importance of oral history from a feminist point of view.[15] Such examples of oral history research in the historiography of Palestine started in the 1970s and expanded from the 1990s onwards, with examples such as Sharif Kanaana,[16] Mustafa Kabha,[17] Adel Abdel-Jawad,[18] Sherna Berger Gluck,[19] Nur Masalha,[20] Faiha Abdelhadi[21] and Lina Miari's work on Birweh village.[22]

Archives: Primary Resources in the Palestinian Case

'In normal conditions', Suleiman Bashir wrote, 'a document is classified and saved on the day it is published, i.e, before it turns into a "document". In other words, building an archive is normally a question of natural and organic accumulation'.[23] However, 'the process of accumulating the Palestinian archive has been extremely difficult and complicated'.[24] In his description of the scattering of Palestinian documents, he uses the term 'horizontal scattering' to denote the places where 'Palestinian sources are preserved and maintained',[25] highlighting the fact that Palestinian history documents are found, if at all, in many places and different levels of preservation, complicating efforts to organise and categorise them. Kabha notes that the history of the Palestinians has been lost due to the many archives that have been captured by Israeli forces, such as municipal records and those of parties, cultural and social clubs, libraries, law firms and so on.[26] No one raises an eyebrow any more upon hearing or reading that the Israeli authorities have closed archives or extended a confidentiality order.[27]

In essence, the Palestinian archive does not exist. What we have are modest but sincere efforts to save the collective history of the Palestinians by numerous Palestinian academic and non-academic centres, refugee and other NGOs, political parties, research centres, mosques, churches and individuals. Despite these efforts and their limited scope, many researchers base their work on these resources whilst acknowledging their limitations. With this in mind, I need to emphasise the limitations on research on rural Palestinian women, especially given that the British, Israeli and Palestinian Authority archives all lack sections devoted to women. Time-consuming efforts need to be made to seek archived material on or by Palestinian women.

In the course of writing the historical background for my master's degree on Palestinian women in the Israeli labour market,[28] I came across Inger Marie Okkenhaug's research on the English High School for Girls in Haifa and the influence of the Jerusalem and Middle East Church on the education of Palestinians.[29] That is where I connected my new knowledge with my intermediate school teacher, Mrs Heifa Mzighit, who I knew had studied in the high school mentioned in Okkenhaug's work, and how a British lady had sent her to Oxford to study pedagogy. My great-grandparents had also been Protestants who had served the church in Kfar Yasif, and my grandmother and father told us stories of how and why my great-grandfather, 'Abdallah al-Bassit, converted to Protestantism when he found work with the mission that arrived in my village in the middle of the nineteenth century. These fit like pieces of a puzzle in my determination to travel and research the archives on my village and on the English High School where my teacher had learned. Preparing to travel took three months, during which I interviewed more women and men, read more about education in Palestine and studied in detail the contents of the files at St Anthony's College, Oxford, on the Jerusalem and Middle East Mission, where I found a box labelled 'Kfar Yasif Clinic'. Like a lost man who has found his guide, I grew more determined to find information about rural Palestinian working women, not only in the oral histories that I had already collected, but also in primary sources: the documents of teachers, headmistresses and church and missionary women, as well as the pictures or magazine clippings that the online handlist of the mission's archive showed to exist.

Researching Oral Histories

As in any rural community, in Palestinian farming families, women constitute an important workforce. To the Palestinian peasant, labour was a way of life and a precondition of survival, and the market was a place where they could sell the surplus of their own or their family's work. However, under certain political and economic conditions, large groups had to sell their labour power as well, which is why we also find Palestinian peasants in factories, workshops, domestic service and other jobs. This research does not aim to provide evidence on women's work in agriculture or other fields of work per se, but to bring their past economic role and experiences into the spotlight. While studying their role, we learn that these women did not see their lives as divided into separate public and private spheres, as conventional economic models show, but as one continuous existence, mostly in farm and domestic work, as well as in other fields.

Researchers of women's work patterns from a sociological perspective have examined the determinants that lead to differing levels of engagement in labour. These include age, marital status, number of children, education, culture and religiosity. Contreras and Plaza point to culture and internalised conservative values as depressive factors.[30] In the case of rural Palestinian women, although living in a socially conservative and patriarchal society, work was the culture of their daily life – in other words, they were part of the collective family and community effort to till the land, process its crops and deal with the surplus. Theoretically, I argue that using the terminology of classic economic research to understand the undocumented and/or unpaid economic activity of women can be misleading. Hence, oral narratives and primary sources provide knowledge that would be obscured if retrieved using only quantitative research methods. Humphries and Sarasúa show that conceptualising low rates of women's work participation is 'in part statistically manufactured by uncritical reliance on official sources that systematically undercount women workers'.[31] Previous research using oral resources includes that on elite women active in national, charity and feminist spheres, such as those studied by Ellen Fleischmann.[32] Here, in contrast, I base my research on the oral histories of women of whom the majority were illiterate and whose involvement in charity work or direct nationalist activity was minor. The educated women whom I interviewed or who were mentioned in the oral narratives were only partly active in political or social activities.

Sun, Thorns and Mud: Physical Pain and Body Image in Women's Labour

On asking female and male interviewees about the challenges that working women, especially married ones, faced during the years before and immediately after the Nakba, physical pain was a constant theme. Hard work and physical pain were frequently referred to as an integral part of peasant life. In order to help the women remember long-forgotten details of their or others' experiences, I purposely formulated the question with superlative adjectives such as the most difficult, hardest or easiest, or asked: 'Which women worked the most or spent most of their time at work?' or, 'Of all women you used to know, who had the most difficult life? Who was the most successful?' Stories about earning a living the hard way poured out, painting a harsh image of village life under poverty, colonialism and economic instability.

Mrs Tuma, also known as Umm Ibrahim, related the pain she suffered as result of her working conditions:

> What was the most difficult thing for me? Harvesting! We were poor. I didn't have any choice. I had to work from sunrise to sunset. Thorns? Don't ask! Back pain? All day! And my hands, especially my little fingers, were all wounded and never healed. But I was young and strong, not like today.[33]

Umm Hasib, or Mrs Dawood, answering a question about a hard-working woman described by another interviewee as the woman who suffered the most to earn her family's living, said:

> Yes, I know Umm Saleem. We used to live next door. Oh!! How hard this woman worked! No one worked as much as she did! Her husband was thirty years older than her, and he was handicapped. This is the reason why she was poor. Can you imagine? Every day, she used to walk from our village to Al-Birwei or I'bilin [30 km] to work in the harvest. Her children? She used to give each [female] neighbour one of them; one here, one there until she came back with sunset . . . poor woman.[34]

Mrs Dawood also related the story of H. J.:

> She was the woman who worked most. She worked in anything you wanted. She even worked in construction. When a group of men wanted to build the roof of a house, they would send for H. J. to bring the water on her head from the fountain and pour it on the cement. She was the only one who could do that physically. She was full of power . . . like a man. She also worked in the olive seasons. She had a big family, and her husband was 'ajjal'; how could he earn enough and support his family?[35] So, she had to work in anything. If she hadn't, her children would have died. Dear daughter! If women who had better lives worked, do you think poorer ones wouldn't have?[36]

As mentioned, pain caused by carrying heavy burdens on the head or back was not looked upon as something that needed special care. In all my interviews, women talked about pain as a normal feature of life. The testimony of sons, such as Mr Sae'd, Mr Nasra and Mr Murkus, does acknowledge the pain and hardship that their mothers suffered, at least in retrospect. In the testimony of Mrs Yusrah Snuno (seventy-one years old) for Zochrot's website, she describes the work that the women of her village, Kuwaykat, performed:

> The whole work fell on the shoulders of women. Women worked just as men did, woke up very early and worked in the fields, planted, harvested, or packed. Our village had many *labbanat* (female dairy sellers). Women who had cattle used to hire a woman to carry the yoghurt or the cheese for them from the village to Acre. They used to pay her two pennies or two and a half. They would start at dawn and make a seven-hour walk to Acre. There, a dairy merchant would be waiting for them and buy the yoghurt. Before leaving Acre the two women would go into the market and buy spices and yeast and come back home before dark.[37]

Mr Wafiq Nasra of Kuwaykat testifies to his mother's work during the Mandate, but with reference to the hardship and pain she suffered:

> My mother was assisted by three women. Each woman got three pennies for every tin she carried on her head. There were neither work hours nor clocks. They would wake up with the morning star. When they saw it, they started their march towards Acre. My mother worked a lot. We were seven or eight persons. She used to make bread, wash clothes, cook and sweep under the goats till sunset. Then she would fall asleep exhausted in the early evening.[38]

The same experience is seen in the description by Mr Murkus, aged eighty-two, of his mother's and other women's work:

> We didn't have a difficult life like other peasants in the village, and my father was considered middle class, and he owned lands and cattle. However, the majority of the village had economic hardship, and women were the main victims. You must imagine how they woke up at dawn to do everything in their houses and then go to work in all seasons, hot or cold, sunny, or rainy, on the landlords' property. Don't think they went alone. Their husbands went with them too and worked in anything they could get. Salary? No! They earned food, seeds, olives, oil, wheat, etc. No one was spoiled.[39]

Other physical hardship was downplayed during the interviews. For example, Umm Atef testifies that, during the tobacco season, a woman had to fill four to five containers of water a day, each holding twelve gallons. This was water they drew from the village well, so they needed to walk back and forth several times. Then they had to walk into the hills to reach the planting areas. All this had to be done before six a.m. The men would carry these containers on the horses, mules or donkeys and head to the mountainous areas. Women in Al-Buqei'a/Peqiin and

Jish said that it was usual for two or three women to plant two *dunums* a day with tobacco seedlings, starting and finishing with the sun. However, despite these burdens, to Umm Atef the never-ending workload at home and in the field was just part of an ordinary village day, as it is evident in the following conversation:

> Interviewer: ... so you are telling me that a woman didn't consider the physical hardship as such?
> Interviewee (holding her hand up to gesture 'no'): It was her job.
> Interviewer: You mean a part of her life?
> Interviewee: Yes, and of the whole family's life.
> Interviewer: Didn't anyone complain?
> Interviewee (now with a serious look on her face, again gesturing 'no'): 'N ... ot even one! This was their shape of life, that's it.
> Interviewer: That's it!
> Interviewee (smiling): What do you think? That they were like you today? All you do is sending your sons, daughters and grandchildren to schools ... and that woman with nails this length [points at her nails to mock women's manicure fashions], all this did not exist during our time, my dear. ...'[40]

Physical pain at work, and not magnifying it as reason for laziness, was often illustrated by my interlocutors by comparing the interviewee's time with my time, with a hint of mockery towards 'you women of today' on the part of the interviewee:

> The women of my time just murmured 'Ayy', and the baby was out! Women of the past used to give birth while gathering wood, while picking olives ... there was that woman who gave birth in an area called Tayyuni, and since then people call her Tayyuni. No one knows that her real name is Suheila. Women of the past used to walk a lot, and so the baby inside the womb was free to move till the head would be in the proper place, not like women of today. You all give birth under surgery. Why?? Because you sit too much, and the baby doesn't turn around. Oh! Now this will be in the recording [laughs out loud].[41]

Umm Habeeb described how she lost her first baby girl in the seventh month of her pregnancy while she was gathering wood for cooking with a group of village women:

> Inteviewee: I was gathering wood from Jabal el-Jarmaq, there, you know, where there are radars today [pointing at an Israeli military base opposite her window]. It was the second time that day that I made the journey and carried a bundle of branches and roots on my head. She died inside.

Interviewer:	How did you know she died?
Interviewee:	She stopped moving, and I felt as if someone dropped a heavy stone inside of me. It remained like this for twenty days, and then I gave birth to the dead baby girl.
Interviewer:	Didn't you have fever? Bleeding, anything?
Interviewee:	No . . . just like that. I had contractions and she came out . . . dead.
Interviewer:	Oh . . . that is so painful. You must have gone through a lot of suffering.
Interviewee:	That was our time, my daughter! If the women hadn't suffered, they wouldn't have lived. Women had to work, like you do. Don't you work and suffer today? The married and the single are working. Everybody works.[42]

The focus on suffering as an integral part of people's work is reflected in the way in which Mrs Jibran considered it an inescapable rule of life, not an exceptional occurrence. Mrs S. of Kisra village had fourteen pregnancies, of which only four babies survived. She explained that this was due to her hard work in the fields:

> I used to cry for months after every miscarriage. I got sick of that. It happened because of the heat and the tobacco plantation. I had to pull very hard to uproot the tobacco plants and roots so that I could plant again next season. I used to see the blood coming out. Oh! They didn't care for the pregnant woman. She worked as much as the others. Society did not have mercy on her.[43]

Fellahat between the Village and the City

The significance of Safad, Acre and Haifa constituted a theme in all the oral narratives for this research. The proximity of the villages to these towns allowed women to commute there with their agricultural, dairy and artisanal products. The three towns also provided the rural communities of the Upper and Western Galilees with administrative, educational, cultural and economic services. Before the Nakba, there were ninety Palestinian villages in the Safad District (compared to only five following 1948),[44] and seventy-eight per cent of the district's inhabitants lived in villages. However, they all, to a large extent, were dependent on the urban leadership of rich and notable Palestinians, who owned twenty-two per cent of the district area. Jewish immigration and settlement, which had been on the rise for some years, also increased the villagers' dependence and fragile economic status.[45]

Archival resources, such as the files on the Safad District's female rural teachers, demonstrate the linkages between village life in the Galilee and these regional hubs. Women teachers, as we see from these files, used to deal with the Anglo-Palestine Bank in Safad, where their salaries were deposited.[46] Women from the village of Jish spoke about their families' need to travel to Safad as a trade centre. Mrs Jibran used to ride the mule which her father loaded with vegetables to send her to the *hisbi*, Safad's vegetable wholesaler. She would deliver the vegetables or the grains to the owners of the *hisbi*, two brothers from the Qaddura family, get the money and ride back to the village.[47] In her narrative she described how the village crops were brought to the *hisbi* every day, and that she used to see single and married women in the *suq* or market where the *hisbi* was based.

The city and plain of Acre were also central to the rural Palestinian economy. The Mandate government invested in agricultural education, and Acre's significance to the Mandate's agricultural policies can be seen in the fact that the largest agricultural station (including the British administration's stud farm) in Palestine was in Acre and the highest number of training gardens was in this district.[48] Although the development of Haifa's port and railway network weakened the status of Acre as an administrative centre, the city remained vital for the Western and Upper Galilee, as oral narratives show. There were fifty-two Arab villages in the district of Acre during the Mandate period, along with eight Bedouin tribes and nine Jewish settlements. Tarshiha was the biggest village, with a population of 3,830 in 1945, followed by al-Bassa with 2,950 and al-Zeeb and al-Manawat with 1,910 persons each. In 1930–31, there were twenty-three schools in the whole district, increasing in number to thirty-one in 1937–38, including girls' schools in Kfar Yasif, al-Rama, Julis and Tarshiha.[49] Nimer Morkus' memoirs show that villagers depended tremendously on the town.[50] Kfar Yasif and its surrounding villages also related to Acre as an economic centre:

> Our village owned many camels, owned by five or six physically strong men. The camels were used for carrying wheat, barley, white maze, *kursanni*,[51] sesame and watermelons from the village to Acre's merchants and markets. These camels were used for bringing the village's supplies of salt, rice, coffee and more from the town.[52]

Haifa, meanwhile, was one of the most vibrant urban centres in Palestine. It has thus been the focus of considerable research on its urban nature and development as result of structural and administrative changes under British economic and military policies. Increased levels of class and national awareness here translated into workers' unions and cultural and political clubs and societies, as numerous scholars have shown.[53] Many others have written about Haifa as an urban centre that attracted villagers and turned them into migrant workers.[54] Haifa-based pre-1948 newspapers and weekly publications provide rich primary materials on these changes and on rural-urban economic activity during the Mandate. The Union of Arab Workers Societies and Trade Unions reported in *al-Ittihad* newspaper that 'the low farming season was the main reason for the movement of *fellahin* from their villages searching for work'.[55] These *fellahin* (and *fellahat*?) came from different regions of Palestine, including Nazareth, Safad, Jenin, Nablus, Ramallah and Jerusalem and their surrounding districts.[56] Awni Faris' article on female workers from the village of Silwad (in the district of Ramallah) to work in Haifa in the early 1930s sheds light on their life and on Haifa as a town that provided work opportunities.[57] Taken together, such research provides important information on the work that women and villagers in general found in the city, as unskilled labourers, pedlars, service providers and low-status clerics.[58] Women worked mainly in domestic services such as laundry and cleaning, or as market workers selling vegetables and herbs.[59]

Commuting for work between rural areas and Haifa continued even during periods of political turbulence and national resistance, such as the 1936–39 Palestinian Revolt. This continued activity can be seen as part of what Sarah Irving describes as the 'complexity of life in which relations between Palestinian Mandate, Arabs and Jews and members of the British administration overlapped on a daily basis'; such a reality can defy 'clear lines and easy ex-post-facto assumptions about personal and professional relations between the different communities'.[60] Rural women took active roles in the anti-colonial resistance; the case of Aziza Hamed, a pedlar in Haifa's market, is one such example. 'Awni Faris describes how, during the 1936 revolt, a bomb exploded at Al-Jreini, one of Haifa's markets, and that one of the casualties was a Palestinian pedlar:

> The incident in which Aziza Muhammad Hamed fell a martyr in Al-Jreini Market in Haifa is an example of the sacrifice that Palestinian rural women made. This woman had to bear and suffer to secure a living for her family. Aziza worked in many of the available jobs that were open to villagers like her, such as wood gatherers who collected wood from Mount Carmel and sold it to the bakeries in the town.[61]

Rarely were rural Palestinian women considered as migrant workers in these major changes, and their social and economic history is rarely written. Awni Faris is one of the few researchers to note that village women were also attracted to the new work opportunities created in Haifa. According to Faris, most of these women came with their husbands or brothers. Whole families from Silwad walked from their village to Nablus and then took the bus to Haifa.[62]

An Indispensable Work Force

The extent of rural women's work in agriculture was never shown in censuses or official surveys because rural women, who constituted the majority of the labour force, were considered housewives. The same goes for teenage girls and children. This under-representation portrays women as immobile, passive and unproductive.

This differs radically from the image found in oral histories gathered from people who lived in the Mandate period. Interviews with both women and men from the Galilee show that women walked or rode long distances to find work opportunities. I thus argue that, where work opportunities existed or appeared, Palestinian women followed them and were proactive in enhancing their chances of employment. Mrs Banna, for instance, described how she became a waged worker:

> I was thirteen when I found out that the Spinney's Soda Factory in Acre hired workers. I was good at English because I went to school and even joined the boys' school because there was no schooling for girls after the fourth grade. My job at Spinney's was to put the stickers on the soda bottles. We used to work for eight hours, and the workday would end at three p.m. When I turned fifteen, I rented a room in Acre and used to return to my village once a week, on foot, with other women who came to sell yogurt in the *suq*. I worked for nine years in the factory; later, at twenty-two, I got bored. Then I bought a sewing machine and started working at home, and then I got married.[63]

Mrs Banna's elementary-level education and her knowledge of English from Kfar Yasif's Sunday school, run by British women, boosted her chances of finding long-term, secure work, a chance that was not available for non-educated women who needed to develop their economic chances with their own hands, such as the women of the Bedouin village of al-Ramel on the road between Acre and Haifa. Mrs Sweity of al-Ramel described to me how women in her village saw British soldiers who passed by the village as an opportunity, boiling coffee and tea and baking bread to sell to them.[64] Village women who lived in Haifa went to the railway station, where they would wait for the arrival of British soldiers and take their clothes to their shacks, wash them and return them within a day or two.[65]

Rural Palestinian Women in Education

A letter sent by the village *mukhtar* and church head of Kafr Bir'im, in the district of Safad, dated September 1946, shows the Mandate government's neglect of the Arab education system. The letter reads: 'We have lost all patience, having waited for over three years for your financial assistance [. . .] with a negative result'. The author of the letter added that the village had raised the 2,000 pounds required by the Education Department, despite the local community comprising mainly people earning 'a trivial income', and that they were willing to 'pay the salary of one teacher and the rental for the school rooms and expenses'.[66] Internal office correspondence shows that the Mandate government refused to carry on discussing the issue 'due to stubbornness of the villagers', adding that 'it was a waste of time'.[67] The archived file also shows that, as of July 1947, the school had not been built and the villagers were still pleading for it, explaining that they were 'very poor' and very much regretted that they 'could not contribute more for this school', but that they 'trusted the Government' to help them.[68]

Across Palestine, parents paid from their own money to build schools for girls and for the salaries of one or two female teachers. The same went for boys' schools.[69] Schneider writes that, 'because police and "security" spending was disproportionately high, few resources remained for education' and that the 'immediate consequence was that public education was consistently and dramatically underfinanced'.[70] As result, the government did not offer educational services to the majority of the Arab population throughout the Mandate period.[71]

Despite this, the number of girls' schools rose, and the entry of qualified Arab teachers and headmistresses into the teaching system can be traced.[72] Primary sources used in my research, such as female teachers' work files, shows how teaching was regulated by law, including employees' rights and duties, wages and promotion scale.[73] Rural women studied and trained in teachers' seminaries such as the Rural Teachers Seminar in Ramallah, then colleges in Jerusalem and Nazareth. Most of these had been established by German and Russian missionary groups.[74]

By studying thirty files of Arab teachers who worked between 1932 and 1948, selecting those from the Galilee, I found that one of the factors that helped Palestinian girls to stay in school until the eighth or ninth year and thus be qualified to join a teacher's seminary was the freedom to move from their villages to other places. Such spatial mobility between the Western and Upper Galilees and Ramallah to receive their teachers' license allowed young village women to secure jobs in the Mandate education system.

The broader picture that we receive from analysing the letters that these teachers wrote to inspectors and officials, as well as the oral narratives gathered for this research, allows me to claim that the support of significant male family members, structural factors such as frequent transportation, and a supportive community were behind the rising popularity and acceptance of education as a profession for rural women. Their letters to inspectors, for example, show that women rented houses or rooms outside their villages and lived independently or semi-independently, such as with relatives. Oral narratives show that staying in the job, professional advancement and coping with challenges were linked to the presence of supportive male family members and social networks. Supportive male family members are described as those who 'did not object' or did not disapprove of their daughters' or sisters' decisions to study teaching. However, in most cases, it was the father who decided and encouraged them. The oral narratives show examples of this support, such as fathers renting the car that took their daughters to the town where the teaching college was based, carrying their bags, accompanying them to rent and furnish their rooms in their distant workplaces and visiting them with food supplies. All interviewees mentioned paternal rather than maternal support, but this does not mean that mothers objected. It may be that the traditional role of the father as head of the family and decision-maker was more dominant in the narrators' memories.

Given that transportation between the villages and the major towns in the north of Palestine was irregular and slow in the 1920s and 1930s, and that freedom was needed to travel to distant towns to acquire jobs such as teaching, nursing or midwifery, it is thus clear that Palestinian rural women grasped whatever opportunities they saw to improve their social and economic status.

Oral histories also show the sad moments when young women had to comply with society's gender restrictions and limitations. Palestinian women demanded to stay in or beyond elementary school, but parental disapproval sometimes prevented them. This is seen in almost all the interviews. Women whose mothers or fathers took them out of school cried when remembering these events, sometimes blaming their fathers or both parents for preventing them from becoming teachers. They mentioned the names of village teachers of the same age who they claimed were less clever than they themselves back in their schooldays.[75] Mrs Farraj of Rama village would have 'loved from the bottom of [her] heart' to continue beyond the fourth year of school, but was taken out of school to help her mother with her new-born brothers and sisters.[76] However, some succeeded in convincing their fathers, such as Mrs Gazali Bishara, who not only managed to 'study further with the boys, but also got higher grades than them all',[77] and Mrs Deebi Banna, who asked to join the Amiri Boys' School in Kfar Yasif and because of her 'cleverness and active learning' managed to learn to read and write very well and found a job in a British factory in Acre.[78]

Epilogue

In this chapter, I have showed women's economic roles and contribution in rural areas in Pre-Nakba Palestine, taking the Western and Upper regions of the Galilee as a research field. I showed how feminist methodology, oral history and use of primary sources help to explain the histories of women's working lives at the intersections of gender and race, under colonial power. What I presented as individual voices on personal economic contributions to private households is in fact the collective narration of Palestinian rural women's collective labour for the welfare and the well-being of entire villages or communities. The roles performed by women, as individuals and as a collective, were determined by social and political structures that dictated the shape, size and economic value of their work. These approaches, alongside the work of the scholars mentioned above, are the beginning of making the barrier between our understanding and the lives of rural working Palestinian women less opaque.

Notes

1. Humphries and Sarasúa, 'Off the Record', p. 40.
2. Ben Ze'ev, 'Returning for a Visit', p. 81.
3. Tamari, 'Hidden Gems', p. 135.
4. Abu Lughod, 'Introduction'.
5. Miari, 'Adwar al-nisaa'', p. VI.
6. Sayigh, *Peasants to Revolutionaries*.
7. Abdelhadi, *Bibliography*.
8. Ben Ze'ev, 'Returning for a Visit'.
9. Interviews with Mrs Dawood and Mrs Nasra.
10. Josselson, 'Hermeneutics of Faith'; Spector-Mersel, 'Narrative Enquiry'.
11. Masalha, *Palestine Nakba*; Abdo and Masalha, *An Oral History*.
12. Interviews with Mr Nimer Morkus and Mr Michael Makhouli.
13. Yahya, 'Oral History and Dual Marginalization', p. 96.
14. Ibid., p. 97.
15. Ibid.
16. Muhawi and Kanaana, *Speak Bird*.
17. Kabha, *Thawrat 1936*.
18. Abdel-Jawad, 'Limatha la nastati'a'.
19. Gluck, 'Palestinian Women'; 'Advocacy Oral History'.
20. Masalha, *Palestine Nakba*.
21. Abdel-Hadi, *Bibliography*.
22. Miari, 'Adwar al-nisaa''.
23. Bashir, *Khazanat al-watha'iq*, p. 24.
24. Ibid., p. 25.
25. Ibid.
26. Kabha, 'Problematics'.
27. Akevot, 'Draft Bill'.
28. Morkus-Makhoul, 'Israeli Labour Market'.
29. Okkenhaug, *Quality of Heroic Women*.
30. Contreras and Plaza, 'Cultural Factors'.
31. Humphries and Sarasúa, 'Off the Record', p. 39.
32. Fleischmann, *The Nation and its New Women*.
33. Mrs Tuma, 2015.
34. Mrs Dawood, 2012.
35. An *'ajjal* was a shepherd helper, the lowest rank of agrarian service or job a man would have performed. It required taking the cattle out to the field in the morning and bringing them back in the afternoon. From the interviews, we can conclude that this job was not only ill-paid, but also undesirable for a decent man.
36. Mrs Dawood, 2012.

37. Zochrot, Testimony of Yusra Snunu.
38. Zochrot, 2008 Testimonies.
39. Mr Morkus, 2008.
40. Mrs Khreish, Umm Atef, 2017.
41. Umm Habeeb, Mrs Jibran 2014.
42. Mrs Jibran, 2014.
43. Mrs S. of Kisra, 2017.
44. Abbasi, 'Tsfat vi Izorah'.
45. Ibid., p. 123.
46. Balqis Ghannum to Education Inspector, 4 February 1942, p. 32; Israel State
     Archives.
47. Mrs Jibran, 2014.
48. El-Eini, 'British Forestry Policy'.
49. Al-Dabbagh, 'Acre'.
50. Morkus, *Stronger than Forgetfulness*.
51. *Vicia erilia* or bitter vetch, a Mediterranean crop legume grown for thousands
     of years.
52. Morkus, *Stronger than Forgetfulness*, p. 21.
53. See, for example, Budeiri, *Tatawwur al-haraka*; Farah, *Min al-uthmaniyya*; Seikaly,
     Haifa; De Vries, 'Proletarianization'; Yazbek, 'Immigrants, Elites'; Hasan, 'Hidden
     from Sight'; Mansour, 'Hijaz-Palestine Railway'; and Ben-Ze'ev, 'Returning for
     a Visit'.
54. See, for example, work by Deborah Bernstein, Mahmud Yazbek, David de
     Vreis, Manar Hasan, Ami Ayalon, Johnny Mansour and Na'ama Ben Ze'ev.
55. *Al-Ittihad*, 23 July 1944, p. 4.
56. Mansour, *Haifa*.
57. Faris, 'Adeebi Al-Halaj'.
58. Mansour, *Haifa*, p. 290.
59. Ibid.
60. Irving, 'A Young Man of Promise', p. 42.
61. Faris, 'Adeebi Al-Halaj'.
62. Ibid.
63. Mrs D. Banna, 2011.
64. Haji Umm Khalil Al-Taye'-Sweity, 2016.
65. Mrs Nazmiyya el-Kilani, 2014.
66. Letter from Khoury Yousef and Abdullah Jubran, 23 September 1946, ISA
     2682/29-M.
67. Letter from Department of Education to Chief Secretary, 25 June 1947, ISA
     2682/29-M.
68. Letter from El Khoury Yousuf Elias to Chief Secretary, Government of Palestine,
     31 July 1947, ISA 2682/29-M.
69. Dabbagh, 'Acre'; Tibawi, *Arab Education*.

70. Schneider, *Mandatory Separation*.
71. Ibid.
72. Okkenhaug, *Quality of Heroic Women*; Greenberg, 'Between Hardships'; Stockdale, *Colonial Encounters*; and Tibawi, *Arab Education*.
73. For more, see Furas 'Old Arabs, New Arabs'.
74. Agsous, 'Making Stage'.
75. Mrs Khoury-Sakkas, 2016; Mrs Dawood, 2012; Mrs Tuma, 2012.
76. Mrs Farraj, 2015.
77. Mrs Bishara, 2017.
78. Mrs Banna, 2011.

Bibliography

Archives

State Archive of Israel, Jerusalem.
Zochrot online interview archive.

Interviewees

Mrs Deebi Ghattas Banna (90), Kfar Yasif, July 2011.
Mrs Gazali Bishara (87), Tarshiha, 2017.
Mrs Farraj, S. Al-Rameh, July 2015.
Mrs Katar Jubran, Al-Jish, February 2014.
Haji Umm Khalil Al-Taye'-Sweity, Al-Ramel, Jiddin, Abu Snan, 2016.
Mrs Mary Khriesh, Um 'Atef (87), Al-Jish, February 2014.
Mrs Miriam Abu 'Akel Tuma, Kfar Yasif, April 2012.
Mrs Munira Dawood (80), Kfar Yasif, 2012
Mr Nazmiyi Mihyi ed-Deen el-Kilany-Ali, Safad/Akko, August 2014.
Mr Nimer Murkus (78), Kfar Yasif, 2008, 2012.
Mrs S., Kisra Village, July 2015.
Mrs Saleema Khouri-Sakkas (82), Al-Birwi/Kfar Yasif, August 2016.
Mr Shehadi Makhouli (88), Kfar Yasif, October 2013.

Secondary Sources

Abbasi, Mustafa. 'Tsfat vi Izorah ha-Kafri (Safad and its Rural Region during the Mandate Period: Attitudes and Tensions)'. *Cathedra* 99 (2001): pp. 115–38.
Abdel-Jawad, Saleh. 'Limatha la nastati'a kitabat tarikhana al-mua'aser min dun istikhdam al-masader al-shafawiyya (Why Can't We Write Our History without Oral Sources?)'. In *Towards a Historical Narrative of the Nakba: Complexities and Challenges*, edited by Mustafa Kabha, pp. 26–55. Haifa: Mada al-Carmel Arab Centre for Applied Social Research, 2006.

Abdelhadi, Faiha. *A Bibliography of Palestinian Oral History, with a Special Focus on Women's Issues*. Ramallah: PNA and Ministry for International Planning and Collaboration, 1999.

Abdo, Nahla and Nur Masalha. *An Oral History of the Palestinian Nakba*. London: Bloomsbury, 2018.

Abu Lughud, Ibrahim. 'Introduction'. In *Palestinians: From Peasants to Revolutionaries*, by Rosemary Sayigh (Arabic version). London: Zed, 1979.

Agsous, Sadia. 'The Making Stage of the Modern Palestinian Arabic Novel in the Experiences of the udabā² Khalīl Baydas (1874–1949) and Iskandar al-Khūri al-BeitJāli (1890–1973)'. In *European Cultural Diplomacy and Arab Christians in Palestine, 1918–1948*, edited by K. Sanches Summerer and S. Zananiri, pp. 63–78. Basingstoke: Palgrave Macmillan, 2021.

Akevot Institute. 'Draft Bill to Extend RAP of Intelligence and Other Security Archives by 20 Years', https://www.akevot.org.il/en/news-item/draft-bill-extend-rap-intelligence-security-archives-20-years/ [accessed 4 October 2018].

Al-Dabbagh, M. 'Acre'. In *Mawsu'at Biladuna Filastin* (Our Country Palestine: An Encyclopaedia), pp. 144–52. Acre: NP, 1988.

Ben Ze'ev, Na'ama. 'Returning for a Visit: Rural Migrants and Social Change in Mandatory Palestine'. *Journal of Levantine Studies* 7, 2 (2017): pp. 79–102.

Bernstein, Deborah. *Constructing Boundaries: Jewish and Arab Workers in Mandatory Palestine*. Albany: SUNY Press, 2000.

Al-Budeiri, Musa. *Tatawwur al-haraka Al-'umaliyya al-'arabiyya fi Filastin* (The Development of the Arab Workers Movement in Palestine). Jerusalem: Dar el-Katib, 1979.

Bashir, S. *Khazanat al-watha'iq al-Filastiniyya: Second Collection 1918–1948*. Jerusalem: Jami'ayyat al-Dirasat al-Arabiyya, 1983.

Contreras, Dante and Gonzalo Plaza. 'Cultural Factors in Women's Labor Force Participation in Chile'. *Feminist Economics* 16, 2 (2010): pp. 27–46.

De Vries, David. 'Proletarianization and National Segregation: Haifa in the 1920s'. *Middle Eastern Studies* 30, 4 (1994): pp. 860–82, doi: 10.1080/00263209408701026.

Doumani, Beshara. 'Rediscovering Ottoman Palestine: Writing Palestinians into History'. *Journal of Palestine Studies* 21, 2 (1992): pp. 5–28.

El-Eini, Roza. I. M. 'British Forestry Policy in Mandate Palestine, 1929–48: Aims and Realities'. *Middle Eastern Studies* 35, 3 (1999): pp. 72–155.

Farah, Bulos. *Min al-uthmaniyya ila al-dawla al-ibriyya* (From the Ottoman to the Hebrew State). Nazareth: NP, 1985.

Faris, A. 'Adeebi Al-Halaj: Hayat Rifiyyat Filistiniyyat fi Haifa 1930–1948 (Adeebi al-Halaj: The Life of Rural Palestinian Women in Haifa 1930–1948)'. *Hawliyyat Al-Quds* 10 (2010): pp. 66–75.

Fleischmann, Ellen. *The Nation and Its New Women: The Palestinian Women's Movement, 1920–1948*. Berkeley: University of California Press, 2003.

Furas, Yoni. 'Old Arabs, New Arabs: Debating Palestinian Pedagogy during the Mandate'. *Middle Eastern Studies* 56, 2 (2020): pp. 257–73.

Gluck, Sherna. 'Palestinian Women: Gender Politics and Nationalism'. *Journal of Palestine Studies* 24, 3 (1995): pp. 5–15.

Gluck, Sherna. 'Advocacy Oral History: Palestinian Women in Resistance'. In *Women's Words: The Feminist Practice of Oral History*, edited by Sherna Gluck and Daphne Patai, pp. 205–20. New York: Routledge, 1991.

Greenberg, Ela. 'Between Hardships and Respect: A Collective Biography of Arab Women Teachers in British-Ruled Palestine'. *Journal of Women of the Middle East and the Islamic World* 6 (2008): pp. 284–314.

Hasan, Manar. 'Palestine's Absent Cities: Gender, Memoricide and the Silencing of Urban Palestinian Memory'. *Journal of Holy Land and Palestine Studies* 18, 1 (2019): pp. 1–20.

Hasan, Manar. *Hidden from Sight: Women and the Palestinian Towns (Smoyot Mi-Ha'ayen)*. Jerusalem: Van Leer Institute, 2017.

Humphries, Jane and Sarasúa, Carmen. 'Off the Record: Reconstructing Women's Labor Force Participation in the European Past'. *Feminist Economics* 18, 4 (2012): pp. 39–67.

Irving, Sarah. '"A Young Man of Promise": Finding a Place for Stephan Hanna Stephan in the History of Mandate Palestine'. *Jerusalem Quarterly* 73 (2018): pp. 42–62.

Josselson, Ruthellen. 'The Hermeneutics of Faith and the Hermeneutics of Suspicion'. *Narrative Inquiry* 14, 1 (2004): pp. 1–28.

Kabha, Mustafa. *Thawrat 1936 al-Kubra* (The Great Revolt of 1936). Nazareth: Maktabat al-Qabs, 1988.

Kabha, Mustafa. 'The Problematics of Writing Palestinian History and the Need for the Formulation of a Comprehensive Historical Narrative'. In *Towards a Historical Narrative of the Nakba: Complexities and Challenges*, edited by Mustafa Kabha, pp. 25–55. Haifa: Mada al-Carmel: Arab Centre for Applied Social Research, 2006.

Mansour, Johnny. *Haifa: The Word That Became a Town*. Haifa: [sel-published], 2015.

Mansour, Johnny. 'The Hijaz-Palestine Railway and the Development of Haifa'. *Jerusalem Quarterly* 28 (2006): pp. 5–21.

Masalha, Nur. *The Palestine Nakba: Decolonising History, Narrating the Subaltern, Reclaiming Memory*. London: Zed, 2012.

Miari, L. 'Adwar al-nisaa' Al-filastiniyyat Areifiyat b-boadayha al-Iqtisadi w-al-T'akafi bayna L'Aawam 1930-1960: Qaryat el Birwi Namuzajan (The Roles of Palestinian Rural Women in its two Dimensions: The Economic and the Cultural: The Case of Al-Birwi Village)'. Unpubl. PhD dissertation. Bir Zeit University, 2005.

Morkus, N. *Stronger than Forgetfulness: A Letter to My Daughter*. Tarshiha: privately published, 2000.

Morkus-Makhoul, Rawda. 'Palestinian Women in the Israeli Labour Market: Challenges and Coping Strategies'. Unpubl. MA Thesis. Tel Aviv University, 2008.

Muhawi, Ibrahim and Sharif Kanaana. *Speak, Bird, Speak Again: Palestinian Arab Folktales*. Berkeley: University of California Press, 1989.

Okkenhaug, Inger Marie. *The Quality of Heroic Living, of High Endeavour and Adventure: Anglican Mission, Women and Education in Palestine, 1888–1948*. Leiden: Brill, 2002.

Qudsiyyi, L. *Safad: The Town of Zaher al-Omar al-Zidani*. Amman: Al-ahlia l-il-nashr wal-tawzia', 2016.

Sayigh, Rosemary. *Palestinians: From Peasants to Revolutionaries*. London: Zed, 1979.

Schneider, Suzanne. *Mandatory Separation: Religion, Education, and Mass Politics in Palestine*. Palo Alto: Stanford University Press, 2018.

Seikaly, May. *Haifa: Transformation of a Palestinian Arab Society, 1918–1939*. London: I. B. Tauris, 1995.

Spector-Mersel, Gabriela. 'Guest Editor Introduction: Narrative Inquiry in Israeli Society'. *Israel Studies in Language and Society* 11, 2 (2018): pp. 20–35.

Stockdale, Nancy. *Colonial Encounters among English and Palestinian Women, 1800–1948*. Gainesville: University Press of Florida, 2007.

Tamari, Salim. 'JPS "Hidden Gems" and "Greatest Hits": Fifty Years of Ottoman Studies of Palestine'. *Journal of Palestinian Studies* 50, 2 (2021): pp. 133–37.

Tamari, Salim. *The Great War and the Remaking of Palestine*. Berkeley: University of California Press, 2017.

Tamari, Salim. *Mountain Against Sea*. Berkeley: University of California Press, 2009.

Tibawi, Abdul Latif. *Arab Education in Mandatory Palestine: A Study of Three Decades of British Administration*. London: Luzac, 1956.

Yahya, Abbad. 'Oral History and Dual Marginalization: Palestinian Peasant Women and Nakba Narratives'. *Jerusalem Quarterly* 70 (2017): pp. 96–110.

Yazbek, Mahmoud. 'Immigrants, Elites, and Popular Organisations among the Arab Society of Haifa from the British Conquest to 1939' [in Hebrew]. In *Economy and Society in Mandatory Palestine, 1918-1948*, edited by Avi Bareli and Nahum Karlinsky, pp. 367–94. Sde Boqer: Ben Gurion Research Centre, 2003, http://in.bgu.ac.il/bgi/iyunim/DocLib4/content.pdf

Ethnographies of Madness: Père Antonin Jaussen, Shaykh Sa'ad al-Din and the Management of Mental Illness in Mandate-era Nablus

Chris Sandal-Wilson

A traveller arriving in Nablus in the early 1920s not through the old east gate, but rather looping down from the north by a new route skirting the slopes of Jabal Ebal, may have had their eye caught by a curious sight. If, passing the Nadi al-'Arabi – the headquarters of the town's vigorous branch of the Arab Club – this traveller happened to throw a glance to the left before entering under the archway which opened onto the town's thronging marketplaces, they would have perhaps paused for a moment to take in the scene: a courtyard, shaded by a majestic mulberry tree; an old divan, on which lay scattered sheets of paper, writing equipment and a Qur'an; three or four people, waiting nervously on an uncomfortable bench; and at the centre, a portly man with a short beard, wearing a long gown and a white turban – Shaykh Sa'ad al-Din.

This daily spectacle aroused the curiosity of Père Antonin Jaussen, Dominican priest, ethnographer and sometime spy. In August 1923, on one of the many occasions on which he took this route into town, Jaussen ventured into the courtyard, having learnt that the shaykh had a reputation as a healer of sicknesses and an exorcist of jinn, including those responsible for states of madness. A series of interviews with the shaykh resulted in an article for the *Journal of the Palestine Oriental Society* (JPOS), which was written and published with remarkable speed, appearing later that year; the same material was reproduced in Jaussen's substantial ethnographic study of Nablus, *Coutumes Palestiniennes: Naplouse et son district*.[1]

Jaussen was far from unique in his ethnographic interest in Palestinian 'folk' beliefs around mental illness and its treatment. As Salim Tamari highlighted nearly two decades ago, madness was a recurring fascination for those concerned with documenting Palestinian folk culture, notably Tawfik Canaan and Stephan Hanna Stephan.[2] Tamari's account of the work of this group of Palestinian ethnographers – which included Khalil Totah, Omar Saleh al-Barghouti and Elias Haddad – has since been developed in several directions by studies which trace the extent to which these figures engaged in multiple intellectual endeavours and important contemporary debates.[3] While this means that we now know much about the activities and ideas of these key Palestinian figures, the attention paid by Tamari to the production of ethnographic knowledge on madness has been less readily taken forward. Canaan and Stephan were not the only ethnographers writing about madness in the pages of *JPOS*. Indeed, Jaussen's own account was published a year before Canaan took up this question in the first part of his magnum opus, *Mohammedan Saints and Sanctuaries in Palestine*, which was serialised before being published separately in 1927.

This chapter treats Jaussen's account as an overlooked element within the ethnographic study of madness in Mandate Palestine. Setting Jaussen's account alongside the writings of Canaan and Stephan makes clear its distinctively ambivalent understanding of the relationship between madness and possession, as well as its value as a close study, based on Jaussen's observations and interviews, of madness and possession handled in a single context – Nablus – by a single individual – Shaykh Sa'ad al-Din.[4] In addition to extending his work on the ethnography of madness, this chapter uses Jaussen and Sa'ad al-Din to think through a further question central to parts of Tamari's oeuvre, above all *Mountain against the Sea*: that of the social and cultural gulf between the coastal plains and hilly interior of Palestine.[5] Taking the picture painted by Jaussen of local reliance on Sa'ad al-Din to treat mental illness as its starting point, this chapter explores the integration – or not – of Nablus into the health services of the British Mandate, in particular how Nabulsis engaged with government provision for the mentally ill from the end of World War I until the Nakba in 1948. While Jaussen himself insisted that the arrival of the British marked a decisive transition from older, superstitious approaches to madness towards more medicalised understandings and treatments, both the detail of his account and the records of the Mandate's department of health suggest a more complex picture, in which religious and medical options were often pursued alongside one another by Nabulsis across the interwar decades and beyond. Before zooming out to these broader issues, however, we start by focusing on the two principal characters in this story: Père Jaussen, and Shaykh Sa'ad al-Din.

The Dominican and the Shaykh

Joseph-Marie, known as Antonin, Jaussen had arrived in Palestine decades before his fieldwork in Nablus in the 1920s. Like many of his contemporaries in French religious orders, the young Jaussen had begun his novitiate at Lyon before being forced abroad by the anti-clerical legislation of the time. After a brief sojourn in the Netherlands, Jaussen arrived in Jerusalem in 1890, at the age of nineteen. His arrival at the Saint-Étienne Dominican convent coincided with the establishment of the École pratique d'Études bibliques, or École biblique, which had as its purpose the study of the Bible in the context in which it had been written. Founded by Père Marie-Joseph Lagrange, the École biblique embraced all scholarly disciplines – archaeology, epigraphy, history, geography and philology – which, in Lagrange's words, might 'illuminate and authenticate the Biblical past'.[6] Jaussen, like other seminarians who found themselves at Saint-Étienne and the École biblique in the 1890s, thus received a wide-ranging scholarly education. Passing his final exams in 1896, he settled into teaching Arabic, Aramaic and the theology of Thomas Aquinas, but the central themes of his publications were Semitic epigraphy, Biblical geography and Arab customs.[7]

Before World War I, Jaussen had published extensively on archaeology,[8] but – more pertinent for our discussion – he had also published the better-known precursor to his study of Nablus, *Coutumes des Arabes au pays de Moab*, which appeared in 1908 and was based on fieldwork in the area east of the Jordan, around Madaba. Jaussen shared Lagrange's Orientalist conviction that the Holy Land had changed so little over the centuries that it could shed light on the Biblical past.[9] But this was accompanied by an increasing sense of urgency in his ethnographic fieldwork, particularly that undertaken in the Hijaz in the years before World War I: for Jaussen, changes driven by the Ottoman government – most obviously the construction of the Hijaz railway – threatened to transform, and thus consign to the dustbin of history, ways of life that had been preserved by the desert.[10] It was this 'on the ground' experience which made him so attractive to British and then French intelligence once war with the Ottoman Empire broke out in 1914; deported to Cairo, Jaussen was recruited to coordinate intelligence operations in Palestine and Transjordan, before eventually being frozen out as not quite trustworthy.[11] The feeling was likely reciprocated: disillusioned with the British policies of side-lining the French and encouraging the Zionist movement in Palestine, Jaussen left for Egypt in 1928, where he remained almost until his death in 1962.

Jaussen's study of Nablus was thus his last major work on Palestine before his departure. He had visited Nablus twice in 1914, just before the outbreak of the war, and returned in 1923 – when he interviewed Shaykh Sa'ad al-Din – and 1924. Both before and after the war, he had lodged with the Sisters of Saint Joseph, who had established a dispensary to the north of the town in 1904; based there, his route into Nablus proper passed by the shaded courtyard in which Shaykh Sa'ad al-Din received his petitioners.[12] For Jaussen, the reason for studying Nablus was a simple yet compelling one. Tucked away in the mountainous interior of Palestine, Nablus was perceived as having been largely sheltered from outside influences.[13] In that respect, there was a clear continuity of thinking with his earlier ethnographic study of Biblical Moab, as well as with the original mission of the École biblique: here was a place seemingly cut off from the modern world where ancient – even Biblical – ways of working could be observed.[14] But at the same time, what was distinctive about Nablus was not just its putative isolation from the outside world. It was also, above all, a Muslim town. And this, too, is reflected in his work: a full third of his text is given over to describing Islam in Nablus.[15]

It might seem difficult to reconcile Jaussen's attention to Islam with an interest in studying Palestine in order to shed light on, if not substantiate, Biblical accounts. Yet, with his focus on observing and documenting the religiosity and belief patterns of ordinary Nabulsis, rather than on scripture or 'official' versions of Islam, Jaussen's Islam is one arrived at via the 'living content of everyday religion', as James Grehan has put it; everyday religiosity which defied neat categorisation as Islamic, Christian, or Jewish.[16] Jaussen was not unique in this respect. As Tamari highlights, popular religiosity and beliefs were also a preoccupation of Tawfiq Canaan's ethnographic work: Canaan's *Muhammadan Saints and Sanctuaries in Palestine* – published in the same year, 1927, as Jaussen's study of Nablus – approached popular religion in Palestine not through the categories of Islam, Christianity, or Judaism, but as localised adaptations which had remained virtually unchanged for thousands of years, stretching back to pre-Biblical times.[17] 'Even the great revolutions produced by the three great monotheistic religions', Canaan wrote, 'whose cradle lay in or near Palestine, were not able to suppress all primitive beliefs'.[18] This shared belief in the usefulness of ethnography in understanding the distant past was no coincidence: it was a belief which defined the Palestine Oriental Society, to which both Jaussen and Canaan belonged and contributed, from its beginnings in 1920, and was articulated by its first president, Père Lagrange himself.

But the similarities between Jaussen's project and those of Canaan, Stephan and the wider circle of Palestinian ethnographers should not be overstated; there were important differences, in aim as well as focus. Jaussen, like Lagrange before him, turned to ethnography for evidence which could be used to test and sift the accuracy of Biblical historical accounts. Canaan and contemporary 'nativist ethnographers', by contrast, looked to the peasantry of Palestine as the depository of the national soul, particularly as evidencing the depth and authenticity of Palestinian roots in the land, at a time when that claim was challenged by the Zionist movement.[19] And while Canaan and Stephan's ethnographies of madness embraced the full breadth of Palestine, taking in healing shrines everywhere from Mount Carmel to the Pools of Solomon and centring on the peasantry as a whole, Jaussen's focus was squarely on Nablus and its inhabitants. In that respect, Jaussen's contribution was distinctive, albeit inseparable from his paternalism and Orientalism. Jaussen may have differed from some of his European Orientalist predecessors and contemporaries in his 'external' method – guided by his own research in the field, rather than literary sources.[20] But his insistence on the antiquity of the social and cultural practices of the living people he encountered, as well as slips like his wartime treatment of Algerian intelligence agents as interchangeable with other 'Arabs' and so suited to deployment in Syria,[21] make clear that Orientalist assumptions informed his worldview and, particularly, his ethnographic research.

Jaussen may have presented his decision to focus on Nablus in terms of its isolation from the currents of the modern world and its almost unchanged character across the centuries, but that was a misrepresentation in several ways. Certainly, Nablus lagged behind other cities in terms of demographic growth in the interwar years. In the crude first census taken by the British in 1922, Nablus had a recorded population of 15,947, making it the sixth-largest municipality in Palestine;[22] by the second census of 1931 it had grown by just 7.8 per cent, to 17,189 – slow when compared to the staggering rates in Jerusalem, Haifa or Tel Aviv.[23] In terms of infrastructure, it was never connected to Mandate Palestine's electrical grid.[24] A not unrelated feature peculiar to Nablus, like other inland areas, was its relative insulation from the most obvious transformations that convulsed Palestine over the first half of the century – that is, European Jewish immigration and Zionist land purchasing. This relative insulation appeared to extend its long history of separateness, evident in Nabulsi resistance to Ottoman centralisation and European missionary activity into the nineteenth century.[25] Yet it is important not to exaggerate the town's isolation. By the second half of the nineteenth century, Ottoman governors and a garrison were firmly ensconced and responsible for the reconstruction of the town inside the walls as well as its extension beyond them;[26] missionary organisations, French as well as the London-based Church Missionary Society, had established a number of schools in the town and the above-mentioned dispensary run by the French Sisters of St Joseph;[27] commercial ties across the Jordan made Nablus a major regional trade centre.[28] And while Nablus may not have been at the epicentre of Zionist land purchasing, unlike the coastal plains, this nonetheless had a knock-on effect on how land was viewed throughout Palestine, such that by the 1930s the number of land transfers around Jabal Nablus among Palestinians also increased dramatically.[29] The list of changes reshaping Nablus and the lives of those who lived in and around the town could go on.[30] Jaussen was not unaware of these transformations; like his Palestinian contemporaries, part of his motivation in undertaking ethnographic fieldwork in the 1920s was precisely a sense that this world would soon be irrecoverably lost, imparting urgency to such work.[31] But for Jaussen, these transformations had not yet buried everyday practices and beliefs which stretched back, so he thought, centuries.

Before turning to Jaussen's account of the healing performed by Shaykh Sa'ad al-Din, it is worth contextualising the shaykh within the wider religious milieu of interwar Nablus. Sa'ad al-Din was not the only shaykh whom Jaussen interviewed during his time there.[32] He also spent time with Shaykh Ali Sharaf, who was in charge of the mosque of al-Khadra, near the western gate of the town, and presented himself as grand master of four Sufi *tariqat* or brotherhoods in Nablus: the Rifa'iyya, Qadiriyya, Badawiyyah and Disuqiyya *tariqat*.[33] While unusual, leadership of a number of *tariqat* simultaneously was not wholly unique.[34] Jaussen recalls how the shaykh showed him his genealogy, with seals appended alongside signatures in testament to its authenticity, as well as *firmans* or decrees from the Ottoman sultan recognising his ancestors' authority over the al-Khadra mosque.[35] Shaykh Ali even allowed Jaussen to copy out the formula that he used for the *mandal*, a rite which was held to divine the truth of a given situation. Used above all to uncover the identity of the author of mischief, such as theft, it could also reveal the nature and cause of illnesses – including mental maladies.[36] Shaykh Sa'ad al-Din apparently knew the same rite but had renounced it, explaining to Jaussen that it was not successful; Jaussen cynically 'translated' this to mean 'it was not lucrative', a point to which we will return.[37]

Unlike Shaykh Ali, and more conventionally, Sa'ad al-Din was head of one *tariqa*, not four: the Sa'diyya. The Sa'diyya *tariqa* had originated in Jabah, a village at the meeting-place of the Hauran and Golan, but had spread throughout Syria, becoming particularly popular in Damascus; it was the only *tariqa* to take part, for instance, in the official celebrations of religious festivals such as *laylat al-qadar* well into the twentieth century.[38] But it spread more widely, including to Nablus by the late seventeenth century,[39] and was best known for the spectacle of the *dawsa* ritual, in which the shaykh would ride a horse over the backs of believers to demonstrate that they were protected from harm.[40] By the nineteenth century, the Sa'diyya lodge in Nablus – like other Sufi lodges – served as a central node within a network knitting together the town and surrounding hinterland; Sufi networks were one of a number – political, economic, as well as religious – which worked to integrate Jabal Nablus.[41] This was reflected, too, in the breadth of supplicants who came to Shaykh Sa'ad al-Din for help in the early twentieth century, as we shall see.

Healing the Sick and Exorcising the Jinn

Predating other attempts in the pages of *JPOS* to explore madness, Jaussen's conversations with Shaykh Sa'ad al-Din were at the heart of an account notable not only for being early, but also for its distinctly oblique approach to the question of madness and its treatment in Mandate Palestine. In contrast to his Palestinian contemporaries Canaan, who wrote freely of the insane and of nervous and mental troubles, and Stephan, who entitled his contribution 'Lunacy in Palestinian Folklore', madness – *la folie* – is a word which appears rarely in Jaussen's account. Sa'ad al-Din, too, may have been surprised by the idea that his wide-ranging conversations with Jaussen, encompassing discussions of natural and supernatural causes and treatments of a whole plethora of conditions, could have formed the basis of any ethnography of madness. It is thus important to consider how both Sa'ad al-Din and Jaussen conceived of illness in general, and mental illness in particular.

For his part, Sa'ad al-Din made clear to Jaussen that there were three groups of causes of illness: first, ordinary, natural causes as with a common cold or fever; second, the evil eye; and third, the jinn. He passed over the first quickly; these could be treated by medical doctors. The second, the evil eye or *darb al-'ain*, he termed a 'pestilence of our town', being at the root of many cases and taking a wide range of forms from sciatica and paralysis to delirium and fever.[42] While the majority of the cases that Sa'ad al-Din healed were caused by the evil eye, it was the third category, possession by jinn, which absorbed Jaussen's attention in both their conversations and his subsequent writing. Shaykh Sa'ad al-Din, Jaussen noted, was particularly celebrated for his power over the jinn; he was able to recognise the symptoms of jinn possession and to drive them out using the names of Allah.[43] But while Canaan and Stephan in their works tended to present possession as a folk explanation of madness, Jaussen was more circumspect, even agnostic: the closest he came to asserting an equivalence between the two was in noting that the symptoms of possession were grave, bordering on madness.[44] Jaussen resisted characterising Sa'ad al-Din as offering a religious kind of mental healthcare, in spite of the fact that many of the symptoms which he listed – sadness, flight from society, agitation, hearing voices and eccentric acts – would have been taken by medical doctors in Mandate Palestine to be symptoms of mental illness. His circumspection notwithstanding, it is clear from the detail of Jaussen's account that others, however, did view the shaykh in exactly this light: both the Ottoman authorities in the past, and the leadership of neighbouring villages in the Mandate era, reportedly sent the mentally ill to him for treatment.

If Jaussen's ambivalence about the relationship between possession and madness distinguished him from his contemporaries, the explanations he recorded from Shaykh Sa'ad al-Din for the causes of possession were more – although not completely – conventional. As in the writings of Canaan, Stephan and others, a host of seemingly innocent acts could trigger the wrath of the jinn and possession: the illustration given by Jaussen was of walking over a jinn in the road, but other examples emerge from the detailed descriptions which Sa'ad al-Din gave of exorcisms he had performed. In one instance, an infant suffering from a violent headache, Sa'ad al-Din interrogated the jinn responsible, who explained that the infant had stepped on him when he was sitting on the doorstep; the possession was an act of revenge.[45] This was a story from many years earlier, as the infant was now, Jaussen reported, a well-known tailor in Nablus, suggesting that Sa'ad al-Din had been performing such exorcisms for decades by the time he spoke with Jaussen in the early 1920s.

While Stephan, in his account of lunacy in Palestinian folklore, emphasised these accidental offences – shouting in a cave or well; coitus under a black fig or carob tree; pouring water over the threshold of the house or on a fire without permission or warning[46] – Jaussen recounted numerous examples in which, on interrogation, Sa'ad al-Din was told by jinn that they had possessed an individual out of love. Indeed, love was described by the shaykh as the most common reason for possession.[47] When male jinn entered the body of a woman, so Sa'ad al-Din told Jaussen, it was not uncommon that conception could ensue; he himself had seen such a case near Salt, across the Jordan. Sa'ad al-Din had been on a tour of the region when a young Bedouin girl was brought to him by her parents. On the day of her wedding, her husband found her 'violated and abandoned'. She told Sa'ad al-Din: 'A strange being has seized my person and has committed, against my will, certain acts'. After exorcising the jinn, the shaykh explained to the husband what had happened, and he took her back. In another instance, a jinn begged Sa'ad al-Din not to exorcise him from the body of his love.[48] All these cases were of male jinn possessing female victims. When, more rarely, men were possessed by jinn, either no explanation was given, or the jinn was simply described as being 'very wicked'.[49] While Stephan noted in passing the legend of the lovers Layla and Majnun, as well as belief in the power of love to drive a person mad,[50] love as a common motive for possession was distinctive to Jaussen's account.

Shaykh Sa'ad al-Din spoke with Jaussen not only about the causes of possession, but also his method of treatment, giving detailed accounts of the exorcisms he had performed. The case of Farizah, a woman in Nablus who had been taken to the town's doctors to no avail before being brought to Sa'ad al-Din, illustrates elements of this treatment: the shaykh wrote out the divine names on the body of the possessed and on paper; a fire was lit and coriander or other plants burned to create fumes; then the shaykh shook the head of the possessed – in spite of his ambivalence about straightforwardly equating possession and madness, Jaussen uses the term 'patient' at this point – and began the interrogation and exorcism, which culminated in commanding the jinn to depart in the name of Allah. The process could take several days; in one case it took nearly three weeks.[51] While Jaussen reported in detail what the shaykh had told him, it is notable that his account omits mention of beatings or physical violence, beyond shaking the head of the possessed to compel the jinn's attention initially. This is in striking contrast to other contemporary writing on the subject, much of which had its own agenda in painting a picture of Oriental obscurantism and dire abuse, but which largely agreed that the treatment meted out to the mentally ill by religious figures – whether Maronite priests in Mount Lebanon, Orthodox monks near Bayt Jala, or Sufi shaykhs in the interior of Palestine – often involved beatings.[52] Given that Jaussen does not appear to have witnessed any exorcism ritual himself, but relied exclusively on Sa'ad al-Din's testimonies, it may well be that the shaykh excluded or minimised mentions of physical violence from his recollection. It is also notable that, although we are told that Farizah had been taken to medical doctors before being brought to the shaykh, this is not a point which Jaussen sought to develop; instead, his focus was fixed on Sa'ad al-Din's ritual practice. As we will see, however, Farizah was far from unique in moving between medical and non-medical contexts of treatment, and in that respect Jaussen's focus on exorcism, as though this and medical treatment took place in hermetically sealed worlds, risks distorting a more fluid reality.

While his focus was firmly on Sa'ad al-Din's ideas and practices, the cases related by Jaussen help us understand how people came before Sa'ad al-Din in the first place, the journeys or experiences that led them to the shaykh, and what this cost them. Supplicants came from Nablus as well as surrounding villages. Not all came to be cured of possession or madness; while he spoke with the shaykh, Jaussen witnessed five women consulting with Sa'ad al-Din on different matters, which he did not disclose, as well as one man – described by Jaussen as a 'fellah', a 'poor peasant' in his glossing – who asked for a remedy for dizziness. All these augmented the shaykh's income, as Jaussen noted: each of the women put between ten and twenty piastres in his hand; the man's cure cost him fifty piastres.[53] Given that one estimate of the annual income and expenditure of an 'ordinary fellah' in Palestine of the late 1920s puts both at around seventy Egyptian pounds,[54] and that before the 1927 currency reform there were one hundred piastres to the Egyptian pound, the sums exchanged were hardly insignificant. And they were not voluntary contributions: Jaussen witnessed Sa'ad al-Din release untreated one 'madman' – the only one he appears to have seen with his own eyes, and a rare use of this language in his account – when promised fees failed to materialise. This is the backdrop, then, to Jaussen's cynical aside that the shaykh, unlike some of his contemporaries, had renounced the *mandal* because it was not lucrative enough.

Therapeutic Pluralism between Empires

In his detailed account of the rituals used by Shaykh Sa'ad al-Din to exorcise jinn and treat the sick, Jaussen presented these practices as unchanging, performed on generations of Nabulsis in unbroken succession. But Jaussen wrote in the wake of the momentous transformations brought about by World War I, as the Ottoman Empire gave way to the British Mandate; even with his focus fixed firmly on Shaykh Sa'ad al-Din and his claim to heal the mentally ill, Jaussen could not but reflect on the impact of that transition from one empire to another. As well as explicitly reflecting on these changes, his account gives a sense of continuities. While people from the Jabal Nablus came to Shaykh Sa'ad al-Din for consultation and cure, he himself travelled, as the story of the young bride whom he treated near Salt suggested. It seems that these tours across the Jordan were relatively regular; they must also have made quite an impression. Sa'ad al-Din claimed that in one such tour he chased jinn from no fewer than six people in Amman and the area around Salt.[55] In the late Ottoman period, Nablus had been the primary trade partner of Salt, then the most important commercial centre on the east bank of the Jordan.[56] Sa'ad al-Din's peregrinations, which by the 1920s took him across not only the river but also the new colonial border separating Palestine and Transjordan, signal at least one continuity with the recent Ottoman past. These tours also add to our understanding of cross-border mobilities in the post-war period. While Toufoul Abou-Hodeib has shown how pilgrimage routes continued to knit together northern Palestine and southern Lebanon into the Mandate period,[57] Sa'ad al-Din's tours around both banks of the Jordan highlight another lived geography which stretched across colonial frontiers, between eastern Palestine and western Transjordan, sustained by a very different kind of religiously inflected movements.

Although Sa'ad al-Din continued to offer his services to those living on either side of the new border, World War I and British occupation had resulted in significant changes to his position and practice, at least in Jaussen's telling. The Ottoman state, Jaussen reported, had actually brought the mad to the shaykh and conferred responsibility for their care on him; they had given him the liberty to practise his exorcisms on these patients. The British did not, as Jaussen put it, 'allow him the same liberty'.[58] Jaussen's account of a sharp rupture between the treatment of the mentally ill under the Ottomans and the British Mandate is typical but should be taken with a healthy dose of scepticism. Whether or not the Ottomans did confer responsibility for the care of the mentally ill on the shaykh, the last decades of the Ottoman Empire had seen a series of developments around the management of the mentally ill. In 1876, most notably, the Ottomans had issued a new law regulating mental asylums which required, amongst other things, that new asylums obtain permission from the state before opening, and that all patients produce formal medical documents in order to be admitted for treatment – measures that seem at odds, on paper at least, with Jaussen's account of the Ottoman government conferring responsibility on Sa'ad al-Din.[59] The impact of these reforms on the provinces and on the frontiers of the Ottoman Empire, in particular, appears to have been limited, however, and so we might well be sceptical of how far these reforms enunciated in Istanbul made a difference in Nablus.[60] Yet more locally, Ottoman authorities supported initiatives such as the Lebanon Hospital for Mental Diseases at 'Asfuriyyeh near Beirut, founded at the turn of the century.[61] Reform by the British should thus be seen within a continuum of earlier efforts at change – however uneven – undertaken or at least supported by the Ottomans, rather than as an abrupt break.

If Jaussen's account of the arrival of the British Mandate overstates the sharpness of this rupture with the past, there is another reason to be cautious about his narrative. Whether starting under the British or the Ottomans, such a narrative gives a sense of direction, if not outright progress, as madness – as Eugene Rogan has put it, with respect to the wider region – journeyed out of the domain of men of religion into that of self-proclaimed men of science.[62] Jaussen the ethnographer, viewing his studies – like his contemporaries, Palestinian and European – as documenting rapidly dying customs and ways of life, seems to have adopted this logic

of transition, with 'superstitious' treatment of the mentally ill fated to be super-
seded by modern medicine. Yet this was far from the only way of conceptualising
the relationship between religion and medicine in the region in these decades;
starting in the 1940s, as Omnia El Shakry has shown, a generation of Egyptian phi-
losophers, psychologists and criminologists sought to cross-fertilise Freud with
pre-analytic Arabic and Islamic traditions, drawing out the resonances between
these systems of thought rather than religion's redundancy in the face of new
bodies of knowledge.[63]

Although Jaussen, like other interwar ethnographers, saw the relationship
between superstitious and medical approaches to madness in terms of transition,
the details of his account jar with this framework. In some cases, as with Farizah
and the infant who grew up to become a well-known tailor, the shaykh appears to
have been consulted after other options – including medical doctors – had been
exhausted.[64] A closer reading, paying attention to the routes taken by those who
came to Shaykh Sa'ad al-Din, suggests that at least some of those who consulted
him did not think of the shaykh and the medical doctor as mutually exclusive;
instead, Nabulsis appear to have gone to both doctors *and* shaykhs, turning to one
when the other failed, shopping around for any treatment which might help ease
their suffering. Not everyone, of course, embraced therapeutic pluralism: Fadwa
Tuqan's memoirs, for instance, make it clear that 'superstition' – including belief
in the jinn, or resorting to amulets or incantations for cure or protection – had
no legitimate place in her family home when she was growing up in interwar
Nablus. Yet even within Tuqan's family, and in the face of disapproval from her
grandmother and mother, her paternal aunt – al-Shaykha – performed healing
rituals, reciting Qur'anic verses and breathing over water to cure sick children.[65]
Coexistence, then, rather than transition, better characterises what was taking
place in early-twentieth-century Nablus.

If Shaykh Sa'ad al-Din still appears to have been taking in cases of 'madness' for
treatment in the early 1920s, this was not wholly overlooked by the British civil
administration established in 1920, in the interim period before the confirmation
of the Mandate for Palestine. In October 1922, attorney-general Norman Bentwich set out legal grounds for prosecuting anyone deemed to be illicitly claiming
the ability to 'cure persons of nervous troubles'; they could be prosecuted under
the Public Health Ordinance for exercising the vocation of a physician without a
licence.[66] While this explanation had been prompted by concerns about hypnotists specifically, the director of the fledgling health department circulated it to
all medical officers, '[a]s questions have from time to time been asked as to what
action, if any, can be taken to restrain "faith-healers", "hypnotists", and such like
persons from indulging in the illegal practice of medicine'.[67]

It appears, then, that hypnotists represented just the tip of the iceberg and
that concerns had been expressed about other groups such as 'faith-healers'.[68]
Indeed, the medical officer at Nablus seems to have had someone particular in

mind when he wrote back to the director of health just a few days after the circular was published to clarify the attorney-general's ruling. He asked if this guidance might 'cover the case of a man who goes around the country professing to cure but who does not take fees or attempt to cure at an "entertainment"', adding, resignedly, 'I presume that such persons cannot be stopped'.[69] While this description certainly fits Jaussen's account of Shaykh Sa'ad al-Din's tours around Jabal Nablus and the east bank of the Jordan, it seems unlikely this is a reference to him – unless a very ill-informed one – given the stress that Jaussen laid on the fees which the shaykh demanded and received for his services. This episode, then, is an important reminder that, in spite of Jaussen's focus on him, Sa'ad al-Din was far from alone in offering relief from madness in 1920s Nablus. More significantly, it returns us to the other side of Jaussen's picture of a sharp rupture with the arrival of the British. The promulgation of ordinances regulating the practice of medicine is in line with Jaussen's conclusion that the British denied figures such as Sa'ad al-Din the 'liberty' – or literally 'licence' – to cure the sick as they had done under the Ottomans. But the underfunding and understaffing which, as we will see, were endemic to the Mandate's Department of Health meant that some kind of accommodation with existing sources of healthcare was often necessary on practical grounds. This was certainly the case with 'unqualified' midwives or *dayat*, as Elise Young has shown;[70] it would be unsurprising if such self-interested leniency was similarly extended, however reluctantly, to other healers, especially given how few specialists in treating mental disease were ever employed by the Mandate's Department of Health.

Nablus and Medical Provision in the Mandate Period

Jaussen's emphasis on Shaykh Sa'ad al-Din's fame as a healer in Nablus and its hinterland, as well as the anecdotal evidence he provides of his continued practice in the 1920s, suggests a local reliance on alternatives to 'medical' or institutional treatments of mental illness. In the final parts of this chapter, we shift gears: having contextualised Jaussen and Shaykh Sa'ad al-Din in relation to ethnographies of madness, our focus now turns to Nablus' integration into the health landscape of Mandate Palestine, in order to better understand the therapeutic options open to the families of the mentally ill.[71] Jaussen's account of the continued popularity of Sa'ad al-Din, especially when set alongside his representation of Nablus more generally as cut off from the wider transformations and currents sweeping Palestine, might be taken to suggest that Nablus was marginal within the health landscape of Mandate Palestine. Yet, colonial archival evidence paints a more nuanced picture, which in turn underlines a key conclusion from the previous section: that medical and 'alternative' treatments, rather than eclipsing one another, coexisted.

At the start of the British occupation of Palestine, the colonial government made much of the fact that there were no government hospitals for the civilian population, in Nablus or elsewhere, in order to trumpet its own modernising sensibilities.[72] But there were certainly hospitals – missionary, voluntary, municipal – across Palestine which predated the British occupation in 1917. Starting in the mid-nineteenth century, missionaries and imperial powers engaged in the almost competitive founding of hospitals, especially around Jerusalem.[73] The city's municipal government, established in the 1860s, was active in this area, with a municipal hospital opening outside the walls of the Old City in 1891.[74] While Nablus, with its lack of both important Christian pilgrimage sites and any sizeable non-Muslim population, was slower to attract the attention of European missionaries,[75] by the early twentieth century both the London-based Church Missionary Society (CMS) and the French Sisters of St Joseph had set up medical services in the town. The CMS had established a hospital at Nablus in 1891,[76] while the Sisters of St Joseph, as we have seen, set up a dispensary in 1904. This dispensary continued to operate even through the war, thanks to protests from the municipality when Ottoman authorities attempted to banish the French Sisters – a reaction suggesting how valued the Sisters had become locally.[77] Predating these missionary foundations was the Watan or National Hospital, established on the slopes of Mount Ebal in 1888 with voluntary contributions from local Nabulsis;[78] initially just a cluster of rooms set in a garden, it formed the nucleus for a greatly expanded hospital in the interwar years.[79]

At the beginning of British rule, then, Nablus was hardly cut off from medical services. While the first High Commissioner of Palestine, Herbert Samuel, boasted that the British government – by contrast to its Ottoman predecessor – was maintaining fifteen hospitals, eight clinics and more than twenty dispensaries by 1921,[80] this was less dramatic a transformation than represented. At Nablus, it translated into the establishment of an ophthalmic clinic and infant welfare centre in the early 1920s.[81] Far from either Samuel or Jaussen's framing of the onset of British rule as marking a moment of disjuncture in health, continuities between the late Ottoman and early Mandate periods far outweighed the discontinuities. The same hospitals and dispensaries continued to provide medical care in the interwar years, as they had before: in 1925 the CMS hospital, with a capacity of forty-five beds, made a total of 851 admissions over the year, while the Watan Hospital, with a capacity of only twenty-five beds, admitted 614.[82] This was in line with the Mandate's wider policy of devolving much of everyday healthcare to other actors, including the municipalities. British spending on health was never large: most years, the proportion of the budget allocated to health was under five per cent,[83] with priority given to 'public health' activities such as combatting malaria.[84] Only in 1935, as part of the gradual reversal of this policy of decentralisation, was the Watan Hospital taken under direct control by the Mandate government.[85]

While the impact of the British Mandate on the provision of everyday health-care in Nablus was far from dramatic, the interwar decades did see the slow and stuttering expansion of the Watan Hospital. It survived the economies inflicted by the government in the early 1920s and again in the wake of the Great Depression after 1929,[86] and even grew over the 1930s: in 1933, an X-ray section was added, making it one of only four hospitals in Palestine to have such a facility;[87] in 1935, when it was taken under direct government control, it was the fourth-largest hospital in Palestine, tied with Jaffa, able to accommodate over sixty general cases and a further twenty in an annexe for infectious diseases.[88] Yet, in view of the fact that the hospital was supposed to provide for the entire population of the Nablus-Tulkarm-Jenin area – which suffered high rates of enteric fever in the summer – this bedstrength was far from adequate. Reports throughout the 1930s make clear the 'gross overcrowding' at the Watan Hospital.[89] But against the backdrop of the great revolt and British counterinsurgency from 1936 to 1939, which had a devastating impact on Nablus as on other towns in Palestine's interior, expansion was slow in coming. In 1939, the bedstrength at the hospital was increased to 113, with forty-six of those beds reserved for infectious cases.[90] This proved timely, as World War II, with its impact on nutrition and precipitation of 'unusual movements of labour to supply military needs', was linked to an enormous jump in the number of admissions to hospitals as a result of enteric fever.[91] The daily average number of patients being treated surpassed one hundred as a result.[92] Enteric fever was not uniquely neglected in Mandate-era Nablus; the Department of Health was similarly slow to invest in the treatment and control of tuberculosis, which it had long recognised as being notably prevalent around Nablus.[93]

Given the scale and urgency of the challenge posed by other health problems and the limited resources marshalled to tackle even these crises, it is perhaps unsurprising that mental illness in Nablus was rarely a priority for colonial authorities. That the government only grudgingly invested in hospital improvements and focused its energies and resources on infectious diseases does not set Nablus apart from wider trends in Mandate health provision, or indeed colonial medicine more broadly: it was typical. In a sense, the inadequate and haphazard provision for the mentally ill specifically in Nablus was also typical. But in one way, Nablus did, in fact, briefly play a more prominent role in the government's plans for managing the mentally ill, when it was mooted – before being dismissed – as a viable option for siting a new, expanded government mental hospital in the late 1920s. This episode proved fruitless in the end, with plans for a new mental hospital anywhere in Palestine scrapped with the onset of the Great Depression, but it nonetheless reveals something of how Nablus figured in the thinking of the Department of Health.

In 1922, the first government mental hospital had opened near Bethlehem, on the site of an orphanage established by a German missionary organisation, the Jerusalemsverein. Just a few years after it had opened, the government began searching for a new site on which to build a larger, permanent mental hospital from scratch, rather than continuing to adapt old buildings on a rented site. One of the criteria for a desirable location was that it be in the hilly interior of Palestine, rather than the coastal plain, 'on account of the great superiority of the hill climate', as a government memorandum from 1928 put it; a second criterion, good access to water, narrowed the choice to Nablus and the Jerusalem area.[94] Here, the division between the hilly interior and the coastal plain which Tamari, among others, has probed, appears in a new guise. While the coastal plain, with its more densely populated cities and cosmopolitan norms, appeared to be the incubator of madness in Palestine, it was to the hills inland, where rates were lower, that the government looked for the site of its mental hospital. Hill sanitaria in nineteenth-century colonial India had established a basic connection between elevation and recuperation.[95] But the decision to search for a hilly site in this instance cannot be taken for granted. As Waltraud Ernst has noted, while hill stations for the mentally ill were mooted in nineteenth-century India, lunatic asylums – along with jails, lock-hospitals and workhouses – were all ultimately relegated to the plains, with the healthful mountain air reserved for those judged more deserving: orphans, convalescent soldiers and the more prosperous classes.[96]

Given how heavily indebted British government in Palestine was to precedents drawn from India,[97] it is thus notable that the coastal plains were not considered in the hunt for a new site. The preference given to the hills in discussions in the late 1920s was not an aberration,[98] but rather continued to inform government thinking across subsequent decades. In 1945, for instance, when plans for a new purpose-built mental hospital were finally revived following a wartime uptick in the economy, the site chosen was to the south of Jerusalem, on a gently inclined limestone hill, with the main building of the proposed hospital on the crown of a hill with views of the surrounding country.[99] Here the government may well have been drawing inspiration from a model closer to hand than any example from India: the Lebanon Hospital for Mental Diseases. This institution – well-known across the region since opening its doors at the turn of the century – was located on a hilltop near Beirut, a site deliberately chosen as a 'salubrious' and 'healthful locality', with a 'varied and cheerful' outlook.[100]

The perception that Nablus and the Jerusalem area were ideal sites for a model mental hospital can be used, then, to tell the story of a wider shift in the history of colonial psychiatry, as nineteenth-century reluctance to afford lunatic asylums prized elevated sites gave way to a twentieth-century embrace of hilltop mental hospitals. Not all, of course, were convinced the mentally ill required or deserved such salubrious settings. When the administration repurposed the Jerusalemsverein's orphanage into the first government hospital in the early 1920s, the move drew sharp criticism from – among others – Near East Relief, who 'expressed themselves rather strongly that the government was taking over, for the benefit of forty insane people, an orphanage which could house two hundred potential useful citizens'.[101] Near East Relief had hoped to take over the Bethlehem site and use it to accommodate Armenian children orphaned in the genocide; their protest is perhaps unsurprising. But the implicit contrast drawn between the 'useless' insane and potentially 'useful' orphans is nonetheless notable, not least because the Department of Health persisted with their plans to convert this site into a mental hospital despite such criticism. Whether in establishing this first government mental hospital, or their plans for a new institution in the late 1920s, the Mandate government seemed willing to assert that the mentally ill deserved the same kind of healthful environment as convalescents or children. Far from being marginal, Nablus proves an instructive site from which to think about broader dynamics in colonial psychiatry.

While both Nablus and the Jerusalem area fulfilled the first two criteria for siting a new mental hospital – the healthy climate of the hilly interior and access to adequate water supply – the Jerusalem area, specifically the area around the existing government mental hospital at Bethlehem, emerged the winner in relation to the third and final consideration: accessibility. 'The Jerusalem area', the 1928 memorandum noted, 'is more accessible from most parts of Palestine and is more suitable for administrative supervision than Nablus', just 'twenty minutes ride by car from Jerusalem and there is a motor bus service available for patients' friends and hospital staff'.[102] In the end, this mental hospital was never built: the Great Depression put a stop to these plans and sent the Department of Health down the road of piece-meal acquisition and conversion of existing sites to meet ever-increasing demand. Nonetheless, the decision to pass over Nablus as too remote for any but the most local of investments in health infrastructure is revealing. At one level, it suggests that a colonial perception of the town as marginal was difficult to shake, notwithstanding the fact that Nablus had the fourth-largest hospital in Palestine. At another level, it helps us understand something of the nature of Mandate governance. The decision to prioritise accessibility and centrality for the proposed hospital is striking, given the Mandate government's policy over the 1920s of decentralisation, devolving responsibility for healthcare to multiple other actors. Viewed from the vantage point of Nablus, the Mandate state's lumpiness, the way it shrugged off direct responsibility in some places and ways, while jealously hoarding its resources for others, is apparent.[103]

Instead of becoming the site of a new government mental hospital, then, medical provision for the mentally ill at Nablus remained haphazard and small-scale across the period. In 1926, the government sanctioned expenditure to convert two small rooms in Nablus' Watan Hospital for the temporary accommodation of patients while they awaited transfer to Bethlehem.[104] Although similar modifications were approved for hospitals in Jerusalem, Jaffa and Haifa in the same year, the mental isolation rooms were only completed in Nablus several years later, in 1929, a delay which suggests a perceived lack of urgency around local provision.[105] Later in the period, indeed, violent or acute cases ended up not in the hospital's isolation cells, but the local lock-up. For example, Hussein A., from north of Nablus, had been serving with the Trans-Jordan Frontier Force when he suffered sunstroke. This – according to his father Ali – 'severely affected his nerves and brains' and led to his discharge from the force. Ali arranged for his son's admission to the renowned and expensive private mental hospital established by Kurt Blumenthal on Mount Carmel, Haifa; while at first the treatment appeared successful, Hussein subsequently relapsed. In a petition to the High Commissioner, his father pleaded for the government to step in and cover the costs of his further treatment:

> I cannot describe his wretched state of affairs and the extent it reached. He is now residing with my family, and is beating the young girls and children. He has only of late beaten his mother and is now detained in the lock-up, Nablus.[106]

In October, the medical superintendent of one of the government mental hospitals examined him, diagnosed him as suffering from 'chronic paranoid schizophrenia' and recommended that he be 'very urgently admitted' to a government mental institution.[107]

While it is not clear whether Hussein had remained in the lock-up throughout the intervening months, this would not have been unprecedented.[108] As well as putting lock-ups to use to detain the mentally ill, mental illness and colonial carceral institutions were linked in other ways in Mandate Nablus. At the end of the period, a thirty-year-old man – Said H., from 'Awlam, near Tiberias – was diagnosed with 'prison psychosis' while serving a sentence for manslaughter in Nablus Central Jail. Described by the examining medical officer as suffering insomnia and hallucinations, reaching 'incorrect judgements about simple matters' and denying his mother and relatives, he was transferred to the lunatic ward of Acre Central Prison in February.[109] While at Acre, his father wrote to the High Commissioner, pleading for clemency: 'He needs sympathy and consideration of his case as he is ill'. The father also noted that 'no enmity' remained between his family and that of his son's victim, attaching to his petition declarations to that effect.[110] But when he was reported to have recovered, Said was sent back to prison in Nablus – the place where he had first developed his 'prison psychosis' – to serve out the remainder of his term.[111] Prisons and lock-ups, as much as mental hospitals and shaykhs, were part of the experience of the mentally ill in Mandate-era Nablus.

'Modern' and 'Vernacular' Registers of Madness

Medical provision for the mentally ill in Nablus was haphazard and uncertain; it was not, as the delay in converting even two small hospital rooms into isolation cells suggests, seen as a priority by the Mandate authorities, because mental illness was not perceived to be a particular problem in Nablus. As historians of colonial psychiatry have long noted, European doctors and others believed in a causal connection between 'civilisation' and 'madness': rates of mental illness rose in line with closer contact with European civilisation, education and modernity.[112] In Mandate Palestine, this way of thinking was most clearly expressed in the census report of 1931. The returns of the 'insane' population were taken as mapping onto the relative progress towards modernity of the three putative communities of Palestine – Muslim, Christian and Jewish – because, as census superintendent Eric Mills put it, 'mental disorder is a disease of modern civilisation'. That the recorded rate of 'insanity' for Muslims was much lower than that among Christians and Jews could thus be explained by Mills on the grounds that 'Muslims, who form the rural population [. . .] live a life of comparative tranquillity engaged in agricultural pursuits which, while not entirely dissociated from anxiety in times of drought or natural phenomena of destructive character, have none of those disturbing factors present in the life of industrial countries'.[113] The apparent divergence between this account of madness – which presented it as a result of modernity and therefore absent in the countryside – and the ethnographic research of Jaussen, Canaan and Stephan – which recorded highly developed ideas and practices around madness in rural as well as urban society – is striking.

This perception was continuously reinforced across the Mandate period by the low number of cases of mental illness reported in Nablus, where the vast majority of the population, as noted, was Muslim. In March 1925, for instance, when two vacancies at the government mental hospital – a rare occurrence – became available for cases to be transferred from the district which included Nablus, Tulkarm and Jenin, the medical officer at Nablus declined to take this opportunity and failed to send any patient on for treatment in Bethlehem. 'The urgency of the cases', as one of his colleagues in Jerusalem noted in response, 'would appear therefore to have been more imaginary than real'.[114] A few years later, in August 1930, over seventy people across Mandate Palestine were registered as requiring urgent treatment at a mental institution: forty of those were from the district of Jerusalem; fifteen and fourteen from Jaffa and Haifa, respectively; and only five were from the district of Nablus.[115] In spite of the steady rise in demand for treatment, the under-representation of patients from Nablus continued until the end of the Mandate: in 1946, the number awaiting admission to a mental institution was over 500, with nearly half from the district of Jerusalem alone – and just fourteen from Nablus.[116]

The under-representation of Nabulsis and others from the hilly interior of Palestine among the mentally ill in the Mandate period can be read in a number of ways. At the time, it was certainly understood by Mandate authorities as reflecting lower rates of mental illness. Another reading, to return to Jaussen and his account of the popularity of Shaykh Sa'ad al-Din into the early 1920s, is that those who might have been considered mentally ill pursued non-medical forms of treatment and thus escaped the attention of Mandate authorities. Rather than contradictory, government perceptions of madness as negligible among Muslims and in rural areas and the hilly interior of Palestine, and ethnographic accounts of the importance of madness and its treatment across Palestinian society, might better be understood as tracking different, almost parallel, registers of madness, modern and vernacular. While this is true for the work of Canaan and Stephan, for whom possession in most cases seemed to be 'misdiagnosed' mental illness, Jaussen's ambivalence about rendering possession as simply the folk understanding of madness made these two registers even more sharply distinct.

Indeed, far from simply recording reality, or a representation of it mediated by Orientalist assumptions, Jaussen's ethnography might itself be taken as playing some role in shaping how madness was approached by the Mandate government in Palestine.[117] As Megan Vaughan and other historians of colonial psychiatry have argued, there was a problem of recognition here: only those cases which conformed to European diagnostic categories, or which incorporated in some shocking way the trace of European influence – which, to cite Vaughan, 'flung back at the conquerors their own images of superiority in disturbingly distorted forms'[118] – compelled the attention of colonial authorities as recognisable instances of mental illness. Those whose madness assumed vernacular form were best left to local institutions and practices. We might well read Jaussen's account of the strength of both existing local understandings of possession and methods of treating it, then, as reinforcing the assumption among Mandate authorities that mental illness – at least in recognisable form – was uncommon amongst the mainly Muslim inhabitants of Nablus and the hilly interior of Palestine. This had the potential to become something of a self-fulfilling prophecy: if mental illness was not a pressing health issue around Nablus, there was no need to invest in local provision for the mentally ill; without much hope of accessing adequate provision, there was little incentive on the part of the families of those thought to be mentally ill to make themselves known to colonial medical authorities.

While it is not the place of the historian to retrospectively diagnose or identify the causes of mental disease, the fallacy of a belief in any straightforwardly causal connection between mental illness on the one hand, and education, modernity and civilisation on the other, is evident when we look at a breakdown of those cases from Nablus which did find themselves awaiting admission to a mental hospital in 1927, the year Jaussen's ethnography of Nablus was published. Out of nearly thirty certified 'lunatics' from the district, nearly twenty came from Nablus itself. The recorded occupations, moreover, of the relatives of a number of those registered suggested that they were from families with relatively high levels of education: revenue and other municipal officials, for instance, as well as merchants. While these cases broadly fit with the prevailing contemporary stress on urban life and education as destabilising factors, many of the other certified 'lunatics' on the list sit less well with that model: there were half a dozen whose relatives were farmers, and others whose relatives were tanners.[119]

In the end, money may have played a greater role in shaping the decisions of families than how educated or 'superstitious' they purportedly were, or to what register, modern or vernacular, observers – whether Mandate officials or ethnographers – believed their madness belonged. We already caught a sense of the importance of finances in the case of Hussein A., whose father sent him for private treatment when he could afford it and then turned to the government for help when he could not. Anxiety about the financial demands of treating the mentally ill permeates petitions on this subject, including from Nablus: in October 1938, to give an example, the family of Badriya S., who was in the government mental hospital at Bethlehem, pleaded with the government for a reduction in hospital fees on the grounds that '[t]he crops season was very bad in this sub-district, and the oranges season is not so very pleasing'.[120] While in this instance the family secured a reduction in fees, the episode highlights how money could constrain possibilities. This was not only true of medical options: Shaykh Sa'ad al-Din, as Jaussen was at pains to point out, did not offer treatments for free either. If, as seems to have been the case, families shopped around in search of relief for (and sometimes, surely, from) mentally ill relatives, without necessarily drawing an uncrossable line between medical and non-medical options, it may well have been questions of cost, rather than judgements about the validity or superiority of particular treatment methods, that played the largest role in shaping those decisions, in Nablus as elsewhere in Mandate Palestine.

Conclusion

Taken together, Jaussen's account from the 1920s of the popularity of Shaykh Sa'ad al-Din and his power over madness-inducing jinn, on the one hand, and colonial archival material – plans, reports, petitions – about medical provision for the mentally ill, on the other, offer a picture of the complex and plural ways in which people in Mandate-era Nablus sought to cope when mental illness appeared in their lives. For Père Antonin Jaussen, the continued resort of Nabulsis to Shaykh Sa'ad al-Din for cure and relief from their maladies was one of any number of practices and beliefs which had endured for centuries, cut off from the changes of the outside world in the isolated interior of Palestine, but which was now, thanks to the arrival of the British, threatened with inexorable decline and extinction. For their part, in the colonial archive we repeatedly encounter the deep-seated belief of medical authorities and others that mental illness was a phenomenon of the coastal plains, not – with the exception of Jerusalem itself – the hilly interior of Palestine. A common thread which can be drawn from a superficial reading of both sets of sources, then, is that psychiatry faced an uphill struggle in establishing its dominion over madness in Mandate-era Nablus.

Yet, a closer reading suggests a more complex picture, decentring – if not destabilising – the notion of any straightforward transition in the management of mental illness, away from religion and towards psychiatry. Reading between the lines of Jaussen's account, it becomes clear that Nabulsis did not necessarily see these forms of treatment as mutually exclusive: they might consult Shaykh Sa'ad al-Din after – or before – going to a doctor. And in spite of the expressed belief of Mandate officials that those on the land lived too 'tranquil' a life to be disturbed by mental illness, patient waiting lists from the Nablus district provide evidence that farmers and tanners, not just merchants and officials, sought to have their relatives treated in government mental hospitals. Rather than occupation or education, what seemed to loom larger in the decisions made by families was the cost of treatment, and here neither mental hospitals nor – as Jaussen emphasises – the shaykh were typically free.

Taken together, the sense emerges that coexistence and not transition might better characterise responses to mental illness in early-twentieth-century Nablus. Far from representing a clear break with the Ottoman past, as Jaussen and others would have it, the Mandate period should instead be seen within the context of a longer history of overlapping approaches to mental illness. Other continuities between the late Ottoman and early Mandate eras come into view thanks to Jaussen's work. While Jaussen, with his focus on one town and one individual, might appear more parochial in his approach than his contemporaries, ethnographers such as Stephan or Canaan who darted up and down the length of Palestine in their writings on lunacy, there is as much – if not more – of a sense of the mobilities that madness might provoke in Jaussen's account: supplicants streaming in from the surrounding countryside to consult Shaykh Sa'ad al-Din; the shaykh's own tours of both banks of the Jordan, looping Nablus and Salt together even into the age of colonial partition. Against the often prejudiced or reductive conclusions reached by both Jaussen and British medical authorities, the detail of their accounts allows for a more complex picture of how Nabulsis reckoned with mental illness.

The question that this conclusion – that no transition from religious to medical approaches to mental illness took place in Mandate-era Nablus – leaves open, of course, is when, if at all, biomedicine overtook alternative understandings and treatments in the interior of Palestine. While this question warrants attention in its own right, it is nonetheless worth raising here, if only because the beginnings of an answer come by way of work done during the 1980s by researchers and participants in the emerging primary health care movement, including Rita Giacaman, Mustafa Barghouthi – and the sociologist Salim Tamari.[121] As Giacaman and Tamari put it in their 1980 study of the village of Zbeidat, east of Nablus in the Jordan Valley, people still relied heavily on 'traditional medicine' and would continue to do so for as long as organised health services remained out of reach for ordinary villagers.[122] Yet, the emergence in the late 1970s and 1980s of a new movement of health professionals and activists who sought to expand basic health care provision to the villages, rural areas and refugee camps meant that, by the time when Giacaman published her study of health in three Palestinian villages near Ramallah towards the end of the 1980s, she could write that, while indigenous means of healing involving herbs, for instance, had adapted successfully to changed conditions, 'spiritual means appear to be on the way to extinction'.[123] Tamari and Giacaman's early work on health in late-twentieth-century Palestine does more than simply fill out our timeline. Their conclusions – that health services would have limited impact until they were genuinely extended beyond select urban centres and that some forms of 'traditional' medicine might well adapt and persist alongside biomedicine – resonate across decades with the picture which emerges from reading between the lines of Jaussen's ethnography and the colonial archive. This picture enriches our sense of the choices and constraints confronting those who cared for the mentally ill in Mandate-era Nablus.

Notes

1. Jaussen, 'Le cheikh Sa'ad ad-din et les djinn', pp. 145–57; Jaussen, *Coutumes Palestiniennes*.
2. Tamari, 'Lepers, Lunatics and Saints', pp. 24–43.
3. This scholarship – some of which predates Tamari's article – has particularly focused on Canaan. See Nashef, 'Tawfiq Canaan', pp. 12–26; Mershen and Hübner, 'Tawfiq Canaan', pp. 250–64; Bourmaud, 'A Son of the Country', pp. 104–24; and Irving, 'A Young Man of Promise', pp. 42–62.
4. For an earlier analysis of Jaussen's interview with Shaykh Sa'ad al-Din, see Bourmaud, 'Ya Doktor', pp. 727–35.
5. Tamari, *Mountain against the Sea*.
6. '. . . qui éclaireraient et authentifieraient le passé biblique'. Sigrist, 'Situation de l'exégèse', pp. 51–64. See also Viviano, 'École Biblique', pp. 160–61.
7. de Tarragon, 'Antonin Jaussen', pp. 13–22.
8. Above all, his multi-volume *Mission archéologique en Arabie*, which was published between 1904 and 1914.
9. de Tarragon, 'Antonin Jaussen', pp. 13–22.
10. Métral, 'Études bibliques, archéologie et ethnographie', pp. 73–96.
11. Mazza, 'For the Love of France', pp. 75–86. See also Mazza and Ouhes, 'For God and *La Patrie*', pp. 145–64.
12. Métral, '*Naplouse et son district*', pp. 121–35.
13. Jaussen, *Naplouse et son district*, p. vii.
14. Ibid., p. 277.
15. A point made by Métral, '*Naplouse et son district*'. The other distinctive feature of Nablus from a religious perspective was its numerically small but significant Samaritan community.

16. Grehan, *Twilight of the Saints*, pp. 4–6.
17. Tamari, 'Lepers, Lunatics, and Saints', pp. 34–35.
18. Canaan, 'Mohammedan Saints . . . (Continued)', p. 1.
19. Tamari, 'Lepers, Lunatics, and Saints', pp. 38–39.
20. Maffi, 'Orientalisme et temporalité de l'Autre', pp. 97–106. See also Mazza and Ouhes, 'For God and *la Patrie*', pp. 150–51.
21. Mazza, 'For the Love of France', pp. 81–82.
22. Barron, *Palestine: Report and General*, Table III.
23. See Graham-Brown, 'Political Economy', p. 110.
24. Meiton, 'Nation or Industry', pp. 8–22.
25. Kushner, 'Zealous Towns', pp. 597–612.
26. Abujidi, *Urbicide in Palestine*, pp. 93–94.
27. Greenberg, *Preparing the Mothers of Tomorrow*, pp. 36–37.
28. Doumani, *Rediscovering Palestine*, p. 47.
29. Graham-Brown, 'Political Economy of Jabal Nablus', pp. 103–4. This process did not start in the twentieth century; as Doumani has shown, the emergence of a market inland in Jabal Nablus predated even the Ottoman 1848 Land Code.
30. Doumani chronicles the multiple layers of the history of integration and centralisation in Jabal Nablus into the nineteenth century. See Doumani, *Rediscovering Palestine.*
31. As Métral points out, Jaussen often had to reach back to the beginning of the century to circumnavigate these transformations; see Métral, '*Naplouse et son district*'. For comparison, see Canaan, 'Mohammedan Saints and Sanctuaries (Continued)', p. 1.
32. Nor was this the first time that Jaussen had deployed this method in his research: he spoke with shaykhs amongst the Bedouin and indeed pressed them with at times disarmingly direct questions during the ethnographic fieldwork for *Coutumes des Arabes au pays de Moab*. See Lancaster and Lancaster, 'On the Nature of Power', pp. 143–75.
33. Jaussen, *Naplouse et son district*, p. 220.
34. de Jong, 'The Sufi Orders', p. 165.
35. Jaussen, *Naplouse et son district*, p. 219.
36. Ibid., p. 215.
37. Ibid., p. 213.
38. de Jong, 'Les confréries mystiques musulmanes', p. 212.
39. Jaussen, 'Le cheikh', p. 146.
40. Hatina, 'Religious Culture Contested', pp. 33–62.
41. Doumani, *Rediscovering Palestine*, pp. 29, 80. See also Grehan, *Twilight of the Saints*, p. 149, drawing on the memoirs of Muhammad 'Izzat Darwaza: 'People used to come from all around the district to kiss the hand of the shaykh [of the Sa'diyya order]'.
42. Jaussen, 'Le cheikh', pp. 146–48.

43. Ibid., pp. 150–52.

44. Ibid., p. 151. ['La presence du djinn dans le corps est toujours suivie d'une indisposition plus ou moins grave, qui confine à la folie'.]

45. Ibid., p. 155.

46. Stephan, 'Lunacy in Palestinian Folklore', pp. 5–6.

47. Jaussen, 'Le cheikh', p. 151.

48. Ibid., pp. 153–54.

49. Ibid., p. 155.

50. Stephan, 'Lunacy', p. 7.

51. Jaussen, 'Le cheikh', pp. 151–53.

52. Rogan, 'Madness and Marginality', pp. 116–19; and Abi-Rached, 'Asfuriyyeh' pp. 24–30. See also Canaan, 'Mohammedan Saints and Sanctuaries (Continued)', pp. 201–2; and Grehan, Twilight of the Saints, p. 149.

53. Jaussen, 'Le cheikh', pp. 156–57.

54. Graham-Brown, 'Political Economy of Jabal Nablus', p. 162.

55. Jaussen, 'Le cheikh', p. 156.

56. Rogan, Frontiers of the State, pp. 28–29.

57. Abou-Hodeib, 'Sanctity across the Border', pp. 383–94.

58. Jaussen, 'Le cheikh', p. 157.

59. See Law Relating to Asylum for Lunatics, Decree of 19 Safar 1293 [1876], amended 3 March 1892, Israel State Archives [ISA] Mandate Series [M] 6555/8.

60. For late Ottoman reforms, see Artvinli, 'Pinel of Istanbul', pp. 424–37. See also Artvinli, 'Insanity, Belonging, and Citizenship', pp. 268–77.

61. Rogan, 'Madness and Marginality', p. 117. For the history of ʿAsfuriyyeh, see Abi-Rached, 'Asfuriyyeh.

62. Rogan, 'Madness and Marginality', pp. 116–19.

63. El Shakry, The Arabic Freud.

64. As Bourmaud points out, Sa'ad al-Din's emphasis here on being consulted *after* medical doctors failed to cure a patient can also be understood as aimed at conferring a certain prestige; *he* is able to solve what these highly qualified, respected doctors cannot. Bourmaud, 'Ya Doktor', pp. 730–31.

65. Tuqan, A Mountainous Journey, pp. 37, 41–42, 31.

66. Norman Bentwich, Attorney General, to Director of Health, 27 October 1922, ISA M 6627/23.

67. Director of Health to Principal Medical Officers, Jerusalem, Jaffa, Haifa and Nablus, 2 November 1922, ISA M 6627/23.

68. 'Faith-healers' was an interesting term, as it was rarely used in discussions of figures such as Shaykh Sa'ad al-Din or the context of Palestine, with contributors to the Journal of the Palestine Oriental Society, including Canaan, Stephan and Jaussen himself, not identifying the healers about whom they wrote in those terms. The term appears to have been more common in relation to developments within European and especially North American Christianity.

69. Principal Medical Officer, Nablus, to Director of Health, 5 November 1922, ISA M 6627/23.

70. Young, *Gender and Nation Building*, pp. 85–87.

71. For the history of health services in Nablus both before and during the British Mandate, see Khater, 'Health Conditions in Nablus' [in Arabic], and Bourmaud, 'Public Space and Private Spheres', pp. 133–50.

72. Samuel, *An Interim Report on the Civil Administration of Palestine*.

73. For the development of hospital provision in Jerusalem during the late Ottoman period, see Schwake, *Die Entwicklung des Krankenhauswesens*. For the Mandate period, see Sufian, 'Healing Jerusalem', pp. 115–38.

74. Lemire, *Jerusalem 1900*, pp. 120–22.

75. Kushner, 'Zealous Towns', pp. 604–5.

76. Frantzman, Glueckstadt and Kark, 'The Anglican Church in Palestine', p. 104.

77. Kushner, 'Zealous Towns', p. 608; Greenberg, *Preparing the Mothers*, p. 37. In part, the decision to allow the French Sisters to continue working in Nablus during World War I seems to have relied on their contribution to staffing the Watan Hospital.

78. Canaan, *An Autobiography*, p. 66.

79. Qamhieh, 'Saving the Old Town of Nablus', p. 41.

80. Samuel, *An Interim Report on the Civil Administration of Palestine*.

81. Annual Report, Palestine Department of Health (1925), pp. 21–22.

82. Ibid., pp. 24–25.

83. Simoni, *A Healthy Nation*, p. 51.

84. See Appendix to Annual Report, Palestine Department of Health (1925).

85. Annual Report, Palestine Department of Health (1935), pp. 11–12.

86. Annual Report, Palestine Department of Health (1931), p. 31. For a graph outlining the fall in expenditure by the department of health across the 1920s, see Simoni, *A Healthy Nation*, p. 74.

87. Annual Report, Palestine Department of Health (1933), p. 40.

88. Annual Report, Palestine Department of Health (1935), pp. 11–12.

89. Annual Report, Palestine Department of Health (1937), p. 47.

90. Annual Report, Palestine Department of Health (1939), p. 63

91. Annual Report, Palestine Department of Health (1942), p. 17.

92. Ibid., p. 9.

93. Annual Report, Palestine Department of Health (1925), p. 8. See Simoni, 'At the Roots of Division', pp. 59–61.

94. Memorandum on Mental Hospital Construction by Director, Department of Public Works and Acting Director, Department of Health, 4 October 1928, British National Archives [BNA] Colonial Office [CO] 733/155/13.

95. Kennedy, *The Magic Mountains*, esp. pp. 20–39.

96. Ernst, *Mad Tales from the Raj*, p. 27.

97. See, for example, Matthews, *Confronting an Empire*, p. 22.

98. While it is true that in the 1940s another government mental hospital was established near Jaffa, this, like the Bethlehem site, was an emergency measure taken to address overcrowding and was not built from scratch.

99. Memorandum by the Director of Medical Services on Plans for a Mental Hospital of 300 beds, enclosed in High Commissioner, Palestine, to Secretary of State for the Colonies, 14 April 1945, BNA CO 733/471/1.

100. First Annual Report of the Lebanon Hospital for Mental Diseases (1898), American University of Beirut, Saab Medical Library, Archives and Special Collections [AUB-SML], pp. 11–13.

101. Extract from Minutes of Weekly Meeting, 25 August 1922, ISA M 4087/6. For more on Near East Relief's care for and education of orphaned children in the wake of World War I, see Watenpaugh, *Bread from Stones*.

102. Memorandum on Mental Hospital Construction by the Director, Department of Public Works and the Acting Director, Department of Health, 4 October 1928, BNA CO 733/155/13.

103. For the 'lumpiness' of imperial formations, see Cooper, *Colonialism in Question*, esp. pp. 91–112, and Benton, *A Search for Sovereignty*.

104. Director of Health to Senior Medical Officers, Jerusalem, Jaffa, Haifa and Nablus, 13 September 1926, ISA M 6549/29.

105. Annual Report, Palestine Department of Health (1929), p. 6.

106. Ali M., Asira ash-Shamaliya, to High Commissioner, 6 August 1946, ISA M 326/51.

107. District Commissioner, Samaria, to Chief Secretary, 22 November 1946, ISA M 326/51.

108. See Wilson, 'Incarcerating the Insane', pp. 39–51.

109. Certificate by Medical Officer, Dr D. K. Mikhail, 25 January 1947, ISA M 350/30.

110. Translation of Petitions regarding Said H., 19 May 1947, ISA M 350/30.

111. Record of Examination, No. P/57, Acre, 8 July 1947, ISA M 350/30.

112. Vaughan, 'Idioms of Madness', p. 230.

113. Mills, *Census of Palestine 1931*, p. 230.

114. Principal Medical Officer, Jerusalem, to Director of Health, 25 March 1925, ISA M 6555/7.

115. Director of Medical Services to Chief Secretary, 16 August 1930, ISA M 6629/22.

116. Annual Report, Palestine Department of Health (1946), Table VII.

117. This is not to unduly exaggerate Jaussen's influence: although he left Palestine just a few years after publishing his ethnography, frustrated by the direction of British policy, the list of subscribers likely to have read his article in *JPOS* was a long and influential one.

118. Vaughan, 'Idioms of Madness', pp. 218–19. See also McCulloch, *Colonial Psychiatry*.

119. List of lunatics certified in Samaria and Galilee district, from Senior Medical Officer Nablus to Director of Health, 29 June 1927, ISA M 6629/6.
120. Medical Officer, Tulkarem, to Senior Medical Officer, Nablus, 15 October 1938, ISA M 6629/14.
121. I am very grateful to the anonymous reviewer for drawing attention to this connection in particular and for their many other helpful suggestions in general.
122. Tamari and Giacaman, *Zbeidat*, p. 125.
123. Giacaman, *Life and Health*, p. 146. For the development of the primary health care movement in the 1970s and 1980s, see Barghouthi and Giacaman, 'The Emergence of an Infrastructure', pp. 73–90.

Bibliography

Abi-Rached, Joelle M. *'Asfuriyyeh: A History of Madness, Modernity, and War in the Middle East.* Cambridge, MA: MIT Press, 2020.

Abou-Hodeib, Toufoul. 'Sanctity across the Border: Pilgrimage Routes and State Control in Mandate Lebanon and Palestine'. In *The Routledge Handbook of the History of the Middle East Mandates*, edited by C. Schayegh and A. Arsan, pp. 383–94. Abingdon: Routledge, 2015.

Abujidi, Nurhan. *Urbicide in Palestine: Spaces of Oppression and Resilience.* Abingdon: Routledge, 2014.

Artvinli, Fatih. '"Pinel of Istanbul": Dr Luigi Mongeri (1815–82) and the Birth of Modern Psychiatry in the Ottoman Empire'. *History of Psychiatry* 29, 4 (2018): pp. 424–37.

Artvinli, Fatih. 'Insanity, Belonging, and Citizenship: Mentally Ill People Who Went to and/or Returned from Europe in the Late Ottoman Era'. *History of Psychiatry* 27, 3 (2016): pp. 268–77.

Barghouthi, Mustafa and Rita Giacaman. 'The Emergence of an Infrastructure of Resistance: The Case of Health'. In *Intifada: Palestine at the Crossroads*, edited by Jamal Nassar and Roger Heacock, pp. 73–90. New York: Praeger, 1990.

Barron, J. B. *Palestine: Report and General Abstracts of the Census of 1922.* Jerusalem: Greek Convent Press, 1922.

Benton, Lauren. *A Search for Sovereignty: Law and Geography in European Empires, 1400–1900.* Cambridge: Cambridge University Press, 2014.

Bourmaud, Philippe. 'Public Space and Private Spheres: The Foundation of St Luke's Hospital of Nablus by the CMS (1891–1901)'. In *New Faith in Ancient Lands: Western Missions in the Middle East in the Nineteenth and Twentieth Centuries*, edited by H. Murre-van den Berg, pp. 133–50. Leiden: Brill, 2006.

Bourmaud, Philippe. '"Ya Doktor": Devenir médecin et exercer son art en "Terre sainte", une experience du pluralisme medical dans l'Empire ottoman finissant (1871–1918)'. Unpubl. PhD Dissertation. University of Aix-Marseille, 2007.

Bourmaud, Philippe. '"A Son of the Country": Dr Tawfiq Canaan, Modernist Physician and Palestinian Ethnographer'. In *Struggle and Survival in Palestine/Israel*, edited by M. LeVine and G. Shafir, pp. 104–24. Berkeley: University of California Press, 2012.

Canaan, Tawfiq. 'Mohammedan Saints and Sanctuaries in Palestine (Continued)'. *Journal of the Palestine Oriental Society* 7 (1927): pp. 1–88.

Canaan, Tawfiq. *An Autobiography*. Edited by M. Raheb. Bethlehem: Diyar Publisher, 2020.

Cooper, Frederick. *Colonialism in Question: Theory, Knowledge, History*. London: University of California Press, 2005.

de Jong, Fred. 'Les confréries mystiques musulmanes au Machreq arabe: Centres de gravité, signes de déclin et de renaissance'. In *Les Ordres Mystiques dans l'Islam: Cheminements et Situation Actuelle*, edited by A. Popovic and G. Veinstein, pp. 205–43. Paris: EHESS, 1986.

de Jong, Fred. 'The Sufi Orders in Nineteenth and Twentieth-Century Palestine: A Preliminary Survey concerning their Identity, Organizational Characteristics, and Continuity'. *Studia Islamica* 58 (1983): pp. 149–81.

de Tarragon, Jean-Michel. 'Antonin Jaussen (1871–1962) parcours biographique d'un religieux'. In *Antonin Jaussen: Sciences sociales occidentales et patrimoine arabe*, edited by G. Chatelard and M. Tarawneh, pp. 13–22. Beirut: Centre d'études et de recherches sur le moyen-orient contemporain, 1999.

Doumani, Beshara. *Rediscovering Palestine: Merchants and Peasants in Jabal Nablus, 1700–1900*. London: University of California Press, 1995.

Dowty, Alan. *Arabs and Jews in Ottoman Palestine: Two Worlds Collide*. Bloomington: Indiana University Press, 2019.

El Shakry, Omnia. *The Arabic Freud: Psychoanalysis and Islam in Modern Egypt*. Oxford: Princeton University Press, 2017.

Ernst, Waltraud. *Mad Tales from the Raj: Colonial Psychiatry in South Asia, 1800–1858*. Abingdon: Routledge, 1991.

Frantzman, Seth, Benjamin Glueckstadt, and Ruth Kark. 'The Anglican Church in Palestine and Israel: Colonialism, Arabisation, and Land Ownership'. *Middle Eastern Studies* 47, 1 (2011): pp. 101–26.

Giacaman, Rita. *Life and Health in Three Palestinian Villages*. Ithaca Press: London, 1988.

Graham-Brown, Sarah. 'The Political Economy of the Jabal Nablus, 1920–48'. In *Studies in the Economic and Social History of Palestine in the Nineteenth and Twentieth Centuries*, edited by R. Owen, pp. 88–176. London and Basingstoke: Macmillan, 1982.

Greenberg, Ela. *Preparing the Mothers of Tomorrow: Education and Islam in Mandate Palestine*. Austin: University of Texas Press, 2010.

Grehan, James. *Twilight of the Saints: Everyday Religion in Ottoman Syria and Palestine*. Oxford: Oxford University Press, 2014.

Hatina, Meir. 'Religious Culture Contested: The Sufi Ritual of Dawsa in Nineteenth-Century Cairo'. *Die Welt des Islams* 47, 1 (2007): pp. 33–62.

Irving, Sarah. '"A Young Man of Promise": Finding a Place for Stephan Hanna Stephan in the History of Mandate Palestine'. *Jerusalem Quarterly File* 73 (2018): pp. 42–62.

Jaussen, J.-A. 'Le cheikh Sa'ad ad-din et les djinn, à Naplouse'. *Journal of the Palestine Oriental Society* 3, 4 (1923): pp. 145–57.

Jaussen. J.-A. *Coutumes Palestiniennes: Naplouse et son district.* Paris: Librairie Orientaliste Paul Geuthner, 1927.

Kennedy, Dane. *The Magic Mountains: Hill Stations and the British Raj.* London: University of California Press, 1996.

Khater, Insaf. 'Health Conditions in Nablus During the British Mandate, 1922–1948'. Unpubl. MA Thesis. An-Najah University, 2000 [in Arabic].

Kushner, David. 'Zealous Towns in Nineteenth-Century Palestine'. *Middle Eastern Studies* 33, 3 (1997): pp. 597–612.

Lancaster, William and Fidelity Lancaster. 'On the Nature of Power in the Works of Orientalist Scholars and its Contribution to a History of Bedouin Society and Nomad-Sedentary Relations in the Bilad ash-Sham'. In *Antonin Jaussen: Sciences sociales occidentales et patrimoine arabe*, edited by G. Chatelard and M. Tarawneh, pp. 143–75. Beirut: Centre d'études et de recherches sur le moyen-orient contemporain, 1999.

Lemire, Vincent. *Jerusalem 1900: The Holy City in an Age of Possibilities.* Translated by C. Tihanyi and L. A. Weiss. London: University of Chicago Press, 2017.

Maffi, Irene. 'Orientalisme et temporalité de l'Autre: Quelques clés pour une lecture de Jaussen et de Robertson-Smith'. In *Antonin Jaussen: Sciences sociales occidentales et patrimoine arabe*, edited by G. Chatelard and M. Tarawneh, pp. 97–106. Beirut: Centre d'études et de recherches sur le moyen-orient contemporain, 1999.

Matthews, Weldon. *Confronting an Empire, Constructing a Nation: Arab Nationalists and Popular Politics in Mandate Palestine.* London: I. B. Tauris, 2006.

Mazza, Roberto and Idir Ouhes. 'For God and *La Patrie*: Antonin Jaussen, Dominican Priest and French Intelligence Agent in the Middle East, 1914–1920'. *First World War Studies* 3, 2 (2012): pp. 145–64.

Mazza, Roberto. 'For the Love of France: Père Antonin Jaussen in Jerusalem, 1914–1920'. *Jerusalem Quarterly File* 66 (2016): pp. 75–86.

McCulloch, Jock. *Colonial Psychiatry and 'the African Mind'.* Cambridge: Cambridge University Press, 1995.

Meiton, Fredrik. 'Nation or Industry: The Non-Electrification of Nablus'. *Jerusalem Quarterly File* 80 (2019): pp. 8–22.

Mershen, Birgit and Ulrich Hübner. 'Tawfiq Canaan and his contribution to the Ethnography of Palestine'. In *Palaestina Exploranda*, edited by U. Hübner, pp. 250–64. Wiesbaden: Harrassowitz Verlag, 2006.

Métral, Françoise. 'Études bibliques, archéologie et ethnographie: Jaussen, un ethnographe chez les bédouins'. In *Antonin Jaussen: sciences sociales occidentales et patrimoine arabe*, edited by G. Chatelard and M. Tarawneh, pp. 73–96. Beirut: Centre d'études et de recherches sur le moyen-orient contemporain, 1999.

Métral, Jean. 'Naplouse et son district: Un essai de monographie urbaine'. In Antonin Jaussen: Sciences sociales occidentales et patrimoine arabe, edited by G. Chatelard and M. Tarawneh, pp. 121–35. Beirut: Centre d'études et de recherches sur le moyen-orient contemporain, 1999.

Mills, Eric. Census of Palestine 1931, Volume I: Part I, Report. Alexandria: Messrs. Whitehead Morris Ltd, 1933.

Nashef, Khaled. 'Tawfiq Canaan: His Life and Works'. Jerusalem Quarterly File 16 (2002): pp. 12–26.

Qamhieh, Khaled Farid. 'Saving the Old Town of Nablus: A Conservation Study'. Unpubl. PhD Dissertation. University of Glasgow, 1992.

Rogan, Eugene. 'Madness and Marginality: The Advent of the Psychiatric Asylum in Egypt and Lebanon'. In Outside In: On the Margins of the Modern Middle East, edited by E. Rogan, pp. 104–25. London: I. B. Tauris, 2002.

Rogan, Eugene. Frontiers of the State in the Late Ottoman Empire: Transjordan, 1850–1921. Cambridge: Cambridge University Press, 1999.

Samuel, Herbert. An Interim Report on the Civil Administration of Palestine, During the Period 1st July 1920 - 30th June 1921. London: His Majesty's Stationery Office, 1921.

Schwake, Norbert. Die Entwicklung des Krankenhauswesens der Stadt Jerusalem vom Ende des 18. bis zum Beginn des 20. Jahrhunderts. Herzogenrath: Murken-Altrogge, 1983.

Sigrist, Marcel. 'Situation de l'exégèse en France au temps du Père Lagrange'. In Antonin Jaussen: Sciences sociales occidentales et patrimoine arabe, edited by G. Chatelard and M. Tarawneh, pp. 51–64. Beirut: Centre d'études et de recherches sur le moyen-orient contemporain, 1999.

Simoni, Marcella. 'At the Roots of Division: A New Perspective on Arabs and Jews, 1930–39'. Middle Eastern Studies 36, 3 (2000): pp. 52–92.

Simoni, Marcella. A Healthy Nation: Zionist Health Policies in British Palestine (1930–1939). Venezia: Cafoscarina, 2010.

Stephan, Stephan H. 'Lunacy in Palestinian Folklore'. Journal of the Palestine Oriental Society 5 (1925): pp. 1–16.

Sufian, Sandy. 'Healing Jerusalem: Colonial Medicine and Arab Health from World War I to al-Nakba'. In Jerusalem Interrupted: Modernity and Colonial Transformation, 1917–Present, edited by L. Jayyusi, pp. 115–38. Northampton: Olive Branch Press, 2015.

Tamari, Salim and Rita Giacaman. Zbeidat: The Social Impact of Agricultural Technology on the Life of a Peasant Community in the Jordan Valley. 2nd ed. Birzeit: Birzeit University, 1997.

Tamari, Salim. 'Lepers, Lunatics and Saints: The Nativist Ethnography of Tawfiq Canaan and his Jerusalem Circle'. Jerusalem Quarterly File 20 (2004): pp. 24–43.

Tamari, Salim. Mountain against the Sea: Essays on Palestinian Society and Culture. London: University of California Press, 2009.

Tuqan, Fadwa. A Mountainous Journey: An Autobiography. Translated by Olive Kenny. St Paul: Graywolf Press, 2013.

Vaughan, Megan. 'Idioms of Madness: Zomba Lunatic Asylum, Nyasaland, in the Colonial Period'. *Journal of Southern African Studies* 9, 2 (1983): pp. 218–38.

Viviano, Benedict T. 'École Biblique et Archaéologique Française de Jérusalem'. *The Biblical Archaeologist* 54, 3 (1991): pp. 160–67.

Watenpaugh, Keith. *Bread from Stones: The Middle East and the Making of Modern Humanitarianism.* London: University of California Press, 2015.

Wilson, Chris. 'Incarcerating the Insane: Debating Responsibility for Criminal Lunatics between Prisons, Hospitals, and Families in British Mandate Palestine'. *Contemporary Levant* 4, 1 (2019): pp. 39–51.

Young, Elise. *Gender and Nation Building in the Middle East: The Political Economy of Health from Mandate Palestine to Refugee Camps in Jordan.* London: I. B. Tauris, 2012.

CHAPTER 8

'Irrespective of Community or Creed': Charity, Solidarity and the 1927 Jericho Earthquake

Sarah Irving

In the months after the Jericho earthquake of July 1927,[1] which killed over 250 people in Mandatory Palestine and Transjordan, tables appeared regularly in the English, Arabic and Hebrew newspapers published in Palestine. The lists named those who had donated to the relief fund for victims of the earthquake, alongside the amounts given. Placing the names and sums of charitable donations in the public domain, especially by listing them in newspapers, was not an uncommon practice at the time and was bound up with issues of personal, familial or institutional prestige. As scholars such as Amy Singer, Melanie Tanielian and Keith David Watenpaugh have shown, in the Middle East, as in other societies and cultures, charity and giving was never neutral, but entangled with social and political power, legitimisation and ideology, although the manner of giving and of displaying one's generosity changed over time and place. A cross-cutting insight is that of Disaster Studies, which proposes that moments of catastrophe, especially rapid and unexpected ones such as an earthquake, offer the chance to observe dynamics in a society which might otherwise lie undiscovered; this chapter thus shifts away from the focus on large-scale poor relief which is the subject especially of Singer and Watenpaugh's research, but looks instead at the comparatively small but discursively significant example of the Jericho earthquake.[2]

In the environment of Mandate Palestine, I argue that the competition not only to donate, but to be seen to donate, carried particular weight. This chapter analyses who donated to the 1927 earthquake fund (and who did not), when and how much they gave, how they chose to present themselves in the process, and how public opinion responded to them. It also considers the donations in the light of behind-the-scenes correspondence and reports which informed both the calls for charity and the way in which money was disbursed. As Watenpaugh outlines, philanthropy and care for those in need had shifted in the nineteenth century, from 'imperial patronage to state function', as the increasingly bureaucratised Ottoman state sought to centralise and standardise its functions.[3] The

British Mandate administration's centralisation of the charitable appeal to help the victims of the 1927 earthquake similarly reflects the assumption that the state should take responsibility for a disaster situation; in this case the fundraising effort also provided an opportunity for the notoriously tight-fisted colonial government to attach to itself credit for the effects of the money disbursed and curry favour with those Palestinians who received funds which they may have been unaware actually came from private donors. But the publication of the donor lists also highlights the myriad ways in which private actors grasped the chance to publicly signal their interests in Palestine and their role in caring for its people and rebuilding its cities.

Many different people and groups – ranging from eminent Egyptian icons of the anti-colonial struggle to British Mandate administration officials, Jewish and Palestinian societies around the world and Protestant clergymen in the Levant – engaged with the emergency fund. As Khatchig Mouradian emphasises in his study of networks who saved and supported Armenians during the genocide, at times activities which might often be subsumed under the heading of aid and charity can, in situations of political conflict, cross into the category of resistance.[4] Whilst the situation of Palestinian donors and recipients of earthquake aid was very different from that of refugees from the mass killing and displacement of Ottoman Armenians, his point highlights the extent to which ostensibly humanitarian acts can be read as highly political in nature, on the part of the giver and the receiver. I thus suggest that the charity lists offer a snapshot of how some of the many interests attempting to embed themselves in Mandate Palestine and to claim allegiances and legitimacy in its political struggles presented themselves and their relationship to the Palestinian people and land in their hour of need. This approach is influenced by works by Salim Tamari such as his study of the Ottoman-sponsored Syrian expedition to Gallipoli during World War I, in which the context, participants and consequences associated with a single event are shown to be closely entangled with a wide range of ideological currents, claims to legitimacy and political positionings.[5] Applying this approach to the analysis of the earthquake appeal reveals that, despite a public rhetoric of neutrality which promised support for the earthquake victims 'irrespective of community or creed', all stages of the process were influenced by racialised assumptions about who had suffered and why, by the desire to project certain images of Palestinian (both Jewish and Arab) society and politics, and by wider networks of identity and solidarity on which all parties drew for support.

Charity and Humanitarianism in the 1920s Levant

Recent studies, particularly those by Keith David Watenpaugh and Melanie Tanielian, have stressed that humanitarianism and charity are never neutral,[6] and that this is perhaps especially true of their manifestations in the Middle East during the era of European and American imperialisms. Providing relief and support to the sick, injured and destitute has since at least the late nineteenth century been a way for actors on multiple levels to send social and political signals, to assert identities and status, and to associate themselves with desirable values and traits. At times this involved direct patronage via control over food or other supplies, but just as often the messages were more implicit, conveyed through symbolic acts or implied choices.

Nation-states have also used food, medicines and other emergency supplies as forms of propaganda; officials in the region's cities have reinforced their places in the social hierarchy by distributing much-needed goods; Ottoman and European colonial governments have sought to assert power and quash opposition through their allocations of vital resources; and religious and political movements have built loyalties and networks via their access to everyday necessities. Amy Singer's work highlights how, throughout the Ottoman Empire, from the sixteenth century onwards the establishment of *waqf*s to feed and otherwise help the poor conveyed multiple political, social and religious messages, especially for the elite women who endowed '*imaret*s like that of Hurrem Sultan in Istanbul and Jerusalem.[7] Tanielian, meanwhile, uncovers the ways in which the Ottoman state, European and American missionaries, Beiruti notables, local politicians and Aleppo grain dealers competed for power and influence during the largely man-made famine which hit Lebanon during World War I. Watenpaugh's seminal volume *Bread from Stones* charts how the ideology of humanitarianism was deployed and spread in the Levant through the actions and ideas of American missionaries and their aid networks.

As is implicit in all of these dynamics, humanitarian relief and charitable giving rarely, if ever, caused significant or lasting change in the welfare of the recipients. It was often not intended to; indeed, if there were any underlying intentions, they were often the reverse – to assert and sustain social hierarchies through the relationship of power and obligation between donor and receiver.[8] This chapter's reading of the variety of appeals and donations made in the wake of the 1927 Jericho earthquake draws on this insight, seeing the act of giving in such instances as more indicative of the aims of the giver than of the fate of the recipient. However, unlike much of the work on charity in the Levant region in the late and post-Ottoman period – including that of Watenpaugh, Tanielian and also Tylor Brand and Graham Auman Pitts for wartime Lebanon, or Anne Irfan and others on relief for Palestinian refugees – this chapter focuses not on wartime and social disasters such as refugee populations and human trafficking,[9] but on a natural disaster taking place during a period of comparative political stability, albeit under a colonial occupation and with increasing tensions.[10] As such, it perhaps has more in common with the tradition of Yaron Ayalon's research on disasters such as plagues and famines, Amy Singer's work on '*imaret*s in earlier periods of the Ottoman Empire, or Matthias Lehmann's study of *halukka* networks and their entanglement of Palestine Sephardic Jews,[11] their millet leadership in Istanbul and the diaspora communities from which they received support.[12] This historiographical context thus highlights the importance of natural disasters for studying peacetime society and politics as well as periods of conflict and turmoil.

The 1927 Earthquake and the Appeal for Aid

The earthquake that hit Palestine on the afternoon of 11 July 1927 had its epicentre in the northern end of the Dead Sea and is estimated to have had a magnitude of around 6.3M_w.[13] In terms of human impact, this meant that in some towns and cities, notably Nablus, Jerusalem, Ramla, Rayna and as-Salt, there was substantial damage and loss of life (amounting to an official death toll of 287), whilst geological variation meant that, just a short distance away, other places escaped unharmed. The tremors occurred just after three o'clock in the afternoon – fortuitous timing, which is thought to have saved lives, as many people would have been outside at this time on a summer's day. Within hours of the tremors – indeed, even before the aftershocks had subsided – they had attracted the attention of news media around the world. Fears of damage to sacred buildings and the presence of foreign tourists and pilgrims provoked coverage out of proportion to the actual events which, although killing several hundred people and injuring and displacing many more, were comparatively minor in terms of both strength and death toll next to tremors in China (over 41,000 deaths), Japan (c. 3,000 dead), Indonesia (magnitude 7.5), Alaska (magnitude 7.3), Chile and Kamchatka (both magnitude 7.2) in the same year.[14]

Within forty-eight hours, news bulletins were also highlighting the donation of 5,000 Egyptian pounds (the currency in use in Palestine at the time) cabled by Nathan Straus, the German-American Jewish owner of two of New York's largest department stores. Despite his fractious and sometimes hostile relationship with the leadership of the political Zionist movement,[15] Straus had been donating to causes in Palestine (as well as Europe and the USA) since well before World War I, with recipients ranging from projects such as a medical institution in Jerusalem and an agricultural station at Athlit, both classic Zionist enterprises aimed at 'upbuilding' Palestine, to institutions supporting the Muslim, Christian and Jewish poor.[16] Straus' cable set the tone for the fundraising effort in two ways: firstly, it specified that the money be spent 'without distinctions [of] race or creed' (implicitly placing the question of identity at the heart of donation to the quake victims); secondly, Straus stated that the money should be used for emergency relief, including his existing soup kitchen and child welfare project and later on 'barracks' for the displaced, and not on repairing damage.[17]

Possibly inspired by Straus' spontaneous generosity, Colonel George Symes, Civil Secretary of the British administration in Palestine and its acting head while the High Commissioner, Lord Plumer, was on leave, launched a public appeal along similar lines. It was formally announced through the official gazette and via cables to the British press,[18] where it rapidly took on political overtones, promoted by groups ranging from the Zionist Organisation to the National League, a conservative British anti-Communist group which supported Arab nationalism, opposed Zionism and was linked to right-wing British anti-Semites.[19] The Mandate administration's stress on the impartiality of the fundraising appeal laid it open to claims by a variety of interests, while the focus on temporary, emergency relief rather than longer-term rebuilding efforts was intended to funnel help to the most needy, although they also provoked dissatisfaction in some quarters, as described below. And, although the public statements surrounding the appeal stressed its neutrality of 'race or creed', behind the scenes its design and operation were predicated on Symes' racialised assumptions about the earthquake's victims and their identities.[20] Jews, Symes believed, by virtue of the modern architecture and building methods of their homes and workplaces, were not amongst those who would need help.[21] Neither were the poorer but 'simpler' and 'more virile' inhabitants of Transjordan, who would get back onto their own two feet with minimal aid.[22] It was an imagined poorer urban Palestinian, living in dangerous and primitive buildings unsuited to the terrain, on whose behalf Symes saw himself as issuing the call for help.

From 1 August 1927 onwards, almost three weeks after the quake, the earthquake fundraising committee published lists of donors and their donations, ordered by the size of the amount given, starting with the largest sums. The information appeared in the Mandate administration's official organ, the *Palestine Gazette*, and its Arabic and Hebrew editions, and was reproduced, either wholly or in part, within commentaries and news stories in the general press. Publishing lists of donors to charity appeals was not unusual in this period, although it may have been spurred by criticisms of the relief effort and calls for quicker aid and more transparency in the Palestinian Arabic press, notably the newspaper *Filastin* in its issues from late July, over two weeks after the quake.[23] This publicity probably contributed to the competitive element which rapidly arose. The public sphere was already a forum for rivalries over land, political legitimacy and modernity between the British administration, the Zionist movement and various Palestinian and Arab nationalist positions; thus, hierarchical lists of those who had stepped up to support the injured and homeless were bound to become forums for competition. Who donated, how much, when, under what name and affiliation, or as a result of having organised which community play, sports match or craft sale were details which, to those reading or hearing the lists read out loud, would have conveyed important messages about relationships and loyalties in a complex colonial setting.[24] The eventual sequence of lists is given in Table 1.

Table 1.1 Total donation sums.

Palestine Gazette issue	Donations list(s)	Official running total in Egyptian pounds
1 August 1927	1 (11–21 July donations)	
	2 (21–27 July)	
16 August	3 (27 July–6 August)	
	4 (6–13 August)	13,319.053
1 September	5 (13–20 August)	
	6 (20–27 August)	14,168.281
16 September	7 (27 August–3 September)	15,526.199
	8 (3–13 September)	16,564.330
1 October	9 (13–29 September)	17,004.243
1 November	10 (29 September–27 October)	17,898.236
16 December	11 (27 October–13 December)	21,401.720

Source: *Palestine Gazette*, August-December 1927.

Shifting Communities of Donation

The first list issued by George Antonius, secretary of the fundraising committee, was topped by Nathan Straus' spectacular gift of 5,000 Egyptian pounds, wired from New York. The rest of the contributors, however, were from closer to home and signalled the desire of members of the British Mandate administration, the Zionist movement and the growing business community in Palestine to assert their positions as beneficent civic actors. Indeed, perhaps applying hindsight, but not inaccurately, the former attorney-general of Palestine and life-long Zionist Norman Bentwich wrote that, as result of the earthquake, 'The Jews were able to further goodwill by their ready help to the Arabs'.[25] Amongst the donors of the largest sums we therefore find Messrs Thomas Cook & Son, the tourism company that had established the first package tours in Palestine in the nineteenth century, which gave 500 Egyptian pounds; Pinhas Rutenberg, who had founded the Palestine Electric Corporation four years previously and gave 200 pounds; and Mr E. Shelley, the Lipton's Teas representative in Palestine, who gave 40 pounds.[26] Smaller local enterprises such as the Palestine Educational Company, founded by Boulos Said, uncle of Edward Said, gave ten pounds, and Messrs S. Awad & Co, engineering and tool merchants, gave five – still not insignificant sums.

Other than this, a significant majority of the seventy or so donors of the first tranche were officials of the mandatory government and related institutions, including Symes, Antonius, Albert Hyamson (Commissioner for Migration), Edward Keith-Roach (Governor of Jerusalem) and Rennie MacInnes (Anglican Bishop of Jerusalem). Expatriate associations and the staff of foreign companies feature strongly, ranging from a freemasons' lodge named Jerusalem 262 to workers at the Jerusalem branch of Barclays Bank. The smaller sums of which the rest of the list is composed came from a wide range of donors: middle- and upper-class Palestinians, mainly Jerusalemites such as Sa'id al-Husayni; and expatriate residents of Jerusalem such as the Hebrew scholar Harold Wiener (who would be killed in the riots of 1929) and lawyer Harry Sacher.

This first list was published on 1 August 1927, with a note stating that it represented contributions made up to and including 21 July – that is, the ten days following the quake. This, I argue, likely skews the way in which different communities are represented within it, under-representing Palestinian Arab donors in favour of those from the Mandate administration, its personnel and its expatriate Jerusalem milieu. Palestinian newspapers and personal accounts suggest that in the worst-hit cities, including Nablus, Jerusalem and Ramla, local Palestinian notables donated money, goods and services to the community surrounding them in the days immediately after the quake had hit; many were embedded in the society, economy and politics of their towns and cities, living amongst those worst effected and indeed suffering damage and injury themselves. Donating to a government fund would, in these initial chaotic days, have made little sense: profound need could be seen first-hand and amongst known individuals. Even if those with the ability to make donations had known about the official charitable appeal, it could hardly have been a priority for them.

The second list, however, had a very different demographic profile, especially in its upper entries. It was published on the same date, as shown in the first table of donations, 1 August, but contained donations made between 22 and 27 July. There had, therefore, been time for people at a greater distance to have heard about the collection, for them to have sent their contributions, and for those who were engaged in local collections to make up their accounts and send larger sums. At the top of the list we thus find Jaffa Municipality contributing 153 Egyptian pounds, followed by a lump sum of 127.540 pounds accumulated by 'Messrs Abdul Rahman Haj Ibrahim, Haj Nimr Abdel Qader, Nafe' Anabtawi and Hassan Hannan'[27] which seems to have been a consortium from Tulkarm, where the first two men of the group were members of the local municipality.[28] The rest of the table, unlike the first list, is characterised by the large number of Arab Palestinian donors, including Nimr Effendi Nabulsi of Nablus, Khalil Effendi Taha of Haifa and Haifa Municipality (each one hundred Egyptian pounds), Taher Effendi Salah (fifty pounds), Hafez Agha Tuqan (forty) and twenty or twenty-five pounds each from Ahmad Effendi Shak'a, Shukri Eff Fakhreddin, Abdul-Rahim

Eff Nabulsi, Messrs Jamal and Majed Nabulsi and Suleiman Bey Nasif. Amongst the smaller donations (of between fifteen pounds and one pound) there are a large number of other Palestinian notables and intelligentsia, especially from Nablus and the surrounding areas: Taufiq Arafat, Farid Anabtawi, the historian Izzat Darwazeh and a number of members of the Tuqan, Abdul Hadi, Shak'a, Tamimi and Masri families, along with Jerusalemites such as Hassan Sidki Dajani and Mahmud and Darwish Daudi. Many of those on the list, such as Abdul Latif Salah or Gregorius Hajjar, the Greek Catholic Bishop of Acre, were associated with strong opposition to the British administration in Palestine, particularly during the 1936–39 uprising, but their places amongst the donors highlights the extent to which, at least at this earlier stage in the politics of the Mandate, a charitable appeal conducted by the British was still something with which they needed to be seen to co-operate.

The second bloc of donations was also when sums from Egypt started to appear, with a substantial donation of one hundred Egyptian pounds from 'Messrs Salem and Said Bazerno' (probably the Yemeni-Egyptian merchants Salem and Sa'id Bazara'a, who owned a khan in Cairo)[29] and another hundred from 'Sa'ad Pasha Zaghlul, Cairo'.[30] The Bazara'a family's enterprises included selling Nabulsi soap in Cairo, which may account for their eagerness to give an impressive sum to the survivors of a disaster in Palestine.[31]

It was Sa'ad Zaghlul's donation, however, which attracted the attention of the Palestinian Arabic-language press in a manner not dissimilar to Nathan Straus' coverage by the English-language newspapers.[32] The veteran Egyptian national-ist statesman, whose Wafd Party had been at the centre of the movement for freedom from British colonialism, was a regular donor to charitable causes, but also a heroic figure to at least some Palestinian intellectuals and politicians. The educator, politician and journalist Akram Zu'aytir's memoirs, for example, fea-ture a tribute to Zaghlul and reflections on his impact on the Palestinian national movement, in a section only one page from Zu'aytir's dramatic account of fleeing his collapsing classroom, along with his students, as the earthquake hit Nablus.[33] Zaghlul died on 23 August 1927, only a few weeks after sending his donation to the fund in Jerusalem, but his and the Bazara'a brothers' were followed by other donations from the Egyptian elite, including the scholar and pan-Arabist Ahmad Zaki Pasha and a substantial sum via the equally scholarly Prince Omar Toussoun from the pan-Eastern Jami'iyyat al-Rabita al-Sharqiyya ('Ar-Rabita esh-Sharkia Society' in the *Gazette*),[34] of which Zaki Pasha was a member.

Finally, the second list also saw the start of a trend that was to become com-mon: departments of the British administration donating *en masse*. In this case, the district staff in Jerusalem's first whip-round brought in 14.350 Egyptian pounds and the 'Haifa staff of the permits section' raised just over three pounds. Whilst these sums may seem small in comparison to some of the grand indi-vidual and collection donations at the head of the lists, it was common for them to be followed by entries for second and third sums from many government departments until December 1927. This generosity undoubtedly represented some genuine solidarity and local feeling; many junior, and some senior, administrators within the British Mandate administration were Palestinian; those in Jerusalem may well have suffered from the earthquake themselves, whilst according to memoirs and letters, even those in offices further afield, such as Haifa, felt the tremors.[35] It may also have reflected a kind of professional pride or group identity, communicated through generosity and community spirit. But it likely also reveals concern by the Mandate administration to be seen to be taking responsibility for the Palestinian population in its time of need, in the eyes of the people themselves, but perhaps more importantly for the British state in a manner visible to the League of Nations and the Permanent Mandates Commission, which oversaw Britain's governance in Palestine and Transjordan. The uniformity of the amounts donated by some administration departments indeed indicates that the amounts were being suggested – with more or less pressure – by senior officials.[36]

To parse the contents of each list in this fashion would be excessive (and dull), but several other individual or groups of donors from the ensuing months are worth commenting on. One of these groups consists of the inhabitants of the town of Kufr Kanna, in the Galilee. The eleventh list, from mid-December 1927, features three sums from the village: one of 12.143 Egyptian pounds from 'Ailut and Kefr Kenna', a second of 9.826 labelled 'Kefr Kenna Village, 2nd donation' and a third of 5.128, the origin of which is specified as the 'Moslem Residents of Kefr Kenna Village'.[37] In 1927 Kufr Kanna was a market town widely associated by outsiders with Cana of Galilee, the scene of Christ's first miracle, but which according to the 1922 and 1931 British censuses was home to a growing majority of Muslims.[38] 'Ailut, the other village named in the first donation, was found by researchers for both censuses to be entirely Muslim,[39] which suggests that the first donation in the list was made by a mixture of Muslims and Christians, very possibly a majority of the former. The practice of collecting donations in both churches and mosques which is revealed by mentions of congregational contributions, as well as of local municipalities centralising collections, suggests that the second donation may well also have come from religiously mixed sources. Why, then, a third donation whose givers felt the need to assert their Muslim identity? The facts are probably lost to time, but a feasible explanation might be that, in the face of an increasingly assertive Christian presence that came first with missionaries and their sponsorship of highly visible landmarks such as the new Catholic church celebrating the miracle of the wedding at Cana,[40] and secondly with Palestine's new Christian rulers and their Biblical obsessions,[41] at least some of the Muslim residents of Kufr Kanna had felt the need to reassert their own presence. The village of Rayna, one of the communities worst hit by the earthquake, is only a few kilometres from Kufr Kanna, and if the latter's Muslim inhabitants had become aware of missionary or state beliefs that credited their donations solely to Christians, a correction might have become a matter of significant local pride and inter-village relations. Although Kufr Kanna itself had escaped serious damage in the 1927 quake, it had suffered in earlier centuries, including the major 1837 tremors which had destroyed much of Safad:[42] for Galileans, both Muslim and Christian, earthquake solidarity must have been a theme in local historical memory. What the donation lists of 1927 show most clearly, then, is that the decision-making of givers and the calculations of those making the appeal draw together a complex web of extremely local considerations and a much broader range of national, colonial and religious issues, and the case of Kufr Kanna is a particularly sharp instance of this.

Another class of donations, which allow a glimpse into the world of Palestine's early diaspora, are the several sums from associations in the Americas. The Centro Social Palestino in Mexico appears in the eighth list as having collected the fairly considerable sum of 135.814 Egyptian pounds;[43] according to Cecilia Baeza, this association in the capital Mexico City was part of a trend during the 1920s of emerging Palestinian identity within the broader Levantine émigré communities in Latin America. In dialogue with political shifts in the 'home country', in this period groups across Latin America started to call themselves Palestinian rather than denoting themselves as Syrian or according to religion or their town of origin.[44] The same dynamic is witnessed in the tenth (late October) list, with a donation of forty-four pounds from the Palestine Fraternal Association in Tampico, Mexico.[45] As Baeza points out, the impacts of the British occupation of Palestine on émigrés in the Americas were considerable, in terms both practical – it inhibited travel and trade – and political, excluding them from the nation and its processes.[46] Donating to an appeal back home thus allowed these Palestinians living abroad to affirm a shared identity within their expatriate communities, to demonstrate their solidarity to their families and contacts in the old country, and to assert a continuing link back to Palestine to the British authorities which, in parallel with the rising politicisation of Jewish immigration, were making it increasingly hard for Muslim and Christian Palestinians to maintain their links. The presence of their donations in the lists, however, emphasises the extent to which the Palestinian diaspora remained connected to the homeland through mechanisms such as money transfers and news wires, as well as identity. Indeed, the same social centres which appear in the donation lists had submitted petitions to the High Commissioner, Lord Plumer, earlier in 1927, protesting the refusal of British Palestinian citizenship to their members.[47] Charitable support for earthquake survivors was, for these Palestinians in Mexico, part of a repertoire of tactics. These also included making political interventions to the Permanent Mandates Commission and other international institutions, reinforcing both their Palestinianness in Mexico and their continued links and rights to Palestine itself in a transnational sense.[48] The donations also hint at other émigré social networks through, for instance, donations from other institutions in the same city, such as that from the Absalom 20 freemasons lodge, also in Tampico, which sent 35.916 pounds, likewise in October 1927.[49]

This diversity of identity and self-representation also appears in other Latin American donations; while the groups mentioned above had followed the trend identified by Baeza of naming themselves as Palestinian, others maintained what she describes as an earlier practice of identifying by town of origin.[50] Key examples are the 'Persons from Beit Jala Residing in Colombia' and the 'Ladies from Bethlehem resident in South America', both of whom sent money (26.530 and 10.923 pounds respectively) in December 1927.[51] Perhaps at this comparatively early stage in the trends identified by Baeza, organisations in Mexico more clearly and assertively saw themselves as Palestinian than those in the Cono Sur; in any case, these examples are a small window onto the ways in which Palestinians across Latin America chose to describe themselves and their communities at this moment in time. Another possibility is that these self-descriptions are from less formal groupings, such as the émigrés 'made good', as charted in the work of Jacob Norris,[52] who may have possessed different priorities of belonging and identity. Or, indeed, the descriptors may not originate with the givers at all but with those through whom the money passed, such as the Mayor of Bethlehem in the second example, receiving money in an informal fashion and taking the opportunity to brand it with the city's name.

Rival Recipients

Although the appeal launched by Symes was billed as a central effort which would ensure that funds were fairly and efficiently distributed to the neediest, not all agreed. In particular, the insistence that money from the official appeal would go to individuals in dire need and not contribute to repairing or replacing public or community buildings ran counter to some expectations, and in ways which highlight the ruptures and continuities in Palestinian society from the Ottoman to the British Mandate periods, one of the key themes of Salim Tamari's work.[53]

The case of the Sephardic community of Jerusalem illustrates this point. After several months of government fundraising and disbursements, community leaders wrote to their fellow Sephardim at the Spanish and Portuguese Congregation in London. They complained that no support had come the way of the Jerusalem Sephardi Jews, and that whilst they appreciated the wish of Nathan Straus and other donors that the money be allocated to the neediest 'without distinctions [of] race or creed', this could not, they believed, have meant that Jews should be excluded from receiving aid. Some of the grounds for this complaint may well have come from statements by Symes and other British officials averring that Jews had been little or un-affected by the earthquake, stemming from British racialised assumptions about Jews as 'modern', European immigrants, thus obscuring the experiences of those Jews who did not fit this description.[54]

Many 'Eastern' Jews, living amongst Christian and Muslim Palestinians and in the same kinds of housing, had indeed suffered, but their chief rabbi was incorrect in claiming that none had received help. Rather, this was a misunderstanding about what kind of support was available, and how it would be allocated.[55] According to the historical norms of disaster relief within the Ottoman Empire and of transnational Jewish support for the Holy Land, the Sephardic community leaders should have been integrated into discussions of who received funds and how they were spent. Charity and aid had been communal affairs, operating within community bounds and often with a sense of reciprocity and/or the kinds of hierarchy described above.[56] The kind of individualised support championed by the Mandate administration thus went under the radar of community leaders; although preconceptions about different 'groups' of people were widely applied by British officials, they were also apparently happy to take this opportunity to undermine collective organising in society. The Sephardim in London were thus at cross-purposes with their Jerusalem brethren for two reasons: the former had indeed contributed a considerable sum to the general appeal and were reassured by British officials that their funds had gone to needy Jews. But perhaps more significantly, the Londoners were backing a generalised model of charity, prioritising the individual and what would come to be called their human rights, over the Jerusalem leadership's belief, founded in centuries of practice, that priority was determined by being part of the same community. The Jerusalemites had hoped to bypass the official appeal's ban on funding repairs to public buildings – in their case, their synagogue and yeshiva – and thought that the London Sephardim's responsibilities lay with this and not with Muslim and Christian victims of the earthquake.[57]

Given the prominence of European and American Christian missionaries in Palestine and the wider Levant, as well as the strength of millenarian Zionism as a belief in some strands of Protestant Christianity, one might have expected to see more missionary institutions amongst donors to the earthquake appeal. This is not to say that foreign Christian individuals, officeholders, congregations and institutions did not donate: many did. They range from the Latin Patriarch Luigi Barlassina to delegates at the ecumenical Lausanne Conference,[58] and senior figures in German Protestant circles in Palestine, such as Theodor Schneller of the Syrian Orphanage and William Hertzberg, provost of the evangelical Deutschen Palästina-Instituts in Jerusalem.[59] But compared to their profile in Mandate Palestinian life, the numbers and the sums involved are often small. This scantness seems to be linked to similar motivations as the Sephardi leadership's complaints to the London congregation. If we look beyond the official earthquake appeal to publications aimed solely at mission supporters, we find numerous advertisements and articles pleading for funds to rebuild or repair mission houses, schools, clinics and other structures which fell outside the remit of the official appeal. Like the Sephardic chief rabbi in Jerusalem, whose vision and remit were focused on his community, the writers and publishers of missionary journals and newsletters such as *Church Missionary Outlook*,[60] *Eastward Ho!*[61] and *The Mission Hospital*,[62] as well as organisations such as the Moravian Missions (in advertisements in *SAMS At Work*),[63] framed a narrow but deep set of priorities, aimed at reconstructing everything needed for their work in all walks of life, in contrast to the broad but shallow official appeal which might help greater numbers of people, but in the short term and with the absolute basics.

Some Conclusions

One of the key ideas behind the development of disaster studies as a field of research has been the assertion that catastrophic events show new aspects of the societies, communities and individuals affected by them via the explanations, reactions and solutions which emerge.[64] In this vein, I argue that observing the myriad outcomes of the 1927 Jericho earthquake can tell us much about Palestinian society in the earlier part of the Mandate period.

Firstly, it emphasises the impacts on policy and practice of the ideas and assumptions embedded in the British mandatory administration's rule in Palestine. The orientalist and racialised views of Arabs and Jews which informed strands of British foreign policy are all too visible in George Symes' confident assertions of which communities did and did not need help after the earthquake. British officials' images of themselves as embodying values such as efficiency, impartiality and organisation led them to centralise charity and solidarity in the belief that they would be bringing drive and fairness to a society which they understood as passive, feckless and conflict-ridden, ignoring existing mechanisms for dealing with disaster which represented a continuity from pre-World War I Ottoman society which the British preferred not to acknowledge.

Secondly, the choice of the British administration to publish the lists of donors to its centralised earthquake appeal highlights the multiple ways in which both donors and recipients, within Palestine and outside it, saw themselves and their relation to the country, and the impact of the press in helping varying interests to push forward their claims. As I argue in this chapter, voices in the Palestinian Arabic-language newspapers used Nathan Straus' initial grand donation as a means to criticise both the British administration and notables in Palestinian society – not necessarily for their inaction, since at least some had engaged in rapid relief and rebuilding efforts on the local scale, but for not making their contributions visible in the same way as international Jewish and Christian donors. Berating others for the absence or smallness of their contributions to the fund provided political leverage to competing interests in Palestinian society. Lost in the tussle to be featured on the donation lists, however, is the fact that the biggest beneficiary of this process was the British Mandate administration and its reputation. Notoriously tight-fisted in its management of the Palestine Mandate, by promoting competitive donation and centralising funds in its hands, it was able to minimise the sums it had to disburse itself, whilst still appearing beneficent to victims of the earthquake.

Thirdly, beyond both the new and old types of notables in Palestinian society, the public nature of the earthquake appeal also created scope for less ordinarily influential voices to make assertions about their identity and presence in the face of internal currents in their own society as well as colonial systems which they rightly feared might lead to them being disenfranchised and denied access to material resources. When the Muslims of Kufr Kanna emphasised that they, as well as their Christian neighbours who were the object of such fascination for foreign visitors, had contributed to the fund, they resisted the categories and assumptions imposed on them by the British and by Euro-American travellers and missionaries. And when groups of emigrants or their offspring living in Mexico sent donations in the name of their Palestinianness, they were deploying a newly popular designation which was entwined with their demands for official recognition and citizenship from the British administration.

All of these threads, I believe, emphasise the complexity of Palestinian allegiances and identities in the early Mandate period, and the contingency of the trajectories which emerged, particularly after the 'year zero' of 1929.[65] As Salim Tamari has highlighted in his many works,[66] Palestinian identity – and the politics which emanated from it – was rich, complicated and diverse, full of shifting patterns of competition and co-operation which, whilst in many cases showing continuity from the Ottoman past,[67] were also reshaped by the colonial present. The oppositional nature of those politics may have hardened in later years, but the cross-section of society revealed by the aftermath of the 1927 earthquake allows a brief view of currents that would later be solidified, and those that were subsumed beneath the surface.

Notes

1. The research on which this paper was based was generously supported by a Leverhulme Trust Early Career Fellowship.
2. For the example of the Ottoman Empire, see Ayalon, *Natural Disasters*.
3. Watenpaugh, *Bread from Stones*, p. 8.
4. Mouradian, *The Resistance Network*.
5. Tamari, 'A "Scientific Expedition" to Gallipoli'; idem, *Great War*.
6. Watenpaugh, *Bread from Stones*; Tanielian, *Charity of War*.
7. Singer, *Constructing Ottoman Beneficence*. An *'imaret* was a public soup kitchen, usually endowed by a *waqf*, which provided food for the poor and sometimes

also for travellers or pilgrims. Larger *'imarets* were often part of complexes including other charitable foundations such as schools or orphanages.

8. See, for example, Tanielian, *Charity of War,* pp. 9, 14–18 et passim; Tanielian, 'Feeding the City'; Pitts, 'A Hungry Population'; Watenpaugh, *Bread from Stones*.

9. Tanielian, *Charity of War*; Watenpaugh, *Bread from Stones*; Brand, 'Some Eat to Remember'; idem, 'That They May Have Life'; Pitts, 'A Hungry Population'.

10. Although locust swarms were certainly one of the causes of the terrible famine which took place in the Levant during World War I, most scholars on the subject argue that the man-made aspects of the situation were at least as, if not more, important in depriving large parts of the population of food. These, varying in focus and conclusion, include: the Allied blockade of the coast; the Ottoman fear of invasion and consequent curtailing of imports; price inflation and widespread unemployment; hoarding and profiteering by local capitalists; the prioritisation of food and other supplies for the army over civilian needs; and competition between military and civilian controllers of resources such as grain and railway transport for it. See Tanielian, *Charity of War*; idem, 'Feeding the City'; Pitts, 'A Hungry Population'; Brand, 'That They May Have Life'.

11. *Halukka* was a system of organised support by Jewish diaspora communities of a Jewish presence in the Holy Land, funding study and prayer as well as supporting the poor.

12. Ayalon, *Natural Disasters*; Lehmann, *Emissaries from the Holy Land*; Singer, *Constructing Ottoman Beneficence*.

13. The Richter scale was not finalised as a tool for measuring the magnitude of earthquakes until 1935, several years after the Jericho quake, but estimates of its scale and location (which was mistakenly thought to be further north, hence the association with Jericho) have been calculated using geological data, damage reports and other types of information.

14. The official death tolls for both Palestine and Transjordan were finalised at 287, although initial estimates were as high as 1,000 and some deaths may have gone unrecorded. For earthquake statistics, see US Geological Service, 'Significant Earthquakes – 1927', https://earthquake.usgs.gov/earthquakes/browse/significant.php?year=1927 [accessed 7 February 2022].

15. Berkowitz, *Western Jewry*.

16. Rosenthal and Rosen, 'Dairy Industry', p. 93; Gal and Ajzenstadt, 'Long Path'.

17. *New York Times*, 14 July 1927, p. 1.

18. *Palestine Gazette*, extraordinary edition, 15 July 1927; *The Times*, 16 July 1927, p. 11.

19. Wagner, *Statecraft by Stealth*; Toczek, *Haters, Baiters and Would-Be Dictators*.

20. Irving, 'Donations and their destinations'.

21. Symes to Colonial Office, 15 July 1927, Kew CO 733/142/13; Symes to 'Sir John', probably Shuckburgh, head of the Middle East division of the Colonial Office 1921–31, 20 July 1927, Kew CO 733/142/13.

22. Symes to Amery, 28 July 1927, Kew CO 733/142/13.

23. *Filastin*, 19 July, 26 July 1927, 29 July 1927.

24. The proceeds of fundraising events appear in the donor lists from August 1927 onwards, usually representing sums of twenty to twenty-five pounds, and include a dance at the Bristol Gardens, a popular Jerusalem café (Third list, *Palestine Gazette*, 16 August 1927), a charity football match by the Maccabee Society (Sixth list, *Palestine Gazette*, 1 September 1927, p. 673), a play by the 'Young Men of Tulkarem' (eighth list, *Palestine Gazette*, 16 September 1927, p. 674) and a 'special entertainment' at the Brummana Tennis Club in Lebanon, where many wealthy Beirutis would have spent their summer months (ninth list, *Palestine Gazette*, 1 October 1927, p. 705). More substantial sums came from larger events such as the Palestine General Agricultural Show, which raised over 137 pounds (ninth list, Palestine Gazette, 1 October 1927, p. 705) and a large craft fair organised in Jerusalem by Helen Bentwich, wife of the Attorney General Norman Bentwich, and others from the social circle of British Mandate officials (Bentwich and Bentwich, *Mandate Memories*, pp. 113–14).

25. Bentwich, *Wanderer Between*, p. 142.

26. *Palestine Gazette*, 1 August 1927, pp. 567–68.

27. *Palestine Gazette*, 1 August 1927, pp. 568–69.

28. *Palestine Blue Book* (London: Government Printing and Stationery Office, 1930), p. 81.

29. I am indebted to Nesrin Amin of the BilMasri podcast for helping me to identify the brothers from the mistyped version in the *Palestine Gazette*.

30. Second List, *Palestine Gazette*, 1 August 1927, p. 568.

31. 'Wikalat Bazara'a', Marefa.org, accessed 8 February 2022, https://www.marefa.org/%D9%88%D9%83%D8%A7%D9%84%D8%A9_%D8%A8%D8%A7%D8%B2%D8%B1%D8%B9%D8%A9/simplified.

32. *Al-Jami'a al-Arabiyya*, for instance, highlighted Zaghlul's donation in a headline which also mentioned Ibn Saud.

33. Akram Zu'aytir, *Bawakir al-nidal*, p. 21–22.

34. Eighth list, *Palestine Gazette*, 16 September 1927, p. 674; tenth list, *Palestine Gazette*, 1 November 1927, p. 752.

35. For example, Ruth Jordan (*Daughter of the Sea*, pp. 40–41) describes a number of watermelons which had been piled up in her kitchen rolling around the floors with the shockwaves.

36. See, for example, Horne, *Job Well Done*, p. 115.

37. *Palestine Gazette*, 16 December 1927, p. 926.

38. Barron, *1922 Census*, p. 38, 51; Mills, *1931 Census*, p. 74.

39. Barron, *1922 Census*, p. 38; Mills, *1931 Census*, p. 73.

40. For example, although there had been a Catholic presence in Kufr Kanna for several centuries, the Franciscan Church of the Wedding was built on

newly acquired land in the 1880s and expanded in the 1890s and early 1900s (Custodia Terrae Sanctae, 'Cana', https://www.custodia.org/en/sanctuaries/cana, accessed 27 February 2022). Even though the identification of Kufr Kanna with the village of Cana from the time of Roman rule in Palestine is disputed, a British writer in 1910 could observe the following: 'To the ordinary tourist in Palestine the site of this place is scarcely a matter of dispute. The carriage road from Nazareth to Tiberias bears him, within the hour, to the picturesque Kefr Kanna (lit. the Village of Kenna) with its Greek and Latin churches, its sacred waterpots – if he wishes to see them – and its undeniably picturesque village fountain' (Masterman, 'Cana of Galilee', p. 79).

41. British military intelligence during World War I believed, for instance, that the residents of Kufr Kanna would be 'friendly or very friendly' to Commonwealth armies, apparently based partly on assumptions about the attitudes of Palestinian Christians (Tamari, 'Shifting Ottoman Conceptions', p. 35).

42. Kárník, *Seismicity*, p. 39.

43. *Palestine Gazette*, 16 September 1927, pp. 674–75.

44. Baeza, 'Palestinians in Latin America', pp. 63–64. Interestingly, this donation names the Centro in Mexico two years earlier than the foundation date cited by Baeza, suggesting that it was perhaps functioning as an informal network before it was officially constituted.

45. *Palestine Gazette*, 16 December 1927, p. 926.

46. Baeza, 'Palestinians in Latin America', p. 63–65; Banko, 'A Stranger from this Homeland'.

47. Bawalsa, 'Citizens from Afar', p. 123.

48. See, for instance, the collection of papers distributed to delegates to the 17th Session of the Permanent Mandates Commission in 1930, which mentions representations by several Mexican-Palestine organisations, including the Associacion Fraternal Palestina mentioned previously and the Committee of Young Palestinians of Parras, Mexico. League of Nations, *Permanent Mandate Commission Seventeenth (Extraordinary) Session of the Commission (Geneva, June 3d-21st 1930), C.355.M.147* (Geneva: League of Nations, 1930), pp. 132–33 (consulted online 10 February 2022, https://biblio-archive.unog.ch /Dateien/CouncilMSD/C-355-M-147-1930-VI_EN.pdf)

49. *Palestine Gazette*, 1 November 1927, pp. 752–53.

50. Baeza, 'Palestinians in Latin America', pp. 63–64.

51. *Palestine Gazette*, 16 December 1927, p. 926.

52. Norris, 'Return Migration'.

53. Tamari, *Year of the Locust; The Great War.*

54. Norris, *Land of Progress*, pp. 65–68, 74–91; Renton, 'Age of Nationality', p. 586.

55. Irving, *Donations and their Destinations.*

56. For the community focus of earlier Ottoman disaster relief, see Ayalon, *Natural Disasters.* For patterns of aid and support from Jews in Europe, Asia, North Africa

and the Americas to those in Palestine (mainly through the *halukka* system), see Lehmann, *Emissaries from the Holy Land*, and Cooper, *Bukharan Jews*.

57. Irving, 'Donations and their Destinations'.

58. Fourth List, *Palestine Gazette*, 16 August 1927; ninth List, *Palestine Gazette*, 1 October 1927, p. 705.

59. Third List, *Palestine Gazette*, 16 August 1927; eleventh list, *Palestine Gazette*, 16 December 1927, p. 926.

60. '£2000 is required by the Palestine Mission to repair damaged buildings', *Church Missionary Outlook* October 1927, p. 210.

61. 'The Earthquake in Palestine', *Eastward Ho!* September 1927, p. 132.

62. 'Editorial Notes', *The Mission Hospital*, September 1927, p. 238; W. Parker Harrison, 'Earthquake Damage at Nablous [sic]', *The Mission Hospital*, September 1927, p. 240.

63. *SAMS At Work*, October 1927, p. 1.

64. Ayalon, *Natural Disasters*, 208 et passim.

65. Cohen, *1929: Year Zero*.

66. Particularly, it might be argued, in the collection *Mountain Against the Sea: Essays on Palestinian Society and Culture* and in *Year of the Locust: A Soldier's Diary and the Erasure of Palestine's Ottoman Past* which, as its title implies, incorporates an emphasis on the importance of the Ottoman period for understanding Palestinian history.

67. As emphasised by Tamari in his introduction to and presentation of Ihsan Turjman's World War I experiences in *Year of the Locust*.

Bibliography

Archives

British National Archives, Kew.
Endangered Archives Project (online; collections 'Filastin', 'Periodical collection of the al-Aqsa Mosque Library', 'Mir'at al-Sharq').
London Metropolitan Archives.
National Library of Israel, Arabic newspaper collection (online).
Yale University Library digital collections.

Secondary Sources

Ayalon, Yaron. *Natural Disasters in the Ottoman Empire: Plague, Famine, and Other Misfortunes*. Cambridge: Cambridge University Press, 2017.
Baeza, Cecilia. 'Palestinians in Latin America: Between Assimilation and Long-Distance Nationalism'. *Journal of Palestine Studies* 43, 2 (2014): pp. 59–72.

Banko, Lauren. '"A Stranger from this Homeland": Deportation and the Ruin of Lives and Livelihoods during the Palestine Mandate'. *Contemporary Levant* 4, 2 (2019): pp. 107–21.

Barron, John B., ed. *Palestine: Report and General Abstracts of the Census of 1922.* Jerusalem: Government of Palestine, 1923.

Bawalsa, Nadim. 'Citizens from Afar: Palestinian Migrants and the New World Order, 1920–1930'. In *The Routledge Handbook of the History of the Middle East Mandates*, edited by Cyrus Schayegh and Andrew Arsan, pp. 123–35. Abingdon: Routledge, 2015.

Bentwich, Norman and Helen Bentwich. *Mandate Memories, 1918–1948.* London: Hogarth Press, 1965.

Bentwich, Norman. *Wanderer Between Two Worlds.* London: Kegan Paul, Trench, Trubner & Co, 1941.

Berkowitz, Michael. *Western Jewry and the Zionist project, 1914–1933.* Cambridge: Cambridge University Press, 1997.

Brand, Tylor. '"That They May Have Life": Balancing Principles and Pragmatism in the Syrian Protestant College's Humanitarian Relief Projects during the Famine of World War I'. In *One Hundred and Fifty*, edited by Nadia Maria El-Cheikh, Lina Choueiri and Bilal Orfali, pp. 51–62. Beirut: American University of Beirut Press, 2016.

Brand, Tylor. 'Some Eat to Remember, Some to Forget: Starving, Eating, and Coping in the Syrian Famine of World War I'. In *Insatiable Appetite: Food as Cultural Signifier in the Middle East and Beyond*, edited by Kirill Dmitriev, Julia Hauser and Bilal Orfali, pp. 319–39. Leiden: Brill, 2019.

Cohen, Hillel. *1929: Year Zero of the Arab-Israeli Conflict.* Waltham: Brandeis University Press, 2015.

Cooper, Alana. *Bukharan Jews and the Dynamics of Global Judaism.* Bloomington: Indiana University Press, 2012.

Gal, John and Mimi Ajzenstadt. 'The Long Path from a Soup Kitchen to a Welfare State in Israel'. *Journal of Policy History* 25, 2 (2013): pp. 240–63.

Horne, Edward. *A Job Well Done: A History of the Palestine Police Force 1920–1948.* Leigh-on-Sea: Palestine Police Old Comrades Benevolent Association, 2003.

Irving, Sarah. 'Donations and their Destinations in the 1927 Palestine Earthquake'. *Revue d'histoire culturelle* 2 (2021), https://revues.mshparisnord.fr/rhc/index. php?id=940.

Jordan, Ruth. *Daughter of the Sea.* New York: Taplinger, 1983.

Kárník, Vit. *Seismicity of the European Area: Part 2.* Dordrecht: D. Reidel Publishing, 1971.

Lehmann, Matthias. *Emissaries from the Holy Land: The Sephardic Diaspora and the Practice of Pan-Judaism in the Eighteenth Century.* Palo Alto: Stanford University Press, 2014.

Masterman, Ernest W. G. 'Cana of Galilee'. *The Biblical World* 36, 2 (1910): pp. 74, 79–92.

Mills, Eric, ed. *Census of Palestine 1931: Population of Villages, Towns and Administrative Areas*. Jerusalem: Government of Palestine, 1932.

Mouradian, Khatchig. *The Resistance Network: The Armenian Genocide and Humanitarianism in Ottoman Syria, 1915–1918*. East Lansing: Michigan State University Press, 2021.

Norris, Jacob. 'Return Migration and the Rise of the Palestinian Nouveaux Riches, 1870–1925'. *Journal of Palestine Studies* 46, 2 (2017): pp. 60–75.

Norris, Jacob. *Land of Progress: Palestine in the Age of Colonial Development, 1905–48*. Oxford: Oxford University Press, 2013.

Pitts, Graham Auman. 'A Hungry Population Stops Thinking About Resistance: Class, Famine, and Lebanon's World War I Legacy'. *Journal of the Ottoman and Turkish Studies Association* 7, 2 (2020): pp. 217–36.

Renton, James. 'The Age of Nationality and the Origins of the Zionist-Palestinian Conflict'. *International History Review* 35, 3 (2013): pp. 576–99.

Rosenthal, Ionel and Baruch Rosen. 'Nathan Straus' Contribution to the Dairy Industry in Palestine'. *Journal of Israeli History* 15, 1 (1994): pp. 91–99.

Singer, Amy. *Constructing Ottoman Beneficence: An Imperial Soup Kitchen in Jerusalem*. Albany: State University of New York Press, 2002.

Tamari, Salim. *Mountain Against the Sea: Essays on Palestinian Society and Culture*. Berkeley: University of California Press, 2008.

Tamari, Salim. 'Shifting Ottoman Conceptions of Palestine, Part 1: Filistin Risalesi and the two Jamals'. *Jerusalem Quarterly* 47 (2011): pp. 28–38.

Tamari, Salim. 'A "Scientific Expedition" to Gallipoli: The Syrian-Palestinian Intelligentsia and the Ottoman Campaign Against Arab Separatism'. *Jerusalem Quarterly* 56–57 (2014): pp. 6–28.

Tamari, Salim. *Year of the Locust: A Soldier's Diary and the Erasure of Palestine's Ottoman Past*. Berkeley: University of California Press, 2015.

Tamari, Salim. *The Great War and the Remaking of Palestine*. Berkeley: University of California Press, 2017.

Tanielian, Melanie S. *The Charity of War: Famine, Humanitarian Aid and World War I in the Middle East*. Palo Alto: Stanford University Press, 2017.

Tanielian, Melanie S. 'Feeding the City: The Beirut Municipality and the Politics of Food During World War I'. *International Journal of Middle East Studies* 46, 4 (2014): pp. 737–58.

Toczek, Nick. *Haters, Baiters and Would-Be Dictators: Anti-Semitism and the UK Far Right*. Abingdon: Routledge, 2015.

Wagner, Steven B. *Statecraft by Stealth: Secret Intelligence and British Rule in Palestine*. Ithaca: Cornell University Press, 2019.

Watenpaugh, Keith David. *Bread from Stones: The Middle East and the Making of Modern Humanitarianism*. Berkeley: University of California Press, 2015.

Zu'aytir, Akram. *Bawakir al-nidal: Min mudhakkirat Akram Zu'aytir, 1909–1935*. Beirut: al-Muassasa al-Arabiya lil-Dirasat wa-al-Nashr, 1994.

CHAPTER 9

Photographing the Palestinian Nakba: Rethinking the Role of Photography in Historical Writing

Issam Nassar

Most historians of the Palestinian catastrophe of 1948, known as the Nakba, and of modern Palestine more generally, conduct their research based on written documents and, in the case of Palestinian historians, to some extent on oral history.[1] We rarely find authors using alternative or additional sources, not just to document events but to try to understand them more deeply, although Salim Tamari, to whom this collection is dedicated, is an honourable exception.[2] Photographs are an important additional resource for studying the history of the Nakba and, although some scholars have used them, they have mainly done so in order to illustrate their books rather than for what the photographs themselves might have to say. In recent times, perhaps due to the internet and social media, the use of images for purposes other than research or documentation has spread, in a way that might be considered nostalgic, since the photographs are often associated with a longing for what users now see as a *belle époque* or golden age, when they are of life in Palestine before the diaspora, or with the arousal of emotions and anger if the pictures are of the victims of Zionism and Israeli violence. This paper takes a different approach, in that it focuses on visual documents as historical documents that can be useful for studying the Palestinian Nakba. Although this chapter discusses specific images, its thrust relates to the possibility of using photographs as documents to study the Nakba, at least from a perspective seven decades after the events of 1947–48.

Although photography was widespread in large Palestinian towns, documenting the events of the Nakba does not appear to have aroused the interest of photographers in general, with some exceptions.[3] We have no evidence that the Arab armies in Palestine made widespread use of photography, unlike the Zionist forces and Israeli army, which used photography to document their activities to a relatively large extent. Some events of the Nakba were recorded by foreign press photographers working for international news agencies. Likewise, in historical research and writing, Arab scholars do not appear to have made substantial use of visual documents. If they used them, it was only to embellish their published work or in their personal memoirs. The question thus arises: why did Arabs, including the Palestinians, make so little use of photographs, especially as the events of World War I in Palestine were widely photographed by local and Ottoman Army photographers,[4] more than three decades before the Palestine war?

Perhaps the biggest problem in studying this subject is that official Arab archives are not available. Where they do exist, they often are not accessible to scholars. The Arab or Palestinian photographs of the 1948 Nakba that we do have come from individual or family sources, such as the Theodorie family collection in Bethlehem, or from Israeli archives such as those of the Government Press Office and Zionist organisation. The only Arab archive that collects photographs from the Arab world is that of the Arab Image Foundation in Beirut, which has focused its interest on photographs and photographers rather than on Palestine and the Nakba, although such photographs do exist in the collection. Most of the pictures on which this paper is based come from two Israeli archives – that of the Israeli War Ministry, which has opened part of its Nakba archive in recent years, and of the Israeli Government Press Office in Jerusalem. The former includes collections of photographs by Palestinian photographers that were appropriated by the state in and after 1948, while the latter does not contain images by Palestinians, whether Arab or Armenian, but photographs by Haganah photographers, or Israeli army photographers after the proclamation of the Israeli state. There are many photographs of the events of the Nakba in international media archives, especially the US magazine *Life*, and some of these may have been taken by Palestinians or Arabs, but we often cannot ascertain that with precision.

Arab Photographers

Knowing the national origin of a particular photographer is not enough for us to assert that their photographs have a special authenticity that distinguishes them from photographs taken by settlers or foreign journalists. It is not national origin that determines the importance of the image or even its basic message. Of course, there are various ways of looking at things and representing them visually or in writing, and ever since photography arrived in the region in 1839 the dominant images of Palestine have been stereotypical representations of the country, whether by photographers, publishers, scholars, or audiences.[5] Photographs of Palestine in the West often still follow Orientalist stereotypes associated with the 'Holy Land', the violence of the indigenous population, or the romance of life in the Orient. Pictures project these stereotypes through their subject matter, the ways in which they are depicted and their captions, whether written by the photographers or by newspaper or book publishers. But the market economy, which cannot be detached from the development of photography as a profession in Palestine or neighbouring countries, usually forced photographers to produce Orientalist images for sale to pilgrims, tourists, or the foreign press,[6] and so the Orientalist style of photography was also produced by Palestinians. At the same time, 'Occidental' photographs of Palestine, like all images, can be re-read in non-Orientalist ways, even in ways that are critical of Orientalism. In other words, they can be liberated from the constraints of the Orientalist perspective, which we will discuss later.

A number of people from Palestine and the neighbouring region photographed the events of the Nakba, and there are probably many others we do not yet know about. As in all historical research, the photographs that are important to the historian of the Nakba cannot be confined to those taken at the time of the event itself; the historian might benefit from photographs that predate or postdate the event. However, in this case, I will restrict the discussion to the portrayal of events in the context of a short period of time – that is, the period between 1947 and the beginning of the 1950s, after displaced Palestinians settled in refugee camps and after Israel demolished most of the villages whose inhabitants were expelled or displaced. The photographers who took pictures of some of these events include Abd al-Salam al-Ujayli (1918–2006), who was a Syrian volunteer in the Arab Liberation Army; the Jerusalemite photographer Hanna Safia (1910–79), who worked for international news agencies; Khalil Rissas (1926–74),[7] also a photographer from Jerusalem; and Abdel Razzaq Badran (1917–2004),[8] who worked for the Egyptian publishing house Dar al-Hilal during the war of 1948 and took photographs of volunteers from the International Red Cross, the US Society of Friends (Quakers) and the UN Relief and Works Agency (UNRWA). From these and other collections we have some photographs of the Nakba period, including those taken in Jerusalem in 1948 by Palestinian-Armenian photographer Antranig Bekeredjian (active between 1950 and 1983), who was known as Tony, pictures by the first Arab photographers in UNRWA, such as the two Lebanese, George Ni'ma (active between 1960 and 1993) and Munir Nasr (dates unknown), and Khalil Rissas' looted photographs that are in the Israeli archives, as well as others.

Some photographs, including examples by the photographers mentioned above, have survived, but others have disappeared for one reason or another. The photographer Hanna Safia went to the village of Deir Yassin to take pictures of the aftermath of the massacre that took place there in April 1948, but these photographs are lost. Hrant Nakashian (1921–91), an Armenian photographer from Jaffa, took pictures when he and others left Jaffa for Gaza as refugees, but these are in the possession of his children and have not yet been seen by specialists. But this paper is not the place to go into more detail about the photographers, a subject we shall treat elsewhere.

The central question in this paper, as indicated above, is how photographs can be used to understand the history of the Nakba and how Arab photographers portrayed the event. The starting point is therefore the question of how we can read photographic images for purposes of historical research. Photographs are the product of an intricate interaction of historical circumstances, including how they were taken, how they were used and their documentary and physical nature. Initially, they captured an event or a scene that the photographer deemed appropriate to record, which reminds us that the event behind the photograph is basically a double event. There is the event that the photographer decided to photograph and the fact that the photographer was present at that time in that place so that they were able to take photographs, and each of these events has its own history. There is the fact that the event took place in front of the photographer's lens, the photographer's decision to capture it in a certain way, from a particular angle, and the way in which the photographer photographed a part of what they could see and left other parts out of the frame. Then there is the reason that led to the presence of the photographer at that moment in particular and in that place and what was behind their presence and motives for taking a picture. A Syrian volunteer in the Arab Liberation Army, for example, may have intended to take souvenir photographs of himself and his friends on their Palestinian adventure. At the same time, another photographer such as Khalil Rissas was invited by one of the military commanders in Jerusalem to take photographs in order to record that officer's heroic defence of the city. Another reason for taking photographs might have been the fact that the photographer was a newspaper journalist, such as Abdel Razzaq Badran at the Egyptian publishing house Dar al-Hilal, or that an international news agency had sent him to cover the foundation of a Zionist state in Palestine, or to document the battles or the British withdrawal from the country, as was the case with John Phillips (1914–96), a photographer for *Life* magazine.[9] Or that the photographer happened to be there by chance or was taking pictures to record relief efforts by the organisation that employed them, as in the case of Myrtle Winter (1915–2008), a photographer for UNRWA.[10] Understanding the reasons that lead a photographer to be there and to take pictures is very important in analysing the photographs that result, but it is not necessarily the most important factor in how we use the images to document the event.

How Should we See Photographs as Documents?

Photographs themselves are material relics that belong to historical time. They are paper on which chemical substances form an image, a historical relic of a kind. What makes the photographic image a strange invention is that the raw materials, as John Berger terms it, are light and time.[11] The image that results from the light and that appears on the surface of the photograph provides us with certain visual information that we have to look at, as it is, before we look into its history or the specifics of the subject matter. There are good photographs, artistic photographs and well-produced photographs, and then there are photographs that are bad by all or some of these criteria. The materials used in forming the image, such as the paper, the way in which the image was photographed and developed, provides us with historical information by which we can to some extent identify the approximate date at which it was produced. The image that appears on the surface gives us a general image of the subject-matter – for example, we might see an image of a certain number of people standing in front of the camera in some way. They may be friends on an outing or doing some kind of work. They might be strangers who have met for the first time when the picture was taken or shortly before. Hence, to some extent the subject of the picture gives us basic but incomplete information about the reason why the photograph was taken. The subject matter is what might determine whether the image is important to our research, but our reading of its subject at the surface level might take us in different directions, based on our previous knowledge of the subject of the image or of what interests us about it. A picture of a group of people might be read anthropologically, as a representation of human relationships, or artistically, in a way related to the way in which the image was photographed and produced. Or we might look at a photograph because we are interested in the way in which people dressed at a certain time, or because we are connected to them as a subject or as particular individuals. But the surface is just one level of viewing the image: the image also has a depth, which is related to the subject-matter, the historical context and the circumstances of its production.

There is also a third dimension associated with the way in which the image has been used and how it takes on various meanings after it has been circulated. Then there is a fourth level, especially important when studying the Nakba, and this relates to the role of the image in the context of the national historical discourse of the state and of the institution that uses it and preserves it in its archives. In this context, the image has another role related to the historian/ critical viewer: the possibility of using the image as a form of sabotage to poke holes into the official discourse of the state or a particular ethnic group, and this makes images an important factor in challenging and critiquing prevailing discourses. This dimension is more closely associated with in-depth rather than superficial readings.

In her well-known essay on photography, Susan Sontag refers to the spread of the use of photography in current times when we compare it with its initial use after its invention in the first half of the nineteenth century. Photography was initially associated with art but later became a kind of social ritual: humans, especially when they are engaged in tourism or doing something they have never done before, came to feel the need to bring their cameras along to record the occasion.[12] In this context, the photographic image concerned is charged with emotion for those who appear in it or those who take it. It might remind them of the feelings they felt when the picture was taken, or of the experience they had at the time. But, according to Sontag, the emotional load gradually diminishes with the passage of time and with the change of generations, so that the picture does not affect the grandchild in the same way as it affected the grandparent who appears in the picture, until it eventually becomes material for nostalgia, lamentation and sorrow because the people in the picture have grown old or passed away. It represents a time that cannot be relived. Eduardo Cadava has written that, in 'photographing someone, we know that the photograph will survive him – it begins, even during his life, to circulate without him, figuring and anticipating his death each time it is looked at'.[13] Thus, the photograph is, in Sontag's words, a memento mori, something preserved to remind us of mortality, whether of the person or of the subject, and this is precisely what makes it possible for photographs of the year of the Nakba to change from being objects of a personal and emotional nature to objects for historical research, as the effect of time, the passing of generations and the change in the people looking at them strips the photographs of many associations.[14] According to Walter Benjamin, 'our sense of perception is determined not only by nature, but by historical circumstances as well',[15] including our previous knowledge of the subject in the photograph.

But even if the personal, emotional attachment to a particular photograph disappears over time, an old photograph has what Walter Benjamin calls an 'aura', which he describes as a mesmeric and phantasmic sense, associated with the amazement and aesthetic pleasure that come over someone when they look at the horizon or some scene from afar. Although Benjamin's aura is associated with a kind of magic in the scene, it is also associated with chronological and geographical distance, and this is the aspect that might be useful to a researcher examining photographs from the time of the Nakba, which is remote from the time of looking at the photographs. Time here creates a distance between the event itself, the time when the picture was taken and the event in the context of Palestinian time particular to the Nakba and associated with what we now know about what happened in general and its historical context.

Semiotic analysis provides us with an additional approach to understanding photographs, in that it links visual representation and linguistic representation, considering that nothing exists outside the text. Jacques Derrida saw all social and cultural phenomena as texts of a kind that could be studied as literature. In his book *De la grammatologie*, he says that the term 'writing' can designate . . .

> . . . not only the physical gestures of literal pictographic or ideographic inscription, but also the totality of what makes it possible [. . .] And thus we say 'writing' for all that gives rise to an inscription in general, whether it is literal or not and even if what it distributes in space is alien to the order of the voice: cinematography, choreography, of course, but also pictorial, musical, sculptural 'writing'.[16]

The science of writing that Derrida proposes is based on reinterpreting the world as a text, indicating that every representation of the world is based on symbols or what he calls 'signs' – a writing process of some kind. But this hypothesis does not always hold true, although the concept of representation in photographs is linked to some extent to the concepts of resemblance and imitation, which are concepts associated with writing. A visible image does not necessarily contain coded signs with an agreed meaning such that the image can be interpreted by decoding them. It is also not like language, which essentially contains rules that are to a large extent fixed, not like words that have clear dictionary definitions, because pictures can carry a large number of meanings and significations. But it is useful to some extent to think of images as a text in general, in the context of our social understanding of subjects that the image might represent. We say, for example, that what we see in front of us is a picture of a woman, or a mother, or a soldier, or a wall, and all these representations have socially and epistemically agreed meanings. This would also apply to the ways of representing the subjects of the image in such a way that we can conclude that what we are looking at are a landscape or a portrait taken in a studio. In other words, we can see in the picture iconic symbols that we can decipher in the same way as we decipher written words. Roland Barthes was the first person to use semiotic analysis to decipher symbols in photographs, in that he tried to analyse the meanings we give to pictures, considering them not as general and fixed inferences from what we see so much as meanings associated with the cognitive experience, which might give them various associations based on how they are used. We might see a picture of food and interpret it as an advertisement for a restaurant, or a picture of an actor and understand it as an advertisement for a movie and so on. Often the caption attached to the photograph helps to clarify the intention.[17]

Since the subject of this paper is the photography of the Nakba, I will not elaborate any further on the theoretical aspect associated with deciphering and analysing historical images as sources for research, despite the importance of the subject. In the following part I move on to analyse particular photographs from this period of history, taking into account the various aspects we have already discussed, but with reference to analysing photographs of the Nakba. But before starting, I think it necessary to address an inevitable question related to the abundance of photographs available these days through social media and digital search sites. The abundance of electronic images and the ease with which they can be copied and distributed, although they are important in expanding knowledge of the picture, also pose a danger, since the pictures are not distributed through archives that have an official status, but through amateurs who sometimes have no knowledge of the nature of the images they are sharing. This aggravates the phenomenon of misinformation and misinterpretations of the photographs. One should handle information that comes from such sources only after checking and research to avoid promulgating false information. Of course, this does not mean that the photographs in official archives always come with correct information because, either through neglect or through interpretations that serve the interests of the national archives, we sometimes find that there is mistaken analysis and generalisations, especially in the Israeli archives on Palestinians.

Photographs from the Nakba Period

We begin our discussion with Figure 9.1, by Abd al-Salam al-Ujayli, a young Syrian activist at the time when he volunteered to join the Arab Liberation Army in Palestine in 1948. Ujayli was not a professional photographer. He was a doctor who became a well-known novelist, a member of the Syrian parliament and a senior official in the Syrian Ministry of Culture. But he was an amateur photographer, and he took a camera with him to Palestine and used it to record his experience in the Arab Liberation Army.[18]

This photograph shows the commander of the Arab Liberation Army, Fawzi al-Qawuqji, and a squadron of the army during its work in Palestine. At the superficial level, the picture shows men in Arab military uniform and a well-known commander standing in front of them. The background shows that they are in a hilly area planted with olive trees. It might be the village of Jaba' in Jenin district, where the Arab Liberation Army had its headquarters. To the general viewer, it is

Figure 9.1   Fawzi al-Qawuqji and a squadron of the Arab Liberation Army. Image courtesy of the Arab Image Foundation.

a photograph of a military unit in training. But if we take a deeper look, we see the picture of a prominent military commander who had fought in the Ottoman Army, in the ranks of Syrian revolutionaries, in Iraq and in Palestine during the Arab Revolt of 1936 and later in the war of 1948. Hence, the photograph documents the fact that Arab volunteers came to Palestine to take part in the fighting, but at the same time it does not give any particular information about whether they fought, what the result of the battle was, or the nature of the events around them. We do not know whether the position in the photograph fell to Zionist fighters, or whether it was close to a village that was wiped out of existence or survived. The picture is commemorative and does not refer to any of the dramatic events that were taking place at that time. Ujayli, the photographer, used it in his autobiography, and it might have been used by Qawuqji himself for reasons related to his role or to document his life. We can imagine the captions that might be put under the photograph if it was published. A caption might say: 'Qawuqji, Heroic Commander in the Palestinian War'. Or it might read: 'A Squadron of Arab Terrorists Preparing to Attack a Peaceful Jewish Community'. In both cases, or with other possible captions, the image can be used to support either the Palestinian, the Syrian, or the Zionist narrative. It can provide evidence for the truth of any one of them.

Let us compare this photograph with a similar one produced by a photographer who accompanied a Haganah unit (Figure 9.2). This picture, which shows soldiers in a non-violent situation, was taken on 1 October 1948. In it we see a group of Israeli

Figure 9.2   Israeli soldiers in Ain Karim, 1 October 1948. Image courtesy of the Government Press Office, Jerusalem.

soldiers moving what appears to be furniture onto a truck. The picture was taken by an Israeli army photographer in the village of Ain Karim, west of Jerusalem, which had been occupied in July 1948 and completely depopulated.

What this photograph does not tell us at the superficial level is that the furniture they are moving is probably from the houses of the inhabitants of the abandoned village. Even if the photograph does not show us the ethnic cleansing of the village by Israeli forces, it does provide evidence that the contents of the Arab houses were confiscated; therefore, it is a photograph that reflects state violence, even if it looks like a peaceful image. If we put it in the context of other photographs from the same period – such as pictures of Palestinian refugee camps being set up in the diaspora, for example – we can extract facts about the fate of the Palestinians at that time. In this sense, studying what we call the depth of the image can give us additional information about the period, especially as we are dealing with clear signs that the soldiers in the picture are not in combat mode – their rifles are stacked around the tree while they carry things to the truck. The only person facing the camera is standing in a relaxed position, holding a pile of papers.

The relaxed atmosphere in this picture leads us to another example of soldiers in a similar situation (Figure 9.3), which was taken by Ujayli. It shows a group of fighters in the Arab Liberation Army, but this time without Qawuqji, the commander. The volunteers are assembled in the traditional pose for a group

Figure 9.3   Arab Salvation Army fighters in Palestine. Image courtesy of the Arab Image Foundation.

photograph, like graduating students. Those at the back are standing, while those at the front are crouching or lying on the ground. They look happy and relaxed, even if some of them are carrying weapons. Was the picture taken as a souvenir of happy times? Or to send to their families in neighbouring countries to show that they were well? Of course, we cannot know the answer without reading the notes that the photographer or one of the fighters in the picture might have written on the back of it. The depth of the picture does not show us details of the period, and since we do not know where they are, or when exactly the picture was taken, it is not possible to generalise. But an important detail emerges through the picture, if we know the names of the people in it – that is, that most of them came from countries outside Palestine. Thus, the picture provides evidence that fellow Arabs did take part in the war of 1948.

But if we put it in the context of two more (Figures 9.4, 9.5) pictures, the first by Western press photographer John Phillips, published in *Life* magazine and showing the British army evacuating Haifa in April 1948, and the second by a Haganah photographer, showing armoured vehicles heading toward Jerusalem, also in April 1948, other meanings behind this image of relaxed, happy Arab troops may emerge.

Figure 9.4   A thirteen-year-old Palestinian boy lying dead on the street of Haifa, British soldiers passing by, April 1948. Photographed by John Phillips. Image courtesy of *Life* magazine photographs.

Figure 9.5   Haganah armoured vehicles on the way from Tel Aviv to Jerusalem. Photographer unknown. Image courtesy of the Government Press Office, Jerusalem.

A comparison with the first photograph seems superficially inappropriate, because one is of fighters in a state of relaxation, while the other is of soldiers walking indifferently past the corpse of a Palestinian in Haifa. But the two photographs are linked, if we look at them in depth. Both of them are pictures of details associated with the Nakba in general, and a deep understanding of both is possible if they are placed in the context of the event. The first shows us that Palestinians and Arab volunteers were preparing to defend themselves and their country. The second shows that the withdrawing British army was not interested in the battles raging between the Zionist forces and the Palestinian Arabs. But a comparison between those two pictures on the one hand and the picture of the Haganah armoured vehicles on the other hand presents us with the possibility that, while the Arab fighters were relaxed and the British were withdrawing and disengaged, the Zionist fighters were engaged in a methodical offensive. It would be hard to be completely sure about this possibility based on the pictures alone, but if we look at the general historical context and find more pictures that are similar in their details, then we may assume that this hypothesis is correct. In other words, photographs, just like written historical documents, have to be understood in the context of other photographs taken in the same historical context.

Of course, what we have referred to does not mean that Arab fighters did not take part in battles, or that Zionist fighters did not appear in souvenir photographs, as much as it indicates that the Haganah forces and then the Israeli army were so well-prepared and well-organised that they recorded their battles in photographs. Among the relatively few photographs that we have of warfare from the Arab side are images of the defence of the old city of Jerusalem by fighters of the Army of the Jihad al-Muqadas, an irregular Palestinian force (Figure 9.6). The picture was taken by Khalil Rissas and formed part of his collection that was looted and placed in the archives of the Israeli Ministry of Defence. As mentioned above, it suggests a way of thinking about the role of photographs on the two sides in the conflict. The Zionist side documents its battles, while the Arab side does not document the battles, but photographs its soldiers in poses that suggest that victory is imminent. The following collection of photographs of fighters by Arab photographers (Figures 9.7, 9.8) shows that the scene is repeated, even if the photographers change.

At the same time there exist a few pictures in which Arab fighters are shown in combat with hostile forces, including in Figure 9.9, by Khalil Rissas.

The photograph above shows Shaykh Yasin al-Bakri, a Muslim cleric (1904–73), pointing out enemy positions to the fighters. The picture is important because of its rarity and because the role of the Army of the Jihad al-Muqadas in defending the old city of Jerusalem is rarely mentioned in Arab studies on the Palestine War. But the picture is stagy and may have been posed. It may not even have been taken during

Figure 9.6   Fighters from al-Jihad al-Muqadas with leader Abdelqader al-Husayni in the middle. Photographer unknown. Image courtesy of *Al-Hadaf* magazine, December, but stated here as January 2008.

Figure 9.7   Arab fighter from al-Jihad al-Muqadas forces with Abdelqader al-Husayni in the middle and to his left Kamel Eriqat. Photographer unknown. Image courtesy of the Institute for Palestine Studies.

Figure 9.8   Syrian volunteers in the Arab Liberation Army. Image courtesy of Syrianhistory.com.

Figure 9.9   Fighters from the Army of the Jihad al-Muqadas defend the Jerusalem citadel, now known as the Tower of David. Photographed by Khalil Rissas. Image courtesy of Central Zionist Archives.

an actual military engagement. The sheikh is standing in a way that suggests that he had no need to take cover from enemy bullets, unlike the fighters holding rifles, and the photographer also appears to have been standing, which would also make him vulnerable to sniper fire if the picture had been taken during a real battle.

But even if posed to highlight the role of Arab fighters or of Sheikh al-Bakri as commander, it is a photograph of historical events that took place, and the same pictures form evidence of those events. By that I mean that there were Arab fighters who defended Jerusalem and that they took part in armed clashes with the enemy. At the same time, photographs such as this are useful in the context of what Ariella Azoulay, a specialist in the Zionist photographic archive, calls 'potential history'.[19] In her theory, she deploys the idea of what Walter Benjamin calls 'incomplete history'. As Azoulay argues, people who study historical photos can imagine alternative histories by studying the conditions that suggest different historical possibilities, those that did not come about because of the dominance of the historical vision of the state that exercised its control, not only through violence practiced in reality, but also through archiving and categorising evidence that it used violence, and putting it in the context of its national discourse.[20] When we look at a photograph in the archives, we find that it has been categorised in some way and has been given a description in the context of the authority of the archive and the institution that stands behind it. An image of Nahr al-Bared camp in north Lebanon (Figure 9.10), a short time after it had been set up in the early

Figure 9.10   Nahr al-Bared camp, 1952. Photograph by Myrtle Winter. Image courtesy of UNRWA.

1950s, helps us to understand this question. The photographer was Myrtle Winter, the founder of UNRWA's photographic archive, and it was this picture that led the agency to set up its own photographic department.

On the surface and without any historical context, this is a beautiful and well-produced photograph, taken with a Leica, one of the best cameras of the time. It shows mountains with snow-capped peaks topped by thick clouds. In front of the hills there are many tents, inhabited at the time by refugees from northern Palestine. The two subjects of the picture divide the frame almost in half, with the top part showing the mountains and the lower part the tents. It is without doubt an extraordinary photograph, but putting it in the context of the Nakba, the expulsion of people from their villages in northern Palestine and their transfer to a refugee camp, puts it in a wider context that gives the photograph completely different and less aesthetic meanings. This is the aspect that is relevant to the depth of the picture and also to the context of its use in the framework of Palestinian nationalist discourse. But we should not overlook the surface of the photograph, because through it we can find things that enrich our knowledge of the historical discourse related to its depth. Let us examine the details of the photograph for a moment: we see three women in the foreground, one of them holding a child and the others empty water jars. We can conclude that the camp is close to a water source, maybe the Bared River itself, after which the camp was named. But why do we not see any men carrying jars? We might conclude from the absence of men that the inhabitants of this camp came from villages in an area where tasks were divided between the genders in such a way that responsibility for housework fell on women. Maybe the fourth woman, who appears in the photograph carrying a large tray on her head and walking in the opposite direction, confirms this theory, especially if she is compared to the old man who appears in the photograph, working in the garden that he has created around his tent.

Between the three women and the fourth behind them we see a boy carrying a school satchel, walking toward the photographer, while in the distance there is what appears to be the school, close to the end of the tents on the right of the picture. Maybe he has finished school and is returning to his family's tent. Also, what looks like fencing around the tents, made of reeds or cane, which may have grown close to the river, gives us the impression that the people in the camp have found ways to create a little privacy by marking off the territory of each tent as if it were their private home. Looking at the details of the picture gives us plenty of information about the lives of the inhabitants, a subject worthy of study to understand how the Palestinian community was fragmented and then reconstructed in exile.

But Myrtle Winter did not take the photograph to analyse the lives of the inhabitants or to explain the tragedy of the Palestinians. She took it to accompany a report on UNRWA's work, to be sent to her bosses at the United Nations. She wrote a caption to the photograph that has been preserved in the agency's archives. In brief, it refers to the agency's efforts to provide services to the refugees and notes that 6,000 refugees living in the camp have benefited from those services. It praises the agency's success in improving living conditions for the refugees. Today, this photograph is one of the best-known images of the refugee camps shortly after the Nakba. It has appeared in the publications of the PLO and other Palestinian institutions. But the major difference is that, when it is used by Palestinians, it has nothing to do with how and why the picture was taken, but with the discourse that puts the refugee camps at the heart of the Nakba as an event, and usually there is no mention of either the name of the photographer or details related to UNRWA's activities.

Thus, the picture above is a historical document that has been used in a number of particular histories. It is a picture of the results of the Nakba in Palestinian discourse and a picture of UNRWA's work in the framework of the history of the institution that took the photograph and owns it. But at the same time, it is a photograph that has meaning for historians if they decide to study it as a historical document, which rarely happens. It includes details that can inform the scholar about social life in the camp. At the same time, it can be put in the context of 'incomplete history', the history of the inhabitants as a group and as individuals, each of whom has their own story and their own history as they try to preserve the social structure of their lives before the dispersal of Palestinians.

There are also photographs in private family collections that can be useful for studying the Nakba. The next photograph (Figure 9.11) is by Daoud Abdo, who worked in West Jerusalem before the Nakba and later moved to Beirut, where he opened a photography studio that bore his name. The photograph is dated 24 April 1948, and superficially it appears to be of a family or group of people standing in their best clothes, as if on their way to a party, in front of a beautiful stone house. But the picture also shows us that they are standing beside numerous baskets and sacks, and in the background, behind the woman on the left of the picture, there seems to be some bedding, which makes it unlikely that they are going to a celebration. The context in which the photograph was taken and later preserved provides us with the historical depth that suggests that it was taken in the Baq'a area of West Jerusalem. The date coincides with the time when this area fell to Palmach Zionist forces and the process of removing the inhabitants began. The people in the picture are members of the photographer's family, standing in front of their house in Baq'a and waiting for the bus that will take them to the part of Jerusalem that was under the control of Arab forces. It is the last picture of them in front of their house, which was confiscated by Israel under the Absentee Property Law of 1950, enabling Israel to confiscate the property of anyone who was not at home between 29 November 1947, when

Figure 9.11 The Abdo and Moushabeck families in Baq'a. Photographed by Daoud Abdo. Theodorie collection. Image courtesy of the Institute for Palestine Studies.

the United Nations General Assembly approved Resolution 181 on the partition of Palestine, and 19 May 1948, the date when Israel's provisional state council declared a state of emergency.[21]

Therefore, what the picture shows us is that the people in it were living their last day as citizens and, when the bus they were awaiting, arrived they became refugees, with no right to go back to their home. The smiles and the generally relaxed atmosphere evident in the picture might reflect their belief at the time that they were leaving for a few days until the fighting stopped. The picture also shows us, based on their clothing, that they were well-off people who lived in the city or, more precisely, its wealthy suburbs. Even if the subject is known to us, it has not received adequate research, compared with that on the rural populations who became refugees living in camps. In this sense, this photograph expands our concept of the victims of the Nakba to include categories of people who were not poor. In the Israeli archives we can see several photographs of the attack on Baq'a by Palmach forces, with the same date as Daoud Abdo's photograph, as in Figures 9.12, 9.13 and 9.14.

Thus, linking the pictures together gives us visual details about the nature of what happened in Baq'a at that time. Similarly, comparing Abdo's photograph, in which we see no compelling evidence of the expulsion of Palestinians, with the

Figure 9.12   Palmach forces attack Baq'a in Jerusalem. Image courtesy of the Israeli Government Press Office.

Figure 9.13   Zionist forces during their attack on West Jerusalem.
Image courtesy of the Israeli Government Press Office.

Figure 9.14   Haganah fighters celebrate fighting off Arab resistance in the
Jerusalem area, April 1948. Image courtesy of the Israeli Government Press Office.

Figure 9.15   Palestinians at the port of Jaffa, waiting for ships to take
them to Acre, April 1948. Photographed by John Phillips.
Image courtesy of *Life* Magazine.

image that press photographer John Phillips took at the same time of evacuees at
the port of Jaffa (Figure 9.15), the resemblance lies in the sacks and baskets in the
two pictures, which helps us to imagine that the first photograph is of Palestinians
leaving their homes and about to become refugees.

What adds to our sense of what the Nakba meant to Palestinians is that Daoud
Abdo's photograph, with two others taken on the same day and of the same group,
were the last photographs in the album kept by the photographer's family – the
album that recorded their lives in Palestine before the Nakba, and this is what
conveys the feeling that, for them, history came to a halt after that.

Did the Arab Press Record the Nakba through Images?

Despite the facts that photography spread early in the Ottoman world (especially
in Istanbul, Palestine and Egypt), that photographers were common in Arab
cities in the first half of the twentieth century and that some Arab and Palestinian
photographers worked for international or Arab news agencies or for newspapers published in Palestine at the time of the Nakba, we rarely find photographs
recording the events of the Nakba. One of the reasons for this may be that those

Palestinian newspapers rarely published photographs in general, except as part of paid advertisements. In *al-Difaa* and *Filastin*, two newspapers published in Jerusalem and Jaffa during the British Mandate period, we do not find news photographs in general. If they do exist, they are portraits of leaders, especially world leaders, and sometimes of Palestinians killed in conflict, or major international events. *Filastin*, for example, published a photograph of the Spanish civil war on 10 January 1937.

In the British Mandate period, Palestine did have some illustrated publications, such as the newspaper *al-Muntada* and *al-Qafila* magazine, which was published by the Palestine Broadcasting Service, commonly known as Jerusalem Calling. *Al-Qafila*, which described itself as an illustrated weekly magazine, was edited at the time by Hassan Mustafa. But the photographs that appeared in these publications were also of a commemorative nature, portraying victories and Arab preparations for battle in Palestine, but not showing the course or results of the battles or the process of driving out the inhabitants. This also applies to the use of pictures from Palestine in Egyptian and other Arab newspapers at the time. The only magazine that published photographs of the ordinary Arab inhabitants of Palestine was *Haqiqat al-Amr*, which was published in Arabic by the Histadrut (the General Federation of Labour in Israel) and which called itself 'an illustrated weekly magazine to promote the principle of fraternity between the two peoples and encourage the unity of the workers in Palestine'. But its alleged commitment to the idea of fraternity, and its Zionist commitment, may explain the fact that it did not publish photographs of the Nakba.

At the same time, we should not forget that some Palestinian newspapers stopped publishing during the height of the conflict, which may explain to some extent why there are so few photographs of the Nakba. Moreover, there may be another reason for the lack of Arab photographic documentation – the fact that Palestinian Arabs and Arab fighters who took part as volunteers, not as regular units with state resources for documenting what happened, had no institutional framework, unlike the Jewish Agency and other Zionist organisations in Palestine. One can generalise by saying that awareness of documentation, or even of international public opinion, was not one of the priorities of the Palestinian or Arab fighters in Palestine.

Conclusion

Although this research suggests that documentation of the events of the Nakba by Palestinians and Arabs was weak, there is still a possibility that unknown collections of photographs exist, or that other photographs by Arab photographers did exist but have gone missing. Yet, the uncertainty about such possibilities makes it hard to speculate about how the Nakba would have been represented if such photographs did exist. This chapter has, however, raised several subjects that help us to think about photographs as historical documents, and this in itself will not be changed by the quantity of photographs available or the fact that other photographs we do not know about might exist. Since our subject was how photographs can be used to understand the nature of the Nakba as a central event, we can say that, based on the photographs that we do have, the way in which the Nakba was documented by Arabs was not at the same level as the way in which Zionism documented its war on Palestinians.

Given that the paper includes a theoretical dimension on how to analyse images by drawing on various ideas, including semiotic theory and history, I hope that it has helped to draw attention to the possibility of rummaging in the photographic archives to expand our knowledge of the events of the Nakba. Let us not forget that absence in itself – and what is meant here is the absence of photographic documentation – might reflect the core of the greater Palestinian problematic, which is Palestine's absence from the map and people's absence from their homes and towns and villages, because the story of the Palestinian Nakba is essentially a story of absence. This does not exempt us, of course, from examining the reasons behind such an absence, not just at the general Palestinian level, but at the specifically photographic level, especially in the Arab context. This might have a number of explanations, some of which have been anticipated in this study, but it might also reflect the lack of seriousness in the Arab military campaign, disorganisation in the Arab army and the weakness of Arab media coverage in general.

In conclusion, I would like to remind the reader that photographs play an important role in shaping the communal imagination of events. At the same time, according to Azoulay, they play a part in forming a 'civil imagination', which she defines as imagination liberated from the constraints of national discourse, which makes it capable of historical imagination outside the official parameters.[22] This is what makes the photographs taken by Zionist photographers, UNRWA photographers or the international media important for understanding the Nakba, if examined outside the specific context of their photographing and of the captions giving to them.

Notes

1. The Arabic original of this chapter will be published in a book on the Palestinian Nakba by the Arab Center for Policy and Research; many thanks to the editors for permission to use this translation and to Jonathan Wright for translating the work.
2. See, for example, chapters in *Mountain Against the Sea, The Great War and the Remaking of Palestine*, and Tamari, Nassar and Sheehi, *Camera Palaestina*.

3. For more detail on the history and spread of photography in Palestine, see Issam Nassar, *Laqatāt Mughāyira, al-Taswīr.*

4. See, for example, Schwake, 'Great War in Palestine', and Nassar, 'John Whiting'.

5. This theme has been addressed by a number of scholars, including Merli, 'A New Art'; de Tarragon, 'Holy Land Pilgrimage'; and Wheatley-Irving, 'Holy Land Photographs'.

6. As discussed also in Zananiri, this volume.

7. Khalil Rissas (1926–74), a Jerusalem photographer who worked in Jerusalem during the British Mandate period and stayed on after the occupation in 1967. His photographs were confiscated by Haganah forces in 1948.

8. Abdel Razzaq Badran (1917–2003), a Palestinian photographer born in Haifa. He migrated to Kuwait and became well-known as the first Arab photographer there.

9. John Phillips (1914–96), a photographer for *Life* magazine from the 1930s to the 1950s. Born in Algiers, he became famous for photographing wars, including World War II, the conflict in Yugoslavia in 1946 and the war in Palestine.

10. Myrtle Winter (later Winter-Chaumeny), an Englishwoman born in 1915, founded the photographic department in UNRWA; she died in France in 2008.

11. Berger, *Understanding a Photograph*, p. 61.

12. Sontag, *On Photography*, pp. 5–15.

13. Cadava, *Word of Light*, p. 11.

14. Sontag, *On Photography*, p. 23–25.

15. Benjamin, *Illuminations*, p. 222.

16. Derrida, *Of Grammatology*, p. 95.

17. Potts, 'Sign', p. 31.

18. Ujayli later held positions at the Syrian foreign ministry and culture ministry. He was one of the first Syrian volunteers in the Yarmuk Brigade in the Arab Liberation Army, which was known as the Intellectuals Brigade. At the time he was a member of parliament. This information about him came to me from fellow scholar Mohammed Jamal Barout, who knew Ujayli well.

19. Azoulay, *Potential History*.

20. Azoulay, *From Palestine to Israel*.

21. For more details and the text of the Absentee Property Law, see the *Palestinian Encyclopaedia*, vol. 1, pp. 302–5.

22. Azoulay, *From Palestine to Israel*, p. 14.

Bibliography

Azoulay, Ariella. *From Palestine to Israel: A Photographic Record of Destruction and State Formation, 1947–1950*. London: Pluto Press, 2011.

Azoulay, Ariella. *Potential History: Unlearning Imperialism*. London: Verso, 2019.

Benjamin, Walter. *Illuminations: Essays and Reflections*. Edited and introduced by Hannah Arendt. New York: Schocken Books, 1969.

Berger, John. *Understanding a Photograph*. London: Penguin Books, 2013.

Cadava, Eduardo. *Word of Light: Theses of the Photography of History*. Princeton: Princeton University Press, 1997.

Derrida, Jacques. *Of Grammatology*. Baltimore: Johns Hopkins University Press, 1976.

Merli, Andrea. 'A New Art in an Ancient Land: Palestine through the Lens of Early European Photographers'. *Jerusalem Quarterly* 50 (2012): pp. 23–36.

Nassar, Issam. *Laqatāt Mughāyira, al-Taswīr al-Fūtūgrāfī fī Filastīn 1850–1948* (Different Snapshots: Early Photography in Palestine, 1850–1948). Ramallah and Beirut, Al-Qattan Foundation and Dar Kutub li-l-Nashr, 2005.

Nassar, Issam. 'John Whiting's Album of the Great War in Palestine'. *Jerusalem Quarterly* 53 (2013): pp. 42–49.

Potts, Alex. 'Sign'. In *Critical Terms for Art History*, edited by Robert S. Nelson and Richard Shiff. London: University of Chicago Press, 1996.

Schwake, Norbert. 'The Great War in Palestine: Dr Tawfiq Canaan's Photographic Album'. *Jerusalem Quarterly* 56 (2014): pp. 140–56.

Sontag, Susan. *On Photography*. New York: Rosetta Books, 2005.

Tamari, Salim, Issam Nassar and Stephen Sheehi. *Camera Palaestina: Photography and Displaced Histories of Palestine*. Oakland: University of California Press, forthcoming 2022.

de Tarragon, Jean-Michel. 'Holy Land Pilgrimage through Historical Photography'. *Jerusalem Quarterly* 78 (2019): pp. 93–111.

The Palestinian Encyclopaedia, general section, 1st ed. Damascus, 1989.

Wheatley-Irving, Linda. 'Holy Land Photographs and Their Worlds: Francis Bedford and the "Tour in the East"'. *Jerusalem Quarterly* 31 (2007): pp. 79–96.

Index